D1552602

Psychotherapy of the
Quiet Borderline Patient

Psychotherapy of the Quiet Borderline Patient
The As-If Personality Revisited

Vance R. Sherwood, Ph.D.
Charles P. Cohen, Ph.D.

JASON ARONSON INC.
Northvale, New Jersey
London

The authors gratefully acknowledge permission to reprint material from the following sources:

From "The Schizoid Personality in Light of Camus's Actor: A Response to Discontinuity," in *Bulletin of the Menninger Clinic*, 51(2): 158–169. Copyright © 1987, The Menninger Foundation.

From "Object Constancy: The Illusion of Being Seen," in *Psychoanalytic Psychology*, vol. 6. Copyright © 1987 by Lawrence Erlbaum Associates.

Production Editor: Judith D. Cohen

This book was set in 11 point Garamond by Lind Graphics of Upper Saddle River, New Jersey, and printed and bound by Haddon Craftsmen of Scranton, Pennsylvania.

Library of Congress Cataloging-in-Publication Data

Sherwood, Vance R.
    Psychotherapy of the quiet borderline patient : the as-if
personality revisited / Vance R. Sherwood, Charles P. Cohen.
        p. cm.
    Includes bibliographical references and index.
    ISBN 1-56821-060-4
    1. Selflessness (Psychology) 2. Borderline personality disorder.
3. Psychotherapy. I. Cohen, Charles P. II. Title. III. Title: As-
if personality revisited.
    [DNLM: 1. Borderline Personality Disorder—therapy.
2. Psychotherapy—methods.   WM 190 S554p 1994]
RC553.S45S48   1994
616.85'8520651—dc20
DNLM/DLC
for Library of Congress   93-46522

Manufactured in the United States of America. Jason Aronson Inc. offers books and cassettes. For information and catalog write to Jason Aronson Inc., 230 Livingston Street, Northvale, New Jersey 07647.

To those who want to maintain the integrity of psychotherapy

Contents

Acknowledgments   xi

Introduction   xiii

Part I: The As-If Personality

1   The Quiet Borderline Patient   3

The Problem of the As-If Personality   5
The Quiet Borderline Patient   12
*Clinical Characteristics of Quiet
    Borderline or As-If Patients*   15

2   Literature Dealing with the As-If Personality   35

Introduction   37
*As-If Phenomena and the Concept of a
    Continuum*   39
*The Question of the Relationship between
    As-If and Schizoid Phenomena*   43
*Further Considerations on the
    Relationship between As-If and
    Schizoid Phenomena*   48

The As-If Personality as a Type of
   Borderline Condition   51
Understanding As-If Conditions from
   the Standpoint of Identity Disturbance   53

3   Etiology of the As-If Personality   57

Introduction   59
Beginnings: The Child's Discovery of
   Self and World   61
Object Constancy: The Illusion of
   Being Seen   65
The Failure of Constancy: The Need
   to Be Seen by Others   70
The Quiet Borderline Patient's
   Adaptation to the Family   76
The Child as Family Protector   83

Part II: Clinical Approaches to As-If Pathology

Introduction   89

4   General Treatment Approach   91

Introduction   93
Getting Started: The Question of
   How Active to Be   95
Moving from Diagnosis to Therapy   101
Taking the Patient Seriously   104
Resisting the Patient's Compliance   113

5   The Appearance of Normalcy   121

Introduction   123
First Impressions   126
Moving toward Diagnosis   132

Final Considerations on the Appearance of Normalcy   *138*
Transcript: As-If Traits in the First Session   *141*

6   Precocious Ego Development   163

The Miniature Adult   *165*
The Appearance of Independence   *172*
The Question of Depending on the Therapist   *175*
Building Dependency on the Therapist   *182*
Transcript: The Need to Be Seen and the Fear of Being Known   *187*

7   The Absence of Identity   207

Identity   *209*
Problems with Aloneness and Relatedness   *216*
Pseudo-Relatedness in the Session   *222*
Therapy of Pseudo-Relatedness   *228*
Further Considerations on Therapy of Pseudo-Relatedness   *233*
Transcript: Identity Issues   *243*

Part III: Broader Concerns

Introduction   265

8   As-If Trends in Culture and Therapy   267

Introduction   *269*
Changing Expectations of Parents   *272*
As-If Therapy   *279*

References   289

Index   295

Acknowledgments

We warmly thank our publisher, Jason Aronson, for continuing to encourage and bring to press works that explore both the inner life and the rich complexities of long term psychotherapy.

We also thank the *Bulletin of the Menninger Clinic* for permission to use portions of Dr. Sherwood's paper "The Schizoid Personality in Light of Camus's Actor" and *Psychoanalytic Psychology* for permission to use portions of his article, "Object Constancy: The Illusion of Being Seen."

We are indebted to Andrew Stewart, M. A., for his invaluable help gathering reference material and for having provided several brief clinical examples.

Finally, we thank the students and friends who graciously let us see and use their work.

Introduction

As-if pathology is essentially imitative, a way of life built on an endless series of transient identifications in which the individual acts as if he or she were sensitive, empathic, conservative, religious, or even rebellious—all dependent on what others want the individual to be. Curiously, most of us who have been through rigorous and personally challenging training have probably gone through a period when we (briefly, we hope) embodied the as-if style. Those of us who remember the trials of being supervised may also recall trying to intuit what a demanding or exciting supervisor wanted and trying then to act as if we were competent to do it, or even trying to act like that supervisor. Presumably, clinicians use their transient identifications to lay down a professional identity that is genuine and built on competence. As-if individuals, by contrast, do not find their transient identifications to be way-stations on the road to a more developed identity but simply their identity for the moment, to be sloughed off for another transient identification later.

As we remark several times throughout this work, the as-if personality has been understudied. The first approach to the topic, which was Deutsch's (1942), led to a dead end. By the metapsychological lights available to Deutsch, it was not at all clear why as-if individuals were not psychotic, or at least incipient schizophrenics. We believe that much more can be done with the as-if concept in our current theoretical climate. The as-if personality seems to us to be a type of borderline pathology, and viewing it from this standpoint causes much more to become visible.

We came to make this study—the first book-length study of this topic and the first to propose a treatment approach—out of our own clinical needs. We have found patients in our case-loads who resemble Deutsch's (1942) as-if individuals, and we have struggled over the years to find a way to understand and treat these patients. There has been relatively little in the literature to help us. If a problem for our first book (Cohen and Sherwood 1991) was the popularity of the subject matter and therefore the sheer weight of positions to be sifted through and considered, the reverse has been the case here. There were virtually no guideposts along the road we wanted to travel.

It is a mixed blessing to be in such a position. On the one hand, we found it a pleasure not to be overly constrained by previous works; on the other hand, we really have no way to tell whether our study is incisive and on target, whether our arguments will still seem sound to us years from now. In large measure, this study will be judged by the directions future analysis of the as-if personality takes. We hope that ours is the first of many intensive studies of this pathology. Even if future works move in different directions than we have gone, we will still be enormously pleased to have done something to awaken interest in a deserving subject.

This work is in three parts. Part I contains three chapters, covering an introduction to the subject, a review of relevant literature, and a study of etiology. These three chapters should acquaint the reader with most of what others have said on this type of pathology and also with the outlines of our perspective on the origins of as-if pathology. The reader will note that Chapters 2 and 3 lay a theoretical foundation for the later, clinical chapters. While the clinical chapters can be read independently, the literature review (Chapter 2) and our study on etiology (Chapter 3) will provide the interested reader the conceptual framework from which the clinical material was developed.

Part II is the clinical section of the book and contains four chapters. The first of these offers a general approach to treatment of as-if patients, while the remaining three cover approaches to different elements of as-if pathology—the appearance of normalcy, a history of precocious ego development and attendant difficulties with dependency, and the virtual absence of a sense of identity. The last three chapters end with commentated transcripts of therapy sessions illustrating points made in the chapter. Part III consists of only one chapter and is perhaps as much social philosophy as psychology. It traces cultural variables that may promote the development of as-if traits and discusses a type of treatment we term as-if therapy, or pseudo-therapy.

As in our other writings, we have tried to be experience-near in the way we present our ideas and material. We avoid metapsychological concepts and overly abstract terminology as much as possible. We favor description over categorization wherever this seems feasible and believe that this is a particularly good practice with a relatively new subject. Where the subject matter is new, there may not be consensus on what exactly is meant by *the negative transference,* for instance, and description of the therapist's or patient's experience may be more revealing than technical language. Our intention has been to discuss our work with as-if patients in such a way that it will be possible for most readers to grasp our meaning, even if the reader has but little acquaintance with these individuals.

Part I

THE AS-IF
PERSONALITY

1

The Quiet Borderline Patient

THE PROBLEM OF THE AS-IF PERSONALITY

A half century ago Deutsch (1942) described a type of patient she called the "as if" personality. It is clear from her article that she was not attempting a thorough exploration of that patient type; she seems to have been offering her early and somewhat sketchy thoughts on an unusual sort of pathology, presumably to provoke further clinical contributions on the subject. She described patients who seemed to be disturbed, but it was not easy to say exactly how. They appeared normal in many ways, and their symptoms were hardly dramatic—it would probably be hard to convince an insurance company reviewer to authorize payment for any of the cases Deutsch presented in that paper. The thing that made them seem in need of a paper and of public discussion was the passively plastic way they went about their lives. These patients seemed void of genuine or deep affect, almost as though they were actors and actresses, lacking in any abiding or rich emotion. While this was the signal feature of as-if patients, Deutsch mentioned several other characteristics: They seldom saw themselves as much disturbed, they tended to blend in by automatically imitating others, and their passivity had completely replaced aggression and its derivatives, such as initiative.

While Deutsch may have hoped to promote public discussion and study, she did not accomplish this goal to any great degree. A literature review on this type of patient would surely be among the shortest any scholar might produce on a diagnostic category that has been known for fifty years. There may be clinical reasons for this absence of study. These are quiet patients, and they can have a knack for making therapists feel positively about the way treatment is going. If the therapist offers a little help or a few clues, they very often produce content that seems important, with the result that therapists may well work with these patients for long stretches of time without realizing how disturbed they are. An unexpected poor outcome after termination or a sudden patient-initiated termination when transference issues are raised may be the therapist's first clue that these patients were not what they seemed to be. Since treatments can (at least appear to) go quite smoothly, then, there has perhaps been little demand for literature on these patients.

In addition to these clinical factors, we believe that there are broader, conceptual reasons for lack of development of the topic. In our view, the patients Deutsch described were almost surely borderline individuals. In a previous work (Cohen and Sherwood 1991) we referred to *noisy* and *quiet* borderline patients, and we believe that as-if patients are the latter. Deutsch regarded these patients as incipient, although not active, psychotics—a natural tendency in the early thirties (when Deutsch actually wrote the paper) and for several decades later, when borderline patients were seen as likely to deteriorate into psychosis (cf. Hoch and Polatin 1949, Zilboorg 1941).

Deutsch leaned toward this view because of the type of identification process she observed in as-if patients. These individuals were not apparently capable of true identification, which entails making one's image of another person part of the very structure of the personality. By contrast, as-if patients stay at the level of primary identification, or fleeting behavioral and manneristic imitations of others. To Deutsch's thinking, a reliance on primary identification amounted to an absence of self-other differentiation, and so, she believed, these patients must be operating at a level not far from schizophrenia. (This is, of course, essentially the same problem later metapsychology had with narcissistic individuals as well, whose capacity for seeing others as extensions of themselves left theorists unsure why narcissists were not psychotic.) Thus, one conceptual factor is that Deutsch lacked the borderline category as a framework for understanding patients whose mental operations are primitive and who are nonetheless not prepsychotic.

A further conceptual problem has to do with the type of psychology at Deutsch's disposal. She worked at a time when Freud's tripartite model of personality was starting to modify the earlier id psychology. Ego psychology was less than one decade old when Deutsch began to develop her thoughts on as-if patients and less than two decades old when she published those ideas in English. As she first thought through the as-if problem, psychoanalytic theory saw the ego's chief function as defense against drive-superego conflict. Deutsch referred to Anna Freud's (1937) *The Ego and the Mechanisms of Defense* in her as-if paper and seemed to have been working with an understanding of the ego consistent with Anna Freud's views, that is, the ego as the agent of intrapsychic defense. We should ask what it meant that Deutsch approached the as-if patient not merely as a Freudian but as what Melanie Klein termed "an Anna Freudian."

The importance of Deutsch's orientation is its influence on how she regarded the as-if patient's shallow and apparently simulated affect. Deutsch (1942) notes "that all the expressions of emotion are formal . . . all inner experience is completely excluded" (p. 303) and "aggressive tendencies are almost completely masked by passivity" (p. 304). She also refers to the "pseudoaffectivity" of as-if patients. It is clear that this impoverishment of the emotional life troubled Deutsch. She rejected the idea that affect was simply repressed with these patients, noting that such repression would have led to hysteria, not to an as-if state. However, when Deutsch rejected repression and other defenses as an explanation, she also lost most of the role usually assigned to the ego at that time. Deutsch was then left with the speculation that as-if patients avoid conflict with the superego through immediate submission to an external authority. Through their characteristic passivity and imitative identifications, as-if patients can thus avoid the intrapsychic conflicts (between id and superego) that would otherwise be in evidence.

This explanation is hardly satisfying. For one thing, it proposes more emotional aliveness to these patients than Deutsch actually had discovered. In spite of the absence of genuinely felt affect in her patients, Deutsch could not bring herself truly to conclude that what she saw was accurate, that the inner life for all intents and purposes did not exist. She assumed that the patient was dissociated from the inner life, that consciousness of that life was excluded, but she clearly assumed that the inner life somehow went on. Deutsch argued that "the scene of all conflicts remains external" (p. 308) to the patient, but it is not clear what led her to believe that there were any pronounced conflicts in these patients.

Thus Deutsch was left to postulate an inner aliveness and intrapsychic conflicts that she could not witness. She really had no choice; her early ego-analytic model viewed affect as the mental expression of a quantity of instinctual energy (Laplanche and Pontalis 1973). Affect was a constant, then, since instinctual energy was always present. From such a standpoint, emotion was a given, and there was simply no way to account for its seeming absence except through the category of defense. From this perspective, the as-if personality seemed to be someone who had defended so well that the psychic life was channeled into external submission.

Working with the metapsychology of her time, Deutsch could not see the internalized object relations aspect of emotion. It is certainly undeniable that there is a physiological basis for affect. However, the development of affect occurs in conjunction with the development of self and object images. That is, affect changes and broadens as our experience of self and other changes and broadens. The principal vehicle for this development appears to be mirroring: Caretakers respond to the young child's moods, urges, and needs by representing in their own faces, voices, and bodily motions the very moods, and so forth, the child appears to be experiencing. We will discuss this process more fully in Chapter 3; for now we want to emphasize that a key principle in the development of affect is that *for a time, the child's inner life is external, on the mother's face and in her voice and movements.* The child organizes experience *in here* by first seeing it *out there,* on the mother's face (Sherwood 1989). Indeed, affect and the inner life do not exist as a constant or given. They are possibilities that unfold only when interactions give them reality. We believe that affect and the inner life may not unfold under certain circumstances or may unfold in extremely limited, truncated ways.

This argument is developed in more detail later in this book. We can, however, sketch it here. We start by asking what happens if the mirroring process should become reversed. There are people who are notoriously poor at mirroring the moods and feelings of others, narcissists, for example, or morbidly depressed and also psychotic individuals, for other examples. What happens when such an individual becomes a parent?

Perhaps we can begin to answer by observing that mirroring is normally reciprocal. Mirroring is a process by which both infant and caretaker are learning to be affectively attuned to each other's moods. Often in the literature one gets the idea that only the caretaker is involved in mirroring. This emphasis on only one side of what by definition is an interaction plays down the significance of what is happening on the child's face. In fact, every parent knows that caretakers take cues from their baby's response to them; parents are alternately organized, encouraged, devastated, and even reinforced by how the baby reacts to them. A responsive and attentive infant can have as strong an impact on a hesitant parent as the reverse.

When the parent is unable to be consistently responsive to the child and fails to carry out the parental part of mirroring, the child's role becomes exaggerated. If the parents are able to mirror only certain selected moods and intentions, the child's responses to the parents lose much of their freedom and range. The baby is faced with the problem of how to make the parents emotionally present or affectively real. The solution of the future as-if individual is to make those responses that the parents can in fact respond to with some consistency. The problem with this solution, of course, is that it changes the focus of mirroring. Whereas ordinarily mirroring mutually affirms both the parents' and the infant's reality, it now becomes the vehicle for maintaining emotional contact. This gives the child's responses to the parents an urgency or drivenness that is abnormal. The child hungrily seeks ways to make the parents react and interact, trying to pick out whatever will be pleasing rather than interacting spontaneously. In a sense, such infants cannot afford to be themselves; these infants must restrict who they will be with the parents, focusing only on what will bring the parents to life.

Our thesis is that under such circumstances the child may become a sensitive but shallow reflection of the fantasies, expectations, and projective identifications of the parent. Our thesis is further that such a child often grows up to become someone whose life is organized around intuiting the expectations of others and then behaving in ways that both arouse those expectations and also create the image of matching up well with them. These individuals are frequently described as perfect children by their parents, and they indeed seem to have assumed adultomorphic traits rather early in life. They are generally somewhat passive and tend to fit in well. If they are rebels or miscreants, it is usually because they have simply fallen in with such people, not because they are committed to an antisocial course. They are, in essence, continuing the task they learned early in life, that of intuiting the feelings and expectations of others and then becoming a living mirror.

Consequently, we see a different approach to the problem of the as-if patient's lack of deep and spontaneous affect than that provided by Deutsch, and we believe that new study is needed. Deutsch defined as-if patients by what seemed to her to be an exclusion or masking of inner experience and the absence of a capacity for internalization. Given her metapsychology, she could hardly have done otherwise. However, the inner life is not masked in the as-if population; it is absent, having been externalized. These patients are properly defined by the virtual reversal of the mirroring process early in life. This reversal keeps their emotional life externalized: As-if patients continue to find their emotional life, motivation, and intentionality in the faces, words, and movements of those around them rather than within themselves. Perhaps in this sense they might be said to have an emotional life; however, they lack a private self.

The literature following Deutsch suggests that very few instances of as-if personality have been seen clinically. Deutsch (Weiss 1966) herself said in the mid-sixties that she had seen only one additional as-if individual in the third of a century following the initial version of her paper. While some thinkers (e.g., Ross 1967, Greenson in Weiss 1966) have tried to broaden the field by suggesting a spectrum of as-if experiences, ranging from the pure as-if character to relatively normal and common as-if states of mind, little has come of the attempt. The clinical literature has generally tried over and over to redis-cover Deutsch's original patients. One fact dramatically illus-trates the field's lack of development: In the entire literature there is virtually no discussion of treatment approaches. The occasional exceptions (e.g., Khan 1960, Meissner 1984, pp. 221, 241, Chase in Weiss 1966) are brief and/or limited to discussion of single cases.

The problem of the as-if personality is that the category has survived, but very few clinicians claim to have treated such a patient. The category has survived because many clinicians feel

that there is some substantial insight into human existence and
psychological functioning in Deutsch's observations (cf. Weiss
1966). We believe that several clinicians (e.g., Ross 1967,
Greenson in Weiss 1966) intuitively feel that there are many
such people, even if they do not think they have treated any of
them. The field has languished for this want of subjects.
Deutsch's observations remain an interesting oddity, included
in edited works (e.g., Stone 1986) and posing intriguing theoretical questions. There has been no bridge whereby study
could progress from the level of an interesting anomaly to the
level of clinical usefulness.

THE QUIET BORDERLINE PATIENT

What has been missing is a viewpoint from which broader
characteristics of the as-if patient can be seen, characteristics
that broaden the clinical picture and allow us to see that there
are far more of these individuals than one would conclude
based on the paucity of literature. We propose viewing those
patients as representatives of a broader class: quiet borderline
patients. Deutsch's as-if label describes this group well if we
add several clinical characteristics of the borderline patient to
her early description. More specifically, we believe that as-if
patients are far more intolerant of aloneness than has usually
been recognized, identity formation is very seriously compro-
mised, and a key factor is their inability to experience themselves as separate individuals.

Looking from this broader viewpoint, we believe many
clinicians will be able to find one or more of these patients in
his or her current or recent caseload. In contrast to the reputed
scarcity of as-if types, we believe that quiet borderline patients
are not at all rare. However, they tend to be mistaken for other,
less severely disturbed individuals due to their ability to match
up well with whatever situation they find themselves in.
Consequently, many such patients are mistaken as mildly depressed but essentially normal individuals or, at worst, unusu-

ally passive hysterics. These are cases that may last a fairly long time but never seem to be going anywhere; usually they simply fizzle out at some point. Therapists are left wondering what they missed and what could have been done differently. Generally, they have a hard time answering this question.

The chances are good that the diagnosis will be missed at the outset due to vague presenting complaints that leave the therapist wondering whether the patient is ill at all. The as-if patient often does not seem to know why he or she has come for treatment, and whatever problems are articulated are generally offered in a rote and resigned manner, not with relevant emotion or obvious investment. Even when as-if patients can present a specific and defined complaint (possibly the result of previous therapy or a self-help book), they cannot discuss it very far. They bog down fast after they say why they have come; they sometimes appear to be watching the therapist for some clue on what might be an acceptable problem to present.

If therapists get past this shaky beginning, they may work with the patient for a considerable length of time before realizing that nothing is really going on in the treatment. Deutsch herself worked for extended periods of time with these patients before realizing that clinical matters were very different from what she had thought. Many therapists will find among their patients some who have seemed for several months—if not years—to be plowing through an important problem but who have actually just been offering words to the therapist. In fact, this is a hallmark of the as-if patient: Even when they produce rich content, it is produced mechanically, void of personal commitment and strong affect. The therapist could very likely suggest that the patient abruptly change to a completely different subject, and the as-if patient could do so with no noticeable distress. Therapists may find themselves thinking that these patients are just going through the motions. This is correct; they are behaving as if they were patients.

The quiet borderline patient is usually able to pick up clues from the therapist on how to act in sessions. As-if individuals have years of experience studying situations for signs that reveal what the other person might expect of them. They then try to arouse those expectations, helping the other person provide a role for them to play. One therapist commented about an as-if patient, "It's like hearing myself talk. I keep wondering how she knows what I think." These are, after all, individuals who were especially driven to mirror their parents, and by the time they come to treatment they can be adept at sensing the other's (the therapist's) mood, wishes, and needs. The therapist's remarks and interpretations will lead to further developments in the whole business, and soon the as-if patient can sound like a genuine patient. If the therapist offers enough clues, the as-if patient can give good material in return.

The therapist may eventually realize that something is wrong when the patient rather blandly discusses material that should be laden with powerful feelings. The as-if patient may *report* powerful feelings, yet the therapist gradually becomes aware that the patient does not really seem to be feeling anything very deeply, no matter what he or she reports. The therapist may also notice growing unease in these patients when the therapist is fairly quiet and gives little feedback. As-if patients need some definition by the other person, some hint of what is expected so that they can develop and fill the role implied by those expectations. Without these hints and clues, they are at sea and begin to feel slightly disorganized and ill at ease. They may then begin to ask the therapist for direction or help, saying, "I don't know what you want me to do" or "I'm not sure what I should be talking about."

In various ways, then, the therapist can become aware that patients who initially appeared to be relatively intact or, at worst, passive hysterics are in fact merely going through the motions, engaged in a kind of two-person stage play with the therapist in which patient and therapist act as if they were having a therapy session. But it is only an act, and in many ways there may be only one person in the room. The individual who is with the therapist is mostly trying to get through the encounter without being exposed to any overwhelming feeling that might produce a sense of neediness and dependency. This is one reason that the patient stays away from real feeling and lives by imitation—matching up with what is expected by others but without the experience of agency or initiative.

The problem for the therapist is how to work with someone whose seeming cooperation with treatment is itself a resistance designed to keep the therapist away. An onslaught of confrontation and intrusion will not work—these patients are not easy with intimacy, and if the therapist tries to close the distance too early, the as-if patient will probably leave. Thus, there is this dilemma: *If the therapist proceeds with business as usual, nothing will happen, but if the therapist tries very aggressively to point out that nothing is happening, the patient may well leave.* It is worth saying at this early point what clinicians may already suspect, that a successful treatment will not be easy and is probably not the rule.

CLINICAL CHARACTERISTICS OF QUIET BORDERLINE OR AS-IF PATIENTS

These patients are difficult to describe as a group. By definition, they are plastic; they do not always look and sound the same way, and there is very wide variation not only from patient to patient but also for the same patient across time. As-if individuals are so variable and so dependent upon each particular situation that there is no single clinical picture that will hold for all. More than any other patient type, they are defined by broad, underlying traits rather than by observable symptoms.

In the following sections, we describe four clusters of traits typically found in as-if individuals:

- the appearance of normalcy, stemming from an unwillingness to be in conflict with the environment;
- a history of precocious ego development, designed to avoid feelings of weakness, dependency, or interpersonal neediness;

- excessive passivity, plasticity, and a tendency toward pseudo-relatedness and avoidance of intimacy;
- severe identity problems, especially an inability to feel alive and real apart from performing roles given by others.

We believe that all four clusters of traits should be present before a patient is approached as an as-if individual (also see Gardner and Wagner 1986 for possible diagnostic criteria).

The Appearance of Normalcy

The first trait worth noting is that the as-if patient generally appears normal to those who know him or her and may well look fairly normal for a time even in the therapist's office. By normal, we mean well adjusted to the demands of external reality and relatively conflict-free. Indeed, patients who appear anxiety-ridden and clearly distressed in the first encounters with the therapist are not likely to be as-if types. Most quiet borderline patients will seem pleasant and comparatively at ease even in the first session. Their presenting complaints are likely either to be vague or to sound like reality-level problems. As a rule, quiet borderline patients will not come for treatment with problems that imply inner conflicts, and they will not show flagrant symptoms.

There are two significant exceptions to this rule. The first occurs with patients who have been told or have read that they ought to be troubled in some particular way; these individuals may well be able to appear as if they were anxious or otherwise upset, at least to some degree. These patients have usually been in therapy before and use statements from earlier treatments as guidelines for what they ought to talk about. Therapists who listen closely, however, will note a certain flatness and lack of investment in the patient's account of the problem. They may mistakenly suspect that the patient is splitting painful affect off from the topic as a defensive maneuver. In fact, there is no split-off of painful affect because there is no problem; the patient is only talking as if there were a problem.

> An example is a 32-year-old woman who initially said she needed help in dealing with the breakup of her marriage. She quickly began to talk, however, about her relationship with her father. At first, the therapist thought nothing of this, assuming that the topics were related. He noticed, however, that the woman tended to talk blandly about her father. She insisted it was a significant problem, but she talked in a rote and intellec- tualized manner. When the therapist eventually interrupted and questioned the patient about this, the patient said she had been in treatment before, and her first therapist had told her that the relationship with her father was "the key." Even though there was no affect associated with the subject (or, as it turned out, with any other), the patient clearly intended to talk about her father, saying, "Isn't this what you do in therapy?"

The second exception involves the patient's response to the therapist's silence. While it will not be immediately apparent to the therapist, the as-if patient is intolerant of aloneness—this is one of the qualities that distinguish quiet borderline patients from schizoid individuals, with whom they are often confused (e.g., Khan 1960, Sherwood 1987). As-if patients are, in fact, hungry for a role to play or a part to act. They make exceed- ingly quick (and fleeting) identifications with others and with the expectations of others, and without these they may not feel entirely real. The therapist's silence, then, is a very difficult experience, since the as-if patient is without the cues he or she needs in order to know how to fit in. Additionally, there is a nakedness and an intimacy to silence that is hard for these individuals. We believe that as-if patients can often adapt to a therapist's silence once they have heard the ground rules or guidelines that govern therapy; they can frequently (though not always) mold themselves to the therapeutic situation. A thera- pist who is inactive or silent in the first sessions, however, may well see agitation and confusion from as-if patients. It is also doubtful that an as-if patient will return to a therapist who is inactive from the start.

> A 30-year-old single woman came for treatment at the sugges-
> tion of her lover, a married man who was about to break up with
> her. She was upset, she said, about the loss of her lover and
> complained that she had not been able to keep any relationships
> in her life. By the end of the first session, the therapist formed
> the impression that this was essentially an identityless woman
> who was looking for someone to provide definition and direc-
> tion. Not wanting to gratify this wish, he took care to be
> inactive, limiting himself to an occasional reflective remark and
> acknowledging the woman's complaints. The patient seemed to
> have strength enough to withstand this frustration; she was
> bright, showed good social skills, and held a responsible job.
> There were no dramatic symptoms that suggested massive ego
> weaknesses. Near the end of the second session, however, the
> patient was complaining that the therapist's silence was too
> painful for her, and she threatened to end treatment. The
> therapist sympathized that his relative inactivity was probably
> difficult for her but added that he thought it would be better in
> the long run, even if hard in the short run. The patient thought
> about this but at the end of the session announced she was not
> coming back. In this case the therapist had probably correctly
> appraised the patient's need for direction and definition, but he
> had seriously overestimated the patient's ability/willingness to
> function without it. She had seemed much stronger or more
> adaptive than she was.

It may be well to add that these patients appear to have above average verbal skills. This is a trait that makes it easier for the as-if individual to appear intact or without significant pathol-ogy. In our society high verbal ability also predisposes others to want to interact with these individuals, thereby offering them the cues, roles, and feedback they need to mold themselves to the situation.

The appearance of normalcy, however, is just that, an ap-pearance. While these individuals seem to be flexible and adaptive, they are actually the opposite of this—they are compelled to adjust; it is a rigid, automatic reaction. They will mold themselves to virtually any situation with no strong sign of distaste or revulsion. As-if patients cannot allow themselves to experience tension with their surroundings. While a part of normalcy is surely the experience of being at odds with and unable to adapt to some circumstances, as-if individuals flow into the contours of any situation, taking on its shape. They do not, then, make an adaptation in the usual sense of the term. Rather, they simply take their definition entirely from their circumstances.

Precocious Ego Development

As children, quiet borderline individuals moved into a prema- ture attempt at self-sufficiency, a phenomenon Blanck and Blanck (1974) have described as precocious ego development. As the phrase implies, these individuals assumed a stance of mastery and competence toward themselves and the external world long before they could actually be effectual. They avoided expressions of need or longing, and they adopted a manner of unusual maturity and independence. The child's overall intent seems to have been to avoid dependency on the parents. The child was unwilling to place demands on the parents or on the external world; in adulthood this same desire to avoid needing anything from the world becomes the appear- ance of normalcy—which is nothing else but the determination not to call attention to oneself or to express any individualized need or desire.

> One patient had been born with severe facial disfigurement, necessitating several plastic surgeries annually, beginning in infancy and lasting through adolescence. The rules of the hos- pital required parents to leave each evening at six, and so the patient was left alone on the unit, trying to master her anxieties about upcoming surgery or to deal with the pain of recent procedures. She remembered reaching out to nursing staff many

times, crying and asking for comfort. According to her recollections, any evidence of neediness or distress was rebuffed with such comments as, "Don't you trust your doctor?" Over time, the little girl became a caretaker for the other patients. Instead of showing her own pain or fear, she attended to the other children on the unit, tucking them in each night and encouraging them when they were upset. She received much praise for this behavior. By the time she was old enough to begin grade school, she had settled into this pattern, behaving as a surrogate nurse on the unit whenever she was there for one of her many operations and playing a similarly adultomorphic role in social settings. The psychological cost was very high, however; by the time she was an adult she had very little idea what she herself thought or felt about anything. She was especially unable to say that she was hurt or bothered by even the most outrageous events and dealt with dissatisfaction by withdrawing into prolonged dissociated states of mind.

A 7-year-old girl was seen in consultation during a custody dispute. She initially seemed charming, nuzzling up to the therapist as soon as he entered the room. This apparent warmth, however, soon came to seem mechanical and stilted. For example, at the start of their second meeting the child gushed at the therapist, "It's so good to see you again." The child's manner was exaggerated, and she almost seemed to be imitating the hostess at a fashionable party. This girl was the caretaker of her younger sister, who was physically handicapped. She also served as her mother's confidante. As the mother said, "My daughter is my very best friend."

It is not simple to account for this type of development. It is certainly not enough to say vaguely that the parents were unempathic or emotionally unreliable. We have already implied that we think the parents of as-if patients may often have been unempathic and unreliable, and this may be a good place to acknowledge that much more needs to be said. Our impression is that a combination of factors—some from the parents and some from the child—produces this type of pathology. The parents of some of our patients are so obviously disturbed that it is no wonder their children suffer some sort of serious pathology; however, our impression is that sometimes there is simply not a good match between the parents' and the child's temperaments. One might go so far as to say that these individuals just were not lucky, that with a different child the same parents might well have had a very different outcome. The question then arises: What are the key parent-child factors that lead to precocious ego development?

We believe that children who resort to premature self-sufficiency tend to possess a native intelligence that allows for development of good verbal skills. They are also likely to grow up in homes that help them elaborate these skills—it is hard to imagine an illiterate, culturally impoverished family's producing an as-if individual, for instance. Further, we believe that these children possess what we might term a quiet temperament, a temperament that allows the child to scan and be alert for cues on how to fit into the family or match up with the expectations of caretakers. Finally, we believe that these children may have had a heightened sensitivity to abandonment or to being cut off from others. Due to this latter trait, they may have been more likely to experience caretakers as unreliable than other children who were not especially sensitive on this score. These various factors altogether led the child to experience his or her parents as emotionally unreliable and contributed in turn to the solution of precocious ego development.

As children, then, quiet borderline individuals avoided the child's usual dependency on adults. Instead of looking to their parents for caretaking, they looked for ways to create narcissistic gratifications for the adults in their lives. They developed a keen sensitivity to how they would have to behave in order for their parents to feel pleased with the job they (the parents) had done. They then tried to match up with those behaviors and roles that would narcissistically satisfy the parents. In effect, they aroused and engaged the adult's preferred fantasy of the child. As noted, we believe that the parents we are discussing were often narcissistically self-absorbed, depressed, and preoccupied, or otherwise emotionally unreliable; in these cases the parents' preferred image of the child was of someone who needed nothing from them. The parents could feel relieved at the child's self-sufficiency, proud to have reared such a capable little man or woman, or even pleased to have someone who could take care of them (the parents).

Consequently, these children received considerable praise for the appearance of self-sufficiency. It was important to them not to draw criticism from their parents, and in fact the absence of criticism was probably more important to them than the praise they received. They tended to be the proverbial perfect children who behaved with a maturity that was far beyond their years. Needless to say, such maturity was largely make-believe. Lacking in experience, wisdom, and adequate parental models, they presented themselves as if they were competent when they were not.

The negative psychological consequences of such an adaptation are very high. The child does not make an emotional investment in the caretakers (that is, the object is not cathected). Rather, the child focuses on molding his or her behavior to fit in with the family and on creating the *appearance* of acceptable functioning. This limited form of identification makes internalization highly problematic, not only because of the emotional distance from caretakers but, more importantly, because the relationship with caretakers tends to be forced in nature. Thus, the process of internalization does not progress beyond the early stage of imitation. The child feels accepted and reassured of having a place in the family only when playing a precociously mature role. To ensure a position in the family, the child orients to the external world, gradually tuning out any personal wishes or feelings. In effect, the relationship with caretakers remains external and takes on a staged quality. As the process evolves, the sense of personal authenticity slowly diminishes; feelings and relationships are perceived in terms of what is appropriate rather than what is genuine.

Initially, the child may sense the inauthenticity of the roles he or she plays in the family. There is no confidence that any praise or love expressed by caretakers reflects an emotional connection. Confidence in relationships and a sense of personal authenticity cannot develop unless the child has had the experience of being oppositional from time to time and also of having spontaneously expressed negative feelings and having caretakers see these attitudes as legitimate. Children moving toward precocious ego development are not generally found in homes where this happens. Indeed, the display of spontaneous affect in any form is not likely to be an ongoing part of family functioning.

> One 47-year-old patient said, "I can't remember a time while I lived at home that I ever said 'No' to my parents. I was really a good girl until I ran off at 19 to get married." She added that her father had a ferocious temper; while she did not fear physical abuse, she did believe that he would utterly reject her if she ever uttered a contrary or independent opinion. In fact, she ran away to get married at 19 in an attempt to leave before her parents could throw her out. She had lived for some time with a fear that her secret opinions on matters would be discovered and that she would be disowned.

Passivity, Plasticity, and Pseudo-Relatedness

Faced with the dilemma of maintaining a precarious place in the family through inauthenticity, the child adopts a passive stance. In essence, the child adjusts to being used in the service of others, meeting and reflecting the parents' narcissistically driven wishes. Such a strategy can be especially useful when caretakers are narcissistic and present their expectations to the child in a matter-of-fact, self-absorbed manner. In this situation, the child can quickly learn what is expected and provide it without personal investment or resistance.

This latter point is critical to understanding the as-if individual's passivity: There is no experience of conflict nor is there a sense of submitting to the world. Rather, the child takes the world as given, much like an actor who is presented with a script for the role he is to play. In the same way, the as-if individual performs (rather than behaves) entirely according to the cues presented by his or her situation. This type of super-ficial adaptiveness is possible because of an amorphous sense of self (which is all that is possible in the absence of a sense of personal genuineness) and a corresponding readiness to iden-tify briefly and intensely with any person or situation. Again, the identification takes the form of mimicry or imitation; there is little emotional investment involved. The shallowness of the attachment can be seen in the fact that when the person leaves or the situation changes, the identification stops. The latter depends entirely on the ongoing presence of the identification object, which may be idealized at the outset but can be just as quickly devalued and dismissed.

As adults, as-if individuals show remarkable plasticity in their relationships, moving easily from one seemingly dependent attachment to another with no corresponding sense of loss. While they are able to act as if they are intensely attached, they readily surrender current attachments in favor of new ones without evident distress. In a mobile society where there is a diminishing sense of community, the ability to function as an emotional chameleon has some adaptive capacity; relationships can be quickly formed and just as quickly surrendered when circumstances change. Thus, it is an irony of our times that the as-if, or quiet borderline, individual may be better equipped than a healthier person to work for a corporation that routinely moves employees to new cities every few years and may in other ways successfully face the challenges of rapid change. Such change simply replicates the individual's experience as a child, when he or she first learned to provide what others wanted without personal investment or resistance.

While quiet borderline personalities easily exhibit a pseudo-warmth in casual social situations, their adaptation tends to deteriorate as intimacy increases. There is a stilted and wooden quality—of which they are usually completely unaware—that becomes more and more prominent in a potentially intimate relationship. There is a lack of genuine investment that leaves others with the sense that ''no one is there.'' Even behaviors that seem to imply intimacy, such as sexual activity, are typically a set of discrete, isolated actions that do not create or solidify a relationship.

As-if individuals often find that others eventually withdraw from them, feeling that there is an insurmountable barrier to closeness. Other people may complain that the as-if individual does not seem to experience tender feelings or that there is an absence of mutual empathy, even though words have been uttered that would seem to imply tenderness and empathy. In turn, the as-if individual may not feel understood by the other person, and it is certain that the as-if individual does not understand the other. At best, the as-if personality acts as if he or she understands, or tries to use words that would imply understanding. In effect, as-if individuals say what a person who understands would be expected to say. It is hard to escape the conclusion that the as-if individual cannot love or be loved because love makes too much of a demand to be real.

One middle-aged man moved smoothly from one relationship to another, seldom staying with anyone for very long. He was extremely passive and tended to let the woman project her own (usually idealized) fantasies onto him. He did surprisingly little to confirm or disconfirm his partner's fantasies of him, usually doing just enough to sustain the woman's beliefs about him. He was not aware that he was doing this even though his therapist repeatedly pointed it out. He finally noticed that he could not respond honestly when a woman made a demand of him. Indeed, he could not even let himself be aware of what he personally wanted to do in response to the demand—all he could be aware of was the demand and the pressure he felt to match up with it, at least briefly. The result was that his lovers never really knew him; they knew only their fantasies about him. When one particularly aggressive woman pressured him into a quick marriage, the result was disastrous. After two months, she realized that this man was a virtual stranger to her, and a very difficult separation and divorce ensued. Most of his relationships did not get the chance to move toward marriage—

he tended to end relationships as the woman began to pressure him for greater intimacy.

Earlier in this chapter we suggested that the parents of many quiet borderline individuals are likely to suffer some impairment that leaves them unempathic and self-absorbed, and we mentioned narcissism as one such impairment. It is worth mentioning one scenario that is often played out when the mother is narcissistically disturbed. In such a case, the child may in fact succeed in identifying with the mother to some extent. What is then internalized is the image of someone who is preoccupied with appearances, including the child's physical appearance and the appearance of maturity in the child. The maternal emphasis on appearance sows the belief in the child that relationships are essentially matters of appearance. Even though relationships may last, they are not experienced as genuine, and, indeed, there is usually a deep sense that relationships are fraudulent. For such individuals, intimacy is quite disturbing and something that usually evokes flight.

One woman in her thirties had been married for many years and gave no sign of an unhappy or unstable relationship with her husband. However, she had always felt that she was simply going through the motions of the marriage, and she dreaded any experience that might force her to be more involved with her husband, such as sickness or his eventual retirement. In therapy she had trouble believing that the therapist was "for real." She repeatedly asked him, "Who are you trying to be like?" or "What therapist are you really imitating?" After several months of treatment she reported a dream in which her therapist asked for a picture of her. She opened her purse and was surprised to find many different pictures spilling out onto the ground. She tried to gather them up and sort through them in hopes of finding "the right one" to give him. He grew impatient, however, and eventually curtly informed her that "time's up" (a phrase the therapist sometimes used at the end of sessions), at which point the dream ended. Among other things, the dream showed the woman's confusion in trying to tell the therapist who she was or in trying to determine how to be with him. The woman experienced herself as a succession of appearances and was bewildered by the therapeutic relationship, where her usual appearances did not seem sufficient. She both feared and probably hoped that the therapist would dismiss her in impatience.

Pseudo-Differentiation and Identity Diffusion

Strictly speaking, quiet borderline or as-if individuals are able to differentiate themselves from other persons in spite of their tendency toward primitive, imitative identifications. That is simply to say that these patients are not organized at psychotic levels. However, their personal boundaries are fragile, and their sense of self is vague. As children, these individuals lacked the sense of being separate and unique individuals. Indeed, the process of development was one of learning to be separate, but only in the sense of being emotionally unconnected, not in the sense of being unique.

Perhaps it helps to describe the identity deficits these patients carry if we describe them as *reality-bound.* They are utterly trapped within the other person's perspective, becoming an extension of the other's needs, wishes, and expectations. Thus, the sense of self lacks definition and must be revised from situation to situation. This is noticeable in interpersonal interactions, where the as-if individual has no personal perspective to offer and eventually leaves the other person wondering, "Who is this person who is talking to me?"

Glimpses of fragile personal identity can be seen in the as-if individual's sexual history. Often the object of sexual desire seems reversible; it is not at all uncommon for quiet borderline individuals to have sexual involvements with both sexes. Males and females can seemingly be interchanged with no strong preference for one over the other, presumably because the as-if individual has no particular commitment to one sexual orientation over the other. The as-if person is more attuned to what role can be played out with another person than to differences between self and other.

Sexual promiscuity is frequently a part of the as-if patient's history. Deutsch (1942) commented on the way these patients appeared to have no sexual morals and could move from puritanical to promiscuous sexuality and back again, depending on whose company they kept. Deutsch argued that this suggested impaired superego development. While Deutsch was certainly correct in her observations, it may be missing the point to focus on superego formation. As-if patients are compelled to take on the behaviors and mores of those they happen to be with (which is what makes them seem normal most of the time) because they do not believe anyone would tolerate them if they voiced divergent views. Quiet borderline individuals believe they have value for others only to the extent that they are narcissistic extensions of the other person. Thus, they feel their company will be endured only to the extent that their presence is without cost to the other person. The quiet borderline individual's desire to mold the self according to the desires of the other often leads to sexual encounters with no emotional meaning. In our opinion, these sexual traits are simply part of an overall identity diffusion and do not represent a more circumscribed problem.

The quiet borderline individual's identity diffusion is further evident in the way words are used. More specifically, as-if individuals do not actually communicate when they talk. Rather, they string words together in a facile manner, saying a good deal less than is at first apparent. Listeners are left in the position of having to provide the meaning and affect, much as if they were responding to Rorschach cards. As-if individuals are accomplished at presenting themselves in ways that allow others to hear and see what they want or expect to hear and see. It might be said that their speech is an invitation to other persons to project meaning and affect onto the as-if individual, who in turn will identify with the projection. Thus, as-if individuals cannot afford to define themselves too closely when they talk. Essentially, they must leave room for the other person to imagine who they (the as-if individuals) are, thereby providing an image with which to identify or a role to play.

Anyone listening from a more or less objective and detached position may well wonder what an as-if individual actually intended. Strictly speaking, nothing was intended, since intention implies selfhood, and the as-if individual is trying to avoid uniqueness.

One therapist found he had a hard time following an as-if patient. His attention wandered as she talked, and he could seldom recall what she had just said. His impression was that she was simply stringing sentences together with no particular intention to communicate. Finally, he interrupted her and said, "I'm having a hard time following what you've been saying." First the patient looked puzzled and then innocently said, "I am too."

Another as-if patient would often talk of seemingly deep and important matters for much of his session. In spite of the apparent significance of the content, the therapist found himself increasingly distracted and sleepy as the session went on. After this happened several times, the therapist interrupted the patient and mentioned that he felt sleepy. The therapist went on to wonder aloud if this might mean that the patient was only pretending to be present but in fact wanted to keep his distance. The patient seemed delighted and became unexpectedly animated, saying that he had not felt "here" until the therapist's remark. Although he seemed genuinely excited by the therapist's observation (he looked like someone who had just been discovered in a game of hide and seek), the therapist found himself wondering whether the patient was finally present or whether he was merely showing a new disguise.

The quiet borderline individual's relation to work may serve as a final illustration of impaired identity. As-if individuals do not exactly pursue a vocation or line of work; rather they "dabble" in one profession or job before moving on to another. Usually they can fit fairly well into a new work setting or school. Their involvement may be intense at the outset, but their interest tends to be short-lived; once a task is mastered, they often become bored and often find a reason to move on to some new situation. This pattern is similar to what we earlier described as the as-if person's style of dealing with intimate relationships: There is a brief, intense period of idealization, shortly followed by reduced interest, then devaluation, and the capacity to exchange one person for another with no apparent sense of loss. In both situations we see that commitment or emotional investment does not run deep. Even if these individuals stay with a job for many years, it is seldom because they find meaning and deep satisfaction at their work. They are behaving *as if* they were teachers, lawyers, or, for that matter, therapists; but in fact they are chiefly filling time, not developing a sense of definition or identity.

A 38-year-old woman illustrates several of the traits mentioned here. She came for therapy at the suggestion of a supervisor at work, who told her that there "must be something wrong because you take work home with you every night." She was herself unable to articulate any particular problem that had led her to respond to the supervisor's suggestion, and it appeared that she had indeed come largely out of blind compliance. Not surprisingly, she tended to wander from topic to topic, usually asking the therapist for help in deciding what to discuss. She would occasionally ask the therapist whether any progress was being made in treatment; the therapist, in turn, would usually ask the patient what she would like to see happening in therapy, to which the patient generally could only shrug and smile awkwardly. At times the patient, who had never been married, would discuss what she might like in a man. When asked once by the therapist what she would bring to the relationship, she replied, "I wouldn't make any trouble. I'd be willing to go along with whatever he might want." While this response could sound hysteroid, in fact it was not. This woman was not saying that she wanted to please and be a complement to the man; she was simply indicating that she had virtually no power to define what happened and was, in fact, defined entirely by what the other person did. Indeed, her behavior was usually built on imitating others. For instance, she once went on an elaborate trip to Asia. The therapist asked if she had any interest in Asia, and the patient said she did not. She explained that a cousin had taken the same trip, adding, "He liked it, so I guess I would." On another occasion she complained to the therapist that a supervisor at work was sexually harassing her. This complaint arose shortly after Anita Hill's testimony in the Clarence Thomas hearings, and the patient made several references to the hearings. The therapist noted that although the patient spoke at length about the apparent harassment, she talked with almost no feeling at all. The overall impression was of someone imitating what she had seen on television, not of someone producing deeply felt material. A final curious note on this patient is that her therapist almost always felt drowsy during her sessions, which he understood to be a reflection of how little energy and affect the patient produced.

Given this vagueness in the sense of identity and the readiness to become almost a different person as circumstances change, it is remarkable that as-if individuals nonetheless maintain solid reality testing, something commented on by most writers on the topic (cf. Deutsch 1942, Meissner 1984, Weiss 1966). It is interesting to puzzle over how these persons manage consistent contact with external reality given their deficient internal reality. Perhaps the answer to this puzzle lies in the way as-if individuals use external reality: In adapting to some aspect of external reality in a superficial and passive way, these individuals fill up the emptiness of their "interior space." As Pontalis (1981) has suggested, the as-if individual confronts us with the possibility of an absence of that structure we call the self. In a sense we might say that what has been called the psychic space is not developed or organized in the as-if individual; the personality seems to be just an empty wrapping.

This is in contrast to other types of patient. The psychotic patient, for example, presents a fragmented and dissociated or split sense of self, but there is an inner realm with definite content. The acting-out patient, for another example, shows an organized fantasy system that lends coherence and intelligibility to the patient, even while he or she behaves impulsively. The theatrical hysteric similarly presents a recognizable set of intentions and demands, even while behaving dramatically and with seeming wildness. In contrast to all of these, the as-if individual uses the external world to substitute for an inner world. In contrast to Deutsch (1942) we do not believe that the process of mimicry or imitation is defensive in nature, an attempt to stay away from inner conflict or anxiety-laden themes. Rather, we believe that as-if individuals rely heavily on external reality to constitute themselves as persons who are inwardly alive.

In sum, inner emptiness directly relates to identity diffusion and the general poverty of affect found in as-if persons. It is small wonder that emotions are expressed in a formal and stylized manner. There is no internal sense of self that is engaged with others; there is only a system of responses, trying to match up with the external world and provide a transitory sense of aliveness. For this reason (seeking after aliveness) as-if individuals are more dependent and less tolerant of aloneness than one might suppose or indeed than they appear. It is true that as-if individuals do not become deeply attached to any single person, and in fact people tend to be interchangeable for them. However, as-if individuals need to be involved with *someone,* or they feel painfully bored, agitated, and empty.

In spite of the appearance of normalcy, as-if individuals have not achieved psychological separateness. Their seeming differentiation from others is at best a pseudo-differentiation. While there are exceptions, it is hard for as-if individuals to be unattached, even though their attachments are superficial and easily changed. The problem with separateness is that as-if persons cannot define themselves when they are by themselves. In a sense, they may be said to need others in order to know that they exist. Thus, they are not exactly dependent on others; certainly they are not dependent in the sense of a constant, meaningful tie to another person. However, they are dependent on some involvement to give a sense of being alive and real. Far more than is the case with healthy individuals, as-if persons are embedded in their immediate situation for a feeling of being alive and for a part to perform.

One patient was able to function if she was at work, with a friend, or with her husband, but not by herself. She dreaded weekends, since her husband often worked and she was home alone. If she could, she would go to her office to find something to do. Otherwise, she usually sat at home with the blinds drawn for the entire day, generally with no awareness of the passing of time and with no recollection of what happened during the day. She frequently sat down on a chair in the early morning and suddenly became aware that it was night, although she had no sense of the hours' passing during the day. She was in a dissociated state of mind, unable to feel real or alive without a project to propel her. She would say of these times, "I don't know what happens. I'm not there."

A young woman told her therapist that her boyfriend had broken up with her during the week. While she had already replaced him with a new lover, she was bothered, she said, by something her ex-boyfriend had told her. He complained, she said, that "I didn't have any identity—I attached myself to others and assumed theirs and was just using everybody up!" This young woman prided herself on getting other people to tell their life stories and secrets to her. In this way, she felt close to people, and she defined relationships on the basis of whether others did this or not. However, she never shared anything of herself except with the intention of prompting further revelations from others. When her boyfriend realized this, he broke up with her, making the aforementioned remark. He had correctly sensed that she lived vicariously, off the experiences of others.

This chapter has tried to address the problem of the as-if patient, namely the lack of definition to the category and the absence of theoretical literature and clinical lore. Our intention has been to identify as-if patients as part of a larger class, borderline patients, and to offer clusters of traits that will help clinicians begin to identify as-if individuals in their own case-loads. In the following two chapters we intend to elaborate the ideas begun here. The following chapter reviews the literature and points out the (relatively few) salient issues that have been developed over the years. The third chapter relates as-if characteristics to issues more commonly associated with borderline patients, trying to make the connection between as-if and borderline pathology clearer. More specifically, the third chapter addresses the subjects of mirroring and object constancy as the crucial issues in understanding these patients.

2

Literature Dealing with the As-If Personality

INTRODUCTION

The past twenty-five years have witnessed a flood of books and articles studying the borderline patient. Most of these focus on the group we have called noisy borderline patients (Cohen and Sherwood 1991). By contrast, there has been little attention given to quieter, as-if patients. Two factors account for the discrepancy. First, noisy patients are easier to recognize. As the adjective suggests, they are more flamboyant in exhibiting their pathology, and diagnosis can be made fairly early on. Quiet borderline pathology is much more difficult to spot; certainly it does not jump out at the therapist.

Second, the therapist's experience of each type of patient is quite different. Noisy borderline patients create many problems for treatment, and therapists may feel they are on a roller coaster, being carried along for a wild ride rather than directing a therapy. Eventually, they may come to doubt their own abilities, making treatment a painful experience. Quiet borderline patients are very different in this regard. They do not generally make therapists uncomfortable and appear to be cooperative or even grateful. Treatment can appear to be going quite smoothly, and the therapist may feel satisfied with developments in the case. By causing quite a bit of trouble for therapists, noisy borderline patients naturally draw attention in the literature. Similarly, by showing and causing few problems, quiet borderline patients fade into the clinical woodwork, as it were, and call for much less mention in journals and books.

The problem, perhaps, is that as-if patients are too adaptable. They are caricatures of Reisman's (Reisman et al. 1955) other-directed persons and can appear to make quite a healthy adjustment. Until recently, such individuals rarely sought therapy, or, if they did, their problems were not recognized as especially pathological. Yet the past decade has seen them coming for treatment, we believe, in increasing numbers, often with complaints of emptiness (which may be mislabeled as depression), difficulty sustaining intimate relationships, and a sense of aimlessly searching for an identity. These patients frequently feel that their lives lack meaning, and they secretly hope to discover some hidden self. While vague and hard to get hold of, such complaints mask serious pathology, even though that pathology has been screened from study by the very adaptability it fosters.

It is understandable, therefore, that so few works have specifically addressed the as-if personality. It is as though Deutsch's (1942) well-known paper on the subject said all that needed to be said, and later writers contented themselves with defining the issues a bit more closely or restating her concepts. While there are, happily, a few exceptions (e.g., Gardner and Wagner 1986, Ross 1967), the literature has not generally taken the concept further than Deutsch's original paper. Indeed, among the works specifically addressing the as-if personality, we are not aware of any paper that speaks to clinical issues, which suggests that these issues were not felt to be pressing by the clinical community. What few clinical applications can be found in the literature were written by authors who thought they were discussing schizoid patients but who, we believe (and will further argue), were actually discussing quiet border-line individuals.

The literature we are reviewing, then, is sparse as regards papers specifically addressing the as-if personality. Most of the works we will discuss were in fact written to study other psychological conditions and unintentionally shed light on as-if patients. Such a circumstance is not surprising when a subject is in the early stages of study, and, even though the as-if concept has been known for over half a century, it is certainly still in its infancy. At this time, the search for a literature to help define and develop the as-if concept will of necessity be synthetic, a matter of reaching not only into the as-if literature but also into related topics and applying some of what we find there to the subject at hand.

AS-IF PHENOMENA AND THE CONCEPT OF A CONTINUUM

Deutsch's (1942) well-known paper on the "As If Personality" has long been the standard for discussion and defines most of the categories for debate. Deutsch described a type of patient who, at the time, had seldom been seen in therapy and who presented a set of intriguing and puzzling characteristics. This was a patient whose social functioning seemed normal, whose intellectual abilities appeared intact, and whose emotional expressions were by and large appropriate. Nevertheless, some-thing was plainly amiss; Deutsch observed, "the individual's whole relationship to life has something about it which is lacking in genuineness and yet outwardly runs along 'as if' it were complete" (p. 302). Such people seemed to fit into any situation, creating the illusion of involvement when in fact there was an absence of emotional investment. The as-if indi-vidual, as described by Deutsch, appeared outwardly amiable but had no lasting loyalty to persons or principles. Deutsch also observed the absence of a sense of identity. Encounters with them left others with a feeling of strangeness that was hard to define. Nayman (1991) recently described the matter by saying, "something feels staged, yet uncalculated, as if one had walked onto a movie set which the actors take as reality" (p. 492). Inevitably, even lay persons found themselves asking of such individuals, "What is wrong with them?"

Most subsequent writers have thought that there were very few true as-if personalities. We mentioned in the previous chapter that Deutsch herself, a quarter of a century after her original paper, said that she had seen only one additional as-if individual (reported in Weiss 1966). Yet it is hard to account for enduring interest in the as-if concept if the phenomenon is indeed so rare. While there have been very few works that addressed the as-if patient, many works summarize and reference Deutsch's original work on the subject in the process of discussing schizoid, borderline, and schizophrenic patients, and her paper is fairly widely included in collections. How can we understand the popularity of Deutsch's paper and frequent references to it in the literature if there are so few such individuals?

Ross (1967) has been one of the few writers to consider that there may be more true as-if patients than suspected. He suggests, moreover, that the as-if personality not be viewed as a sharply demarcated syndrome; he outlines, instead, a spectrum, with pure as-if personalities at one end, as-if states of mind and pseudo-as-if states in the middle, and as-if phenomena in people who are well functioning at the other end. He reasons that whatever the true number of "pure" cases, "there are as-if states which may occur transiently in a wide spectrum of individual personalities ranging from apparently normal to definitely psychotic" (p. 61).

Greenson's (1958) work on screen identity offers support for Ross's view. Greenson observes that many different character types display as-if phenomena and that we can speak of as-if symptoms, as-if mechanisms, and as-if character traits. These three states have several common features when viewed from a descriptive point of view: a lack of genuineness, transience, and changeability. Greenson believes that true as-if patients are fixated around the age of eighteen months, which would place them in the throes of early individuation from the mother.

Greenson also described patients who resembled as-if personalities but who were not, he felt, as sick. Similar to as-if individuals, these other patients continually sought the company of others, searching for need-satisfying object relationships. These persons were well oriented to reality and usually were socially successful; however, they were incapable of being alone. Similar to the shifting morality of the as-if personality, Greenson noted that their superegos were eminently corruptible. Ross (1967), who later reviewed Greenson's paper, assigned these patients to a pseudo-as-if category (as described by Katan 1958), largely because they showed greater capacity for affect. The pseudo-as-if individual differs from the pure as-if personality in that the former's identifications are of the secondary type; they are identifications with real objects.

Annie Reich (1953) indirectly contributed to the idea of an as-if continuum. In an important paper, she dealt with the various ways a woman could make an object choice at the narcissistic level (i.e., love an object she had once wanted to be). Along with a nonpathological form, Reich discusses two pathological versions of such an object choice, one of which is an as-if object tie. The as-if relationship consists of what Reich calls "transitory pseudo infatuation" (p. 190) and begins with a powerful overvaluation of the man, who is virtually elevated to the status of a deity. During this period of idealization, the woman takes on the man's characteristics and values as if she had no personality of her own. The relationship then suddenly changes, and the formerly idealized object is denigrated, "dropped like a hot potato," as Reich puts it, and usually quickly replaced with a new idealized figure. This sequence often occurs over a few days, and the intensity of affect seemed "spurious and unreal" (p. 192) to Reich. It was the spurious nature of the relationship that led Reich to use the as-if label.

Reich's studies led her to conclude that the mothers of such women were exceedingly narcissistic and overly concerned with what impression their children would make on others. These mothers tended to use their children for exhibitionistic purposes. Their daughters—the as-if individuals—identified in turn with glorified images of their mothers. Curiously, in their later as-if relationships, it seemed as though almost anyone would suffice. While some of these women at least required that other people might perceive the man as valuable, others had no discrimination at all: "Some of them can glorify anything and are ready to identify themselves with anyone happening to enter their sphere of life" (p. 193). The intent appears to be building the other person into a grand figure in order then to identify with him in a primitive, imitative type of identification. Reich did not believe that these women were true as-if personalities, saying that they appeared more affectively alive than the patients Deutsch had described.

At the more normal end of the spectrum, aspects of as-if behavior have been found in the first playful imitations of the parents by the young child (Jacobson 1961). Anna Freud (1937) as well as Reich (1953) has noted as-if features in adolescents whose relationships with peers involved swiftly changing identifications and imitations. As Anna Freud observed, the teenage girl's "violent love fixations" are not object ties but primitive identifications. She believed that these passionate relationships serve a defensive function, bridging the gap to the external world as old relationships are ruptured and reworked. Gardner and Wagner (1986) observe that few would describe these episodes as pathological. Passionate fixations are likely to be viewed as adaptive efforts to "construct a sense of identity as the adolescent separates from the family" (p. 145). This as-if behavior is transient, lasting only as long as it is needed to help negotiate problems in identity formation.

There are other factors that help distinguish as-if phenomena in normal individuals from as-if personalities. In the latter, as-if traits appear before adolescence and do not have the character of defensive structures, according to Reich (1953). Thus, there seem to be some grounds for Ross's (1967) proposal of a continuum embodying a variety of as-if states, and there appear to be grounds for distinguishing nonmalignant as-if states from pathological conditions. In normal individuals, as-if phenomena serve a defensive purpose and are transient, while more purely pathological as-if conditions seem structural in nature and therefore become a way of life.

THE QUESTION OF THE RELATIONSHIP BETWEEN AS-IF AND SCHIZOID PHENOMENA

In her seminal paper, Deutsch (1942) depicts the as-if personality as a type of schizoid individual who behaves as though he or she has normal emotional responses but who is actually affectively empty. Any expression of emotion is formal, and affective engagement with others lacks depth, according to Deutsch. Attachments are rapidly formed but superficial; there is no genuine investment in others, as might be expected of schizoid patients. Later writers (e.g., Khan 1960, Meissner 1984, Millon 1981, Ross 1967) have agreed with Deutsch, either directly by regarding the as-if personality as a subset of schizoid pathology, or indirectly by including cases we would consider to be as-if individuals in discussions of schizoid patients.

Consequently, some very cogent observations about the as-if patient are included in studies of schizoid pathology. A particularly good example is Khan's (1960) important article, "Clinical Aspects of the Schizoid Personality." Khan believed that Fairbairn's (1952) work on schizoid phenomena, Deutsch's (1942) study of the as-if personality, Winnicott's (1955) early thinking on the false self, and Greenson's (1958) already mentioned work on screen identity all address the same type of patient. Following Fairbairn, Khan believed that this patient is properly regarded as a schizoid individual. Since Fairbairn's work forms the foundation for much of contemporary thinking about schizoid pathology, perhaps a brief review of his ideas will help set the stage for an exploration of Khan's paper and for comparing as-if and schizoid patients in general.

Fairbairn (1952) describes a core of intrapsychic tendencies in schizoid patients that apparently derive from the mother-infant relationship in the early oral stage. This core carries three prominent characteristics: (1) an attitude of omnipotence, (2) an attitude of isolation and detachment, and (3) a preoccupation with inner reality. As a consequence of these traits, the schizoid individual has trouble with "that element of giving which is involved in expressing emotion toward others . . ." (p. 15). This difficulty is due to the fantasy that giving means losing and becoming depleted. Emotions are therefore kept inside, in order to avoid their loss, and this causes schizoid persons to appear detached, aloof, and remote. Two basic techniques help such individuals compensate for the missing affects. First, they may take roles, like actors playing on a stage, and, second, they may show a kind of exhibitionism that replaces giving with showing (p. 16).

Fairbairn argues that schizoid individuals are not only afraid of being depleted themselves, they are also afraid that the intensity of their neediness can deplete others. Loving and being loved can both feel dangerous, then, and others are kept at a (safe) distance. Fairbairn describes the process as "depersonalization of the object and de-emotionalization of the object relationship" (p. 15). In addition, Fairbairn traces the source of the schizoid individual's feeling that he or she is different from others, pointing to "an unsatisfactory emotional relationship with [the] parents and particularly with [the] mother." Fairbairn believes that schizoid patients were reared by "the type of mother who fails to convince her child by spontaneous and genuine expressions of affection that she herself loves him as a person. Both possessive and indifferent mothers fall into this category . . ." (p. 13). This troubled maternal relationship is seen as the foundation of the later inability to love and be loved.

From this brief summary, we can see some of the traits that seem to be a bridge between schizoid and as-if pathology. Fairbairn's ideas may be taken as an explanation for the as-if individual's inability to give emotionally, for the patient's tendency to take on and act out roles, and for the ability to enter into and leave relationships fairly speedily, as though people were interchangeable. Given these many traits in common, it is not a farfetched conclusion that as-if pathology can be located along a schizoid continuum (Meissner 1984).

Fairbairn's description of schizoid pathology, however, also contains many elements that are not consistent with the as-if personality. For instance, Fairbairn references the isolation and detachment of the schizoid individual and also that patient's "overvaluation of the internal at the expense of the external world" (p. 23). We have not found either trait in as-if patients and do not believe that these traits are consistent with Deutsch's (1942) description of her patients. By contrast, we believe that as-if patients have trouble being alone or at the very least being out of a relationship through which they can achieve some definition (cf. Meissner 1984, pp. 220, 237) and that they have virtually no inner world to overvalue. Finally, Fairbairn insists on the key role played by secrecy in schizoid patients; he thinks secrecy to be part of a quiet and hidden narcissism in such individuals. While we also believe there is unexpected narcissism in as-if patients (this is discussed in Chapters 3 and 6), we do not believe it is at all as pervasive or important as Fairbairn finds it to be in schizoid individuals, nor do we believe that as-if individuals are typically secretive or deceptive. Those adjectives imply a much more lively inner world than we have found in our patients.

We are therefore strongly inclined to separate schizoid and as-if patients as quite different, and we approach Khan's (1960) important contribution believing that most of what he proposes about schizoid individuals is in fact applicable to as-if patients instead. Some of Khan's findings include the interesting proposition that these patients "tend to provoke or seduce the analyst into a tantalizing relation to their material, e.g., past history or internal reality. Hence the danger of overinterpretation" (p. 433). Khan also notes that these patients "exhibit" rather than communicate psychic contents. In effect, "the patient from the outside in cooperation with the analyst is having a good peep at himself . . . there is an intensive self-engrossment in relation to which the analyst is merely a spectator'' (p. 433).

We believe that this is not a picture of a schizoid patient, but, rather, of an as-if patient, someone *who exists more in the response and interest of the therapist than in his or her own right.* Khan is presupposing more identity and sense of self than is actually there. He writes as though these patients bring to treatment some coherent sense of self—albeit highly damaged—and he believes that the therapist is used to represent and experience aspects of the self that the patient wishes to split off or at least avoid (cf. p. 434). This would make sense if these were schizoid patients; we believe, however, that Khan is in error on this issue, that there is no reliable sense of sameness or continuity in the patients he describes, that they do in fact have identity *only* in the responses, roles, and expectations offered by the other, in this case the therapist. We think that Khan has offered a sensitive description of as-if patients, who manage to make the therapist more invested in their lives than they are, whose psychic contents are more ''in'' the therapist than ''in'' the patient, and who are therefore having a good peep at themselves, although not in the way Khan thought: They are seeing themselves in the response of the therapist, much as infants may catch glimpses of themselves in the mirroring responses of their mothers.

Khan observes the usual primitive defenses in the patients he describes, such as splitting, devaluation of objects (and of emotional experience in general), projective identification, and idealization. However, he sees these as forms of communication and not simply as resistance. They ''carry within them a very true picture of [their] infantile and devalued reality'' (p. 434). Focusing on the use of idealization, Khan arrives at an interesting conclusion about the way these patients can impress therapists as being psychopathic or, at least, amoral. In contrast to other writers, including Deutsch, who see the as-if patient's casual morality as a defect in superego formation, Khan suggests that the behavior is an attempt to fulfill the demands of a highly organized ego ideal. Most intriguing here is that the ego ideal is not built from introjection of idealized parental objects; rather, it is the reverse. The schizoid/as-if patient's ego ideal is a replacement for unsatisfactory primary figures, and idealization is a way of dealing with deprivation from the primary object (cf. Meissner 1984).

One of the most important parts of Khan's (1960) paper is his attention to the nature of the therapeutic task. Except for brief attention the subject receives in Meissner (1984), Khan is alone in addressing this question. He believes that the patient seeks regression "to the primitive stages of dependence and undifferentiated unintegrated affectivity" in therapy and that fear of such a regression constitutes "their most adamant resistance and negativity" (p. 436). The therapeutic task parallels the role of the mother; the therapist must become the "primary environment." That is, these patients must "utterly depend upon [the therapist's] ability to empathize and crystallize this into an affective ego-experience." Khan observes that such dependency may invite the therapist to intervene and offer direction to the patient, but this is not what the patient needs. The actual therapeutic task is "to enable the patient to experience regressively and affectively in the analytic setting the total fragmented reality that he is carrying around under magical control."

Khan makes an additional point that bears on therapy. He observes that these patients rely extensively on the hope they generate in others but that ultimately they "reduce all this to futility and the persons involved feel defeated, demoralized, and rendered inane and useless" (p. 433). This sort of countertransferential response is common in those working with schizoid patients and is less typically associated with as-if patients, since the latter can very often make the therapist feel content with what is happening in treatment. However, once a therapist realizes that his or her patient suffers as-if pathology, such contentment may very well be replaced with the discouragement Khan describes. The meaninglessness of the relationship and the patient's willingness to substitute words for reality may deplete the therapist's reservoir of hope.

We believe, with Khan, that all of this is part of what the patient needs from the therapist. These patients are too fragmented and undifferentiated to experience for long in any organized way such affects as despair, anger, weakness, or need. It falls to the therapist to feel these things on behalf of the patient, as it were. The therapist, that is, will be aware of these feelings as regards the patient long before the patient is. The therapist provides an experiential unity over long periods of time that the patient is not capable of, offering a kind of containment and definition to the patient's affective life before that life is organized enough to be experienced in a coherent way by the patient.

FURTHER CONSIDERATIONS ON THE RELATIONSHIP BETWEEN AS-IF AND SCHIZOID PHENOMENA

In the preceding section, we referred several times to our opinion that there is essentially no inner life or sense of self in the as-if patient. This is an unusual and even an extreme claim (one that is developed further in Chapter 3). It might seem that the category of false self bypasses the need for such an extreme position, since that concept perhaps accounts for the automatic compliance and general superficiality of affect that we attribute to the absence of a sense of self. Thus, we want to pursue the question of whether there can be said to be a false-self organization in as-if patients.

Khan (1960, p. 432) argues that the concept of false self does apply to as-if personalities, and he refers to Winnicott's (1955) paper, "Clinical Varieties of Transference" to describe the false-self process. Winnicott proposes a hidden true self that is protected by the false self from the environment's empathic failures toward the small child. The false self "develops a pattern corresponding to the pattern of environmental failure. In this way the true self is not involved in the reacting and so preserves a continuity of being" (p. 296). The false self, then, is self protective and reflects some self valuation.

Winnicott's thoughts on the false-self adaptation spring from his struggle to understand the schizoid dilemma, in particular how the infant can adapt to an unreliable maternal environment during the holding stage of infancy. When there is a consistent failure to meet the baby's spontaneous gestures empathically—that is, when the mother fails to "decode" the infant's movements or sounds and replaces them with her own attitudes and feelings—the infant presumably experiences anxiety that is strong enough to threaten disintegration. The true self is threatened with engulfment in its relation to objects and withdraws inwardly. As the true self is withdrawn, a false self comes to the fore. The false self responds to the mother through compliance and by splitting off, or dissociating, its original self assertiveness. The false self is engaged in the double task of hiding and caring for the true self, while complying with the outside world's demands. The false self may appear quite normal and adaptive, but it is designed for preservation, not for gratification. The false self cannot experience life and feel real, according to Winnicott. The true self, meanwhile, becomes impoverished as a consequence of being hidden and lacking experience with other people.

The question is whether the false self concept applies to the as-if personality. The false self presumably protects a rudimentary and poorly developed true self from the threat of internal destruction. This is the schizoid adaptation, and its result is a kind of poverty to the emotional life and in relating to others and a fine-tuned excellence at mimicry or false compliance. As with other aspects of schizoid pathology, the false self concept sounds similar to phenomena encountered in as-if patients. But the conclusion that as-if patients demonstrate a false self rests on elevating the false self (and the true self) to the status of agencies or structures within the personality. We do not believe that Winnicott intended these concepts to be used in such a way. Our impression is that he used these terms somewhat poetically, to describe phenomena that could be sensed interpersonally but not quite witnessed. That is, he was not trying to describe an intrapsychic agency but, rather, a manner of relating to oneself and to other people.

Pontalis (1981) makes just this point in an important paper, "The Birth and Recognition of the Self." He says, "the distinction between false and true self is not a *conceptual* one. It is even less aimed at differentiating two *agencies* within the same person" (p. 146). Rather, he says, "true and false are not to be understood as inherent qualities of the individual. . . . They designate movements in a relationship" (p. 147). By relationship, Pontalis refers to the interplay between maturational processes in the young child and the environment's contribution. True and false self, then, describe a child's freedom (or the lack of it) to be spontaneous and genuine in experiencing his or her feelings, wishes, and intentions, and in presenting these to the world. When we say that the schizoid patient shows a false-self organization, we mean to say that the patient seldom if ever proceeds on the basis of his or her genuine preferences and intentions but, by contrast, demonstrates automatic compliance to the apparent expectations of other persons. We mean, in addition, to say that the patient's genuine preferences and intentions, although very poorly developed, have at one time been a feature of relating to the world but are now hidden from both the world's and the patient's view.

We do not believe this describes the as-if patient. Returning again to Pontalis, he speculates that the as-if personality "confronts us with the possibility of an *absence* of the self" (p. 130). Using the metaphor of "an empty psychic space," Pontalis suggests that "psychic space is not constituted [but] is just an empty wrapping" (p. 130) in as-if individuals. Even the psychotic patient does not present such a possibility; in psychosis, says Pontalis, the self is split and dissociated, but it is present. In addition, psychotic individuals seem to have some inner world; they are constantly engaged in ejecting dangerous internal objects, trying to make their private world less menacing and confusing. By contrast, the as-if patient does not appear to be trying to get rid of internal objects; external reality completely replaces an inner, private world. As Pontalis puts it, "we shall say that they find their psychic space in the exterior world, they need a producer to feel alive" (p. 131).

We agree with Pontalis's position. In effect, we believe that there is no false self organization in the as-if individual because there is no true self to protect. As Pontalis put it, the as-if patient's inner world is in the external world, entirely given and held by the expectations and roles offered by others.

THE AS-IF PERSONALITY AS A TYPE OF BORDERLINE CONDITION

In the first chapter, we suggested that Deutsch's as-if patients almost certainly showed borderline pathology, a concept to which Deutsch did not have access at the time she wrote, in the mid-thirties. This suggestion is not original with us; many writers (e.g., Capponi 1979, Dorr, et al. 1983, Gardner and Wagner 1986, Kernberg 1967, Meissner 1984, Modell 1963, Weiss 1966) have noted the connection. For example, in the panel discussion summarized by Weiss (1966), these borderline characteristics were described as typical of the as-if personality: primitive object relations without object constancy; poorly developed superego, prevalence of the primary identification process; absence of a sense of identity; emotional superficiality and poverty of affect, of which the patient is unaware; and lack of insight (cf. Capponi 1979).

The study by Grinker, Werble, and Drye (1968) of fifty-one hospitalized patients is well known, yielding one of the first classifications of borderline conditions. Group III in that study consisted of "adaptive, affectless, defended, as-if patients" (p. 87). Grinker and his colleagues found that these patients showed bland, adaptive, appropriate behavior. They showed little in the way of negative affect or behavior, although they also showed relatively little positive affect. Their relationships tended to be complementary; they changed roles continually depending on the important other to whom they were relating and adapting. Finally, "there is no indication of a well-developed sense of self-identity" (p. 86). Thus, in this study, as-if pathology is seen as a distinct subtype of borderline pathology.

Kernberg (1967), Meissner (1984), and Modell (1963) have regarded the as-if syndrome as part of a borderline spectrum. Kernberg (1975) sees the as-if individual among other "low level" disorders with borderline organization, characterized by disturbed identity in the presence of intact reality testing. Also working with the concept of a borderline continuum, Meissner (1984) suggests that as-if pathology can be located in the area of organization of the self. The patient's as-if mechanisms achieve a transient cohesiveness to the self through superficial, imitative, and idealizing object attachments. The absence of such organization is an important aspect of borderline pathology. It has been described by Green (1977), who speaks of "a lack of cohesiveness, a lack of unity, and above all a lack of coherence and an impression of contradictory sets of relations. . . . This failure in integration gives the observer a feeling of aloofness, an absence of vitality" (p. 37). In words that could have been written about the as-if patient specifically, Green goes on to say that, "The discourse of the borderline is not a chain of words, representations, or affects, but rather—like a pearl necklace without a string—words, representations, affects contiguous in time and space but not in meaning" (p. 37).

In spite of these arguments for regarding as-if pathology as a borderline condition, Gunderson and Singer (1975) have raised an important objection. In their study of borderline psychopathology, they point to the predominance of intense, destructive hostility in borderline patients. Considering this to be one of the key traits shown in borderline states, they exclude as-if patients, noting that the latter simply do not demonstrate intense anger.

We, of course, do not agree with Gunderson and Singer's position. Their objection seems to be a matter of how narrowly the borderline concept should be defined. Gunderson and Singer are clearly referring to what we have called the noisy borderline patient. If intense hostility is a necessary hallmark of all borderline conditions, then two groups from the study by Grinker and his co-workers (1968) would not qualify (in fact, Gunderson and Singer criticize that study), nor would portions of Kernberg's (1967) continuum. We believe that this results in too exclusive a category, one that rests on a few flagrant symptoms rather than on underlying personality structure and dynamics. We therefore agree with those writers who have placed as-if patients along a borderline spectrum.

UNDERSTANDING AS-IF CONDITIONS FROM THE STANDPOINT OF IDENTITY DISTURBANCE

In their incisive paper on the as-if personality, Gardner and Wagner (1986) note that "the disturbance of identity is the prominent clinical feature in the history and presentation of as-if patients that argues for including them in the group of patients with borderline personality organization" (p. 145). They go on to point out that relationships characterized by identification and imitation may suggest identity diffusion (cf. Erikson 1959). Gardner and Wagner also observe that a reliance on imitation allows the as-if individual to look normal but that depending on such a fundamental psychological function reveals the severity of the identity disturbance. They see the as-if patient's identity problems as different from identity disturbances shown by other anxious, impulsive, and labile borderline individuals.

Much of what we now know about identity formation comes from Erikson's (1959) pioneering work on the subject. He speaks of ego-identity, meaning "both a persistent sameness within oneself (selfsameness) and a persistent sharing of some kind of essential character with others" (p. 12). Emphasizing the period of adolescence as crucial for consolidating identity, Erikson believes that adolescents attempt to integrate what they know of themselves and their world into a stable continuum of past knowledge, present experience, and future goals. In striving to develop continuity of character and also inner solidarity with group ideals, adolescents try to elaborate a cohesive sense of personal feeling. As Erikson says, "identity formation begins where the usefulness of multiple identification ends" (p. 122).

Erikson uses the term identity diffusion to describe the adolescent's failure to integrate earlier identifications into a harmonious psychosocial identity. Clinical phenomena associated with identity diffusion include: impaired capacity for intimacy and mutuality, lack of commitment to an occupational choice, and contradictory identifications. These characteristics might be used to describe as-if individuals, and they reveal the reasons for considering as-if pathology from the standpoint of identity disturbance. Difficulties with identity formation underlie the as-if patient's characteristic difficulty in making a commitment to a career line or to long-term attachments.

Meissner (1984) has noted that any intense engagement— whether friendship, competition, sexual involvement, or love—carries with it the threat of fusion and loss of identity. The attempt to avoid such a threat may then lead to "stereotyped or formalized interpersonal relationships, or even the frantic seeking of intimacy with improbable or inappropriate partners. Such attachments, whether as friendships or affairs, become simply attempts to delineate identity by a form of mutual narcissistic mirroring" (p. 221). Similarly, Kernberg (1975) has noted that individuals suffering disturbed identity experience a sense of inner emptiness, and, while they may appear normally sociable and even charming, they have no intimate friends and trust no one. Although they are incapable of experiencing tender feelings for others, they tend to be sexually active to the point of promiscuity, at times approaching a "polymorphous-perverse" type of sexuality. This promiscuity presumably compensates for the absence of genuine love feelings.

Deutsch (1942) noted what might be termed a moral laxness about as-if patients, particularly where sexuality is concerned, and we have already noted that she regarded this as evidence of impaired superego development. We are more inclined to view this trait as a reflection of identity diffusion, which is often accompanied by unstable gender identity. Akhtar (1992) notes that individuals suffering identity diffusion often show a kind of "gender dysphoria." He argues that such persons often have to struggle with their heterosexuality because of weak gender identity, or "they may fail to convey a deep sense of possessing any gender at all, thus displaying a state of psychic eunuchoidism" (p. 36). This suggests that sexual promiscuity in as-if patients may be an attempt to confirm maleness or femaleness in some way.

One of the intriguing issues in identity diffusion is the individual's experience of time. Without a sense of continuity—of intentionality and agency that stretch from the past into the present and toward the future—there is no abiding feeling of selfsameness. In a thought-provoking paper, Nayman (1991) relates the as-if individual's identity diffusion to a disturbed time sense. Nayman describes as-if patients as feeling trapped in an inner void, reaching outside themselves to identify with other groups or persons in hope of finding a sense of self. Thus, "time becomes swallowed into an eternal future, a future that is hopeful because it always promises new objects of identification" (p. 495). Nayman goes on to say that the "as-if personality is grounded by an *imaginary* counterpart: a substantial self lies just ahead, in a future constantly anticipated" (p. 495). As long as the future is effectively cut off from what comes before, a stable sense of personal continuity will be hard to attain.

The as-if concept is relatively undeveloped since Deutsch. What development has occurred has been in the area of describing an as-if continuum and in trying to relate as-if pathology to other disorders, such as schizoid and borderline conditions. There is support in the literature for establishing a continuum of as-if states. With one end defined by the as-if personality, the other end is comprised of normal and transient as-if states, such as those shown by infants and adolescents. Along the continuum are other pathological conditions, all of which involve some plasticity, superficiality in relationships, role playing, and identity disturbance.

Much of the literature assigns as-if pathology to the larger category of schizoid phenomena. The absence of genuine investment in others, shallow and easily exchanged relationships, and affective impoverishment characterize both types of patient. Some writers have assumed the presence of a false self organization in as-if patients, which would further push them toward the schizoid camp. We disagree with the tendency to equate schizoid and as-if patients. We believe that schizoid patients are better organized and present a more coherent sense of self than do as-if patients. We do agree with those who see as-if patients as a subset of borderline pathology, however. Those who take this position point to the presence of fundamental, or primitive, psychological processes and to a lack of cohesiveness in the as-if personality.

Finally, there is wide agreement that as-if pathology involves a severe identity disturbance. The personality is built around primitive types of identification, including imitation, which lends some appearance of normalcy but also prevents a sense of continuity with self across time. Disturbances in sexuality, vocational choice, capacity for interpersonal commitment, and time sense have all been defined as elements of the as-if individual's derailed identity.

What is missing from the literature on the as-if personality is as important as what is present. There is no detailed discussion of etiology, no close description of what exactly goes awry and how. In addition, there is very little clinical literature beyond Deutsch's original cases, and we are unaware of any (even modestly) detailed discussion of treatment principles or technique in any work specifically addressing as-if pathology. It is, in many ways, an unexplored field.

3

Etiology of the As-If Personality

INTRODUCTION

In the previous chapter we noted that little work has been done on the etiology of the as-if personality. We are not aware of any closely reasoned, detailed explanation of the developmental and interpersonal issues involved in as-if pathology or of what turns those issues in an as-if direction. We have also observed that the literature has not elaborated particular clinical approaches to these patients. Doubtless these two problems go together; it will be difficult to decide what clinical approaches might reach as-if pathology until we understand the crucial issues involved in its formation.

In our view, etiology can be profitably explored from two different perspectives. First, we can examine the formation of as-if pathology from the standpoint of the child's internalized object relations. This perspective focuses on the child's private experiences and on the residues of expectation left by those experiences. This approach searches for internalized images of self and other, which, in our view, chiefly refers to the types of interpersonal experiences the child is most likely to create or be receptive to. An object-relations perspective is typically dyadic, focusing on mother–child interactions in the first three to four years of life.

Second, it is possible to look at patterns of interaction within the patient's family. The idea behind such an approach is that as-if pathology, like most pathology, carries a certain logic. Behaviors that seem odd or even insane in a normal setting may well have made some sense in the world in which the patient grew up. From this perspective, pathology does not exist "in" the individual but is more an expression of the social system in which the individual develops. This second perspective, which we associate chiefly with R. D. Laing (cf. Laing and Esterson 1964), differs from the first by its focus on what is happening in the patient's social world rather than in the patient's internal world. Both perspectives, however, are inherently interactional, and we are going to use the second perspective chiefly as an elaboration of the first.

We believe that each approach is useful in the case of the quiet borderline individual, and we propose in this chapter to study etiology from both perspectives, beginning with the internalized object relations approach. From the standpoint of the child's internal world, as-if pathology has its roots in a particular type of breakdown during mother–infant mirroring. We believe that the breakdown that leads to the as-if orientation is not solely the work of the parent or the child but, rather, something to which both parent and child must make a contribution. We noted in Chapter 1 that normal mirroring is an interaction, and so is pathological mirroring.

To put the matter in general terms, we believe that the parental contribution is to be relatively self-absorbed and uninvolved with the young child, failing through that uninvolvement to confirm certain of the child's expanding feelings, needs, and wishes. In particular, the parent seems unable/unwilling to respond to the child's normal but greedy demands for dependency. The child's contribution is to be passive in the face of this failure, not fighting for a more intimate response or protesting the parental detachment. Instead of fighting or protesting, the child accepts and/or creates a reversal of normal mirroring; the child becomes a reflection of the parents' needs and wishes, trying to find ways to bring the parents to life and lead to interaction with them.

Discussion of this set of issues necessarily leads us to the subject of object constancy. We have elsewhere (Cohen and Sherwood 1989, 1991, Sherwood 1989) referred to the importance of object constancy in healthy development and the key role played by its failure in the borderline states. Essentially, the story of object constancy is the story of how the child discovers his or her own reality through the crucible of the relationship to the mother. Thus, in what follows we will trace elements of normal development as we see it, in particular, development of the child's growing sense of his or her own substantiality. We will then turn to what happens when this process goes awry, and we will propose a particular scenario that we believe leads to as-if development. The chapter concludes with a study of what family dynamics the clinician may expect to find and their contribution to the formation of the quiet borderline state.

BEGINNINGS: THE CHILD'S DISCOVERY OF SELF AND WORLD

Very soon after birth, the outside world starts to make an impact. Even the very young infant begins to notice the external world, although at times it may not be a particularly pleasant discovery for the infant or, for that matter, for the world. In place of the relatively tensionless state of life in the womb (cf. Grunberger 1989) there is the rise and fall of instinctual needs, urges, and hungers. The mother responds to these, and the cycle of rising tension followed by satisfaction begins to build a slowly emerging awareness that the child's body is different from the world. In the womb there is no "there," but after birth it is different. As Schachtel (1959) suggests, the infant finds "There is something out there, which has to come, to make me feel good" (p. 255).

Even in the first weeks of life most infants give signs of attending to the outside world by showing a sense of the direction from which lights and noises come. By two months infants can focus on objects visually and can track them. These are early forms of what Schachtel calls focal attention, or the ability to narrow the perceptual beam, filtering out some data and attending to selected elements of what is there. As children come to do this, they move beyond rough impressions of their own comfort/discomfort and, instead, start to construct and interpret a separate reality, the external world.

For the infant, the most important thing to be discovered in the world is surely the mother's face. Of course, the baby notices and responds to the mother's face before focal attention is a possibility. Before two months, however, babies are responding to general shapes, animated movements, and intensities when they notice the mother's face (Sherrod 1981), or to what Stern (1985) calls "the more 'global' qualities of experience" (p. 57). Such fluid scanning of the mother's face changes when the child becomes capable of distance perception, or of directing the focus of seeing and hearing. Infants are then able to focus on the specific features of the mother's face, initially her eyes and later her mouth.

The change has a dramatic impact on mothers, who suddenly feel, "My baby recognizes me!" On the mother's part there is a dramatically heightened sense of personalized interaction (Southwood 1973). Others who know the child can see the change as well and usually alter the way they treat the baby. They start to deal with the child more as a complete person than they did before (Stern 1985, p. 69). We might say that the baby notices the world, and the world responds.

If the change is dramatic for mothers, it is much more so for infants. What infants discover in their mother's faces is— themselves. Winnicott (1967) and Southwood (1973) note that mothers tend to mimic and echo their baby's facial expressions and noises as they play together, an observation confirmed many times by infant researchers as well (e.g., Malatesta and Haviland 1983, Uzgiris 1974, 1984). This mirroring is fairly frequent; Stern (1985, p. 147) reports that mothers make roughly one emotionally attuned reflection of their child's affective displays every minute they play together. As Winnicott (1967) succinctly puts it, "The precursor of the mirror is the mother's face" (p. 26, emphasis deleted).

A number of authors (e.g., Mahler and Furer 1968, Spitz and Wolf 1946, Winnicott 1967) have suggested that this mirroring interaction is one through which mothers give their babies some sense of self. We do not believe this is too extreme a claim. To see its truth, we should look briefly at the subject of perception; it is the child's maturing perceptual apparatus in the first months of life that makes mirroring possible and, in turn, allows the mother to give the baby an early sense of self.

The child's private experience is vague and ill defined as long as near or proximal modes of perception are the chief form of experience (as they are for about the first two months of life). Proximal perception—taste, smell, touch, proprioception—chiefly gives information about our response to a stimulus, but it gives little information about the objective qualities of the stimulus. At most, proximal modes of perception tell us something about the object's interaction with us. As long as the infant must rely on proximal perception, therefore, information about the world will be global, imprecise, and thoroughly egocentric.

By contrast, distal perception—sight and sound—opens up a new world. Sight and sound offer the chance to gain information about the stimulus itself rather than simply our interaction with it. This information is far more detailed and precise than can be gained through proximal forms of perception. The world becomes more textured and differentiated, and, as important, alternate perspectives gradually become available as the child moves away from experiencing objects solely in terms of whether they cause pleasure/unpleasure. This important change in perception, or the capacity for focal attention, takes place at about two months—the same time, as mentioned above, mothers start to have a sense that, "My baby recognizes me!"

Babies seem to "recognize" the mother at this time because they suddenly see *themselves* in her mirroring gaze. Private experience becomes unexpectedly visible when it is reflected in the mother's face, body movements, and sounds. The mother's reflection of the child is not simply one more thing in the steadily enlarging world of out there. Rather, in her reflection the child can join proximal cues with distal perception; proprioceptive feedback from the child's own facial movements, sounds, and visceral reactions are seen and heard in the mother's matching facial movements and sounds. With this, a change of vast significance occurs: *For the first time, there is the possibility of not merely feeling comfortable or uncomfortable but of seeing that I feel comfortable or uncomfortable.*

When babies scowl, grunt, kick, or wave their arms, parents can often determine which affect category the child will experience by responding as if the child were angry, playful, and so forth. The baby can then follow the parental lead and display whatever affect the parents suggested. This is a clear example of the way small children let their parents define private experiences. When older infants are in ambiguous situations, such as taking a slight fall or knocking something over, they frequently look to their mothers and follow her cue on what emotion is appropriate (Stern 1985, p. 132). In short, infants use the mother's responses to interpret and validate what they feel, need, and want. For instance, it is difficult to imagine small children being able to mold the urges and tensions they feel when frustrated into an organized and defined experience of anger without their parent's willingness to see, reflect, and validate that anger first. Children learn to look to the mother's face—and later to her general response—as an explanation or representation of what they themselves are experiencing internally or privately.

Infants start to become visible to themselves in the mother's face and, later, in her other mirroring responses. As infants focus on the mother's face, they discover representations *there* of what they feel *in here*. As long as proprioceptive feedback is the child's primary source of information about feelings, excitements, and appetites, private experience is by necessity ill defined. By contrast, when these private experiences become visible on the mother's face and in her other mirroring responses, they are clarified and defined, like all objects of distal perception. The infant may not be able to distinguish between excitement and hunger, for example, but the mother can gradually intuit the difference and match those different states with differing facial expressions and sounds. Through this type of interaction with the mother and other caretakers, the child comes to distinguish and define private experience. Even though these are the child's own private experiences, they become real to the child as distinct experiences only when the child sees them in distal perception, on the mother's face, while also experiencing them subjectively. Parents thereby play the crucial role in their child's coming to define and separate discrete emotions, needs, and wishes (cf. Miller 1981, pp. 9–10).

Children find that their intentions, emotions, and needs feel real when their experience "in here" is congruent with the parent's response "out there." To put the matter more strongly, nothing about the child feels real to that child until it is first seen by the mother (cf. Basch 1985). The mother does not simply imitate the baby's sounds, gestures, and facial expressions; she intuits the experience behind the child's behavior and finds ways to highlight the private, or internal, experience (cf. Stern 1985, p. 142). Thus, mothers can show their babies whatever they can see there, representing with clarity the private experience the child is able to feel only vaguely and fluidly. As a corollary, what the mother fails to see in her infant will gradually be excluded from the child's experience: What is felt in here must be mirrored out there to become part of the baby's gradually developing sense of personal reality.

OBJECT CONSTANCY: THE ILLUSION OF BEING SEEN

Freud (1920) gave us a dramatic depiction of the way the mother's gaze holds the young child's reality. He described having watched a toddler who was engaged in a game of throwing away and retrieving small objects; Freud identified this game of disappearance and return as one associated with the mother's leaving and coming back. Freud observed that the toddler one day discovered his reflection in a mirror. The mirror was long but did not reach the floor, and the child spent the better part of an afternoon's separation from his mother making his own image appear and disappear by standing in front of the mirror and then crouching below it. When the mother finally returned, the toddler greeted her with the words, "Baby gone!" Freud's own commentary was that the baby tried to master anxiety over separation from the mother through repetitions of the anxiety-producing situation. Laing (1960, pp. 124–128), however, goes further. He notes that if Freud was correct, then fear of disappearing oneself is closely associated with fear of the mother's disappearance. The child did not miss his mother because he could not see her but because she could not see him! The child seems to have concluded that if he was not out there in the mother's gaze, he was objectively gone altogether.

The mirroring interaction gradually comes to hold the child's sense of his or her own reality, then, a sense that at least initially depends to a great degree on the mother's actual presence. Yet there is an irony here: The same infant who is able to define and elaborate private experience precisely because of the mother's mirroring gaze is also in the grip of urges toward independence that gradually lead away from the mother. The drive toward autonomy is well known, as is the senior toddler's marked ambivalence over this drive during what Mahler and her colleagues (1975) called the rapprochement stage of separation-individuation. Those infants who discover themselves in their mother's mirroring gaze early in life (and beyond) must find ways to leave the mother emotionally and forge the beginnings of a separate identity. It is an impressive undertaking: How do we manage to leave someone who has been so massively important?

The first step is dealing with the *mother's* ability to leave.

Before children can leave the mother emotionally they must first deal with her ability to leave them, an ability that is demonstrated in most families on a regular basis. As long as the child's sense of his or her own reality lies in the mother's mirroring gaze and, later, in her whole range of empathic responses, her leaving poses a problem. The problem is whether the child's continuing reality as a real entity in the world can be maintained independently versus whether that reality depends on the comings and goings of the one who sees the child.

This problem underlies the phenomenon commonly called stranger anxiety, in our opinion. It is generally assumed that the absence of the mother's face is the cause of stranger anxiety (Fraiberg 1969, Spitz 1957), but this is an incomplete explanation. We believe it would be more accurate to say that loss of the self is the cause. When the mother's face is replaced with the stranger's, the baby experiences a disruption in what might be termed a primitive sense of self-feeling. The child feels a rudimentary sense of self-continuity while in the mother's gaze, but there is a break in the continuity when the mother's face is replaced with the stranger's. Stranger anxiety signifies the infant's failure to find his or her familiar self in the stranger's face. When strangers look at the child, they reflect back a new image of the infant. The child appears to experience this different reflection as an *alien self,* raising questions for the child, as it were, of what happened to the *familiar me.* The absence of the mother means the absence of the familiar me as well.

Stranger anxiety is part of a larger process in which the toddler confronts loss of self when the mother leaves. For example, McDevitt (1975, pp. 718–719) describes the development of a child, Donna, who was clearly having trouble accepting separateness from the mother. Donna had just learned to stand upright at eight months. When her mother would leave the room, however, Donna could not maintain the upright posture. She did not sit down so much as she deflated into a sitting position as the mother moved out of sight.

Fleming (1975) discusses an adult patient who, apparently struggling with the same set of issues, says, "I need you with me to know how I feel about myself" (p. 754).

If children are to manage their mother's absences, they must come to perform for themselves a task originally belonging to the mother, the task of seeing the child in such a way as to make the child feel real. We have a clue in how children manage this task in their discovery and use of the mirror. Many of Mahler's and McDevitt's case studies indicate that children start to take an interest in their mirror images about the same time they first show stranger anxiety. Children do not seem to recognize their mirror images as their own until around 18 months; however, they seem quite taken with mirrors by 8 months. Bach (1977) makes an interesting comment on this; he proposes that the 8-month-old's jubilation in front of the mirror comes from joining proximal cues with distal perception, from the discovery that "he can act and thereby influence that which he sees at a distance . . ." (p. 214). Surely this process begins much earlier, though, when the infant at 2 months focuses on the mother's face and suddenly finds proprioceptive feedback matched in distal perception. The 8-month-old's discovery of the mirror reproduces this experience at a time when the mother's ability to leave becomes a problem. It does not matter whether babies recognize their mirror images: The joining of proximal cues with distal perception re-creates the mother's mirroring gaze and creates the fantasy of continuing to be seen by the mother. This last element is the key: *The child is learning to create the fantasy of being seen by the mother.*

Between 8 and 18 months the child works to create the illusion of being seen continuously by the mother. The struggles of Donna, the child mentioned previously, whose development was troubled, reveal something of the process of normal development. Early in her second year Donna used the mirror to prepare for her mother's leaving by saying "Bye-bye" to her reflection; after the mother had left, Donna would stand before the mirror and say "Mama" to her reflection. In Donna's case the mirror seems to have replaced the mother after a fashion by allowing the child to retain the experience of being seen by an important other. This implies that toddlers come to manage their mother's absence through forming the illusion that the mother who sees them is constantly available.

One of the common vehicles for developing this illusion is the game of peek-a-boo. Here the parent and child participate in creating anxiety by disappearing from view and then express the joy of reappearance. The child's delight is obvious when he or she is covered with a blanket, listening to the parent ask anxiously, "Where is Billy?" or "Where is Susie?" The child then has the chance to relieve parental anxiety by suddenly throwing off the blanket and announcing, "Here I am!" The child gains a sense of mastery by learning to tolerate temporary separation and not being seen by the parent. A critical aspect of the play is the child's eventually learning to take the active role—hiding from the parent and also making the parent disappear temporarily. (Hide and seek is a later, sublimated version of this game, also aimed at the problem of separation and reunion.)

The name for this overall process is object constancy. Most of those dealing with this topic refer to the internalization of a stable maternal representation in the child's inner world. Presumably this maternal image offers the child the sense of the mother's company even when mother and child are apart. We prefer to avoid classical language in this case and use somewhat more experience-near terms. We prefer to say that, for the senior toddler, the fantasied presence of the mother can often replace her actual, physical presence. We prefer this restatement because it highlights the central issue in object constancy: It is not an image of the mother that is internalized but the experience of being seen by her.

Object constancy is the illusion of the mother's constant availability in her mirroring function. What rests on this illusion is self constancy, the sense that one is really there, or the feeling of being real and substantial. This sense of self originates in the mother's empathic responses to her infant. Such factors as the mother's inevitable occasional empathic failures, her ability to leave the child, the child's periods of anger with the mother, and, finally, the toddler's own growing independence stimulate the child to internalize this maternal function. This internalization becomes the foundation for developing a separate identity. As the child starts to experiment with autonomy, bodily mastery, and rapidly expanding competencies, the illusion of the constant object offers a way to validate independent strivings.

The illusion of object constancy, then, begins in response to the mother's ability to leave the child. Eventually, however, the child uses this illusion as a kind of staging area for his or her own independence from the mother. We believe that the central issue of object constancy is whether the child can leave the mother—by being increasingly competent and independent and therefore needing her less. If constancy is achieved, independence can seem acceptable; the one who sees the child in such a way as to make the child feel real is felt always available to perform this function. The child can travel away emotionally, then, without leaving the self behind. The private, independent self is built on object constancy.

THE FAILURE OF CONSTANCY: THE NEED TO BE SEEN BY OTHERS

When children have not experienced the mother's responses as reflections and elaborations of their own feelings and intentions, a pathological process results. Ordinarily, the sense of private integrity is built on finding that feelings are refined, clarified, and validated in the mother's (and, later, other caretakers') sensitive, affectively attuned responses. But if children cannot feel a congruence between private feelings and the mother's responses to those feelings, the sequence tends to become reversed: *Children then learn to match their feelings, intentions, and wishes to the mother's moods and needs.* Children consequently feel validated and confirmed in their reality when *they* make a successful match. In this case, however, the child's reality depends upon his or her becoming a (pseudo)empathic reflection of the mother rather than vice versa. The child then comes to feel that independence and a separate identity are unacceptable and result in a sense of inner emptiness. In this case, the child's reality becomes underwritten by pseudo-mature compliance rather than by object constancy (cf. Miller 1981, p. 12).

Our impression is that the families of quiet borderline patients have generally been uncomfortable with the future patient's normal demandingness as an infant, with the child's hungry dependency on them for interaction and responsiveness. It was as though caretakers lacked the energy or flexibility to go where the child's needs took them. They could respond only within a narrow range, traveling but a short distance emotionally with the child before becoming unresponsive or responding incongruently. It seems chiefly to have been the child's naturally greedy dependency on them that was most problematic. Certainly, as they grew, these patients came to feel that dependency was an unacceptable or even a dangerous state. Such a feeling was further solidified by the discovery that a pseudo-mature appearance and desire to please the parent could establish a place for the child in the family.

Wright (1991) has described what may be the origins of this situation, referring to patterns of mother–child interaction in which the child is "looked at" rather than "looked after." A child is looked at when the mother sees the child from an emotional distance—in this case perhaps to take distance from the child's neediness. This form of looking is experienced as intrusive and objectifying, not as confirming and validating. The mother is not experienced as feeling with the child; her look from the outside becomes a negation of the child's interiority rather than a complement to it. With the absence of an inside, the self becomes completely defined by the outside, and the gaze of the other freezes and withers the child's spontaneous subjectivity. In such a case, the child simply becomes someone else's object.

In psychological terms, this scenario can be seen as a premature separation from the mother. The child has (been) moved away from the mother emotionally too early, before he or she can carry out important functions independently. There is a sense of dislocation from oneself, from being a center of subjective experience to an external position in which the self is as it appears to others. We might say that such a self has an outside that is defined only by the other's point of view (cf. Pontalis 1981).

Of course, the view of the other impacts all children in the course of development. The issue here is one of timing. Since looking-at seems to generate feelings of separation, the question to be asked is when such a distancing type of interaction can be tolerated. It is premature if there is not a sufficiently clear distinction between self and other to tolerate separation. The child is forced to be on his or her own long before this is psychologically possible, doing damage to the developing sense of self. Wright (1991) notes this, saying, "the substitution of the Other's view for one's own feelings is itself a form of depersonalization" (p. 28).

In Chapter 1 we referred to narcissistic and also depressed parents as among those likely to contribute to as-if pathology in their children. Narcissistic parents may be too indifferent to the child, too self-absorbed, to respond sensitively and more or less consistently. When narcissistic parents are invested in their children, their investment may be for the purpose of exhibition, proudly treating the child as an extension of themselves. Depressed parents may lack the energy the young child needs, or they may fear the child's hungry dependency. We might add to this list parents who are overly afraid of making mistakes and become stiff and arid in their interactions. While none of these styles necessarily causes as-if pathology, they may contribute to such pathology if children give up hope that the world can respond to them and instead set their sights too early on matching up with the world.

We do not mean to imply that parents are always supposed to be attuned with and responsive to their children or that they are supposed to lose their own personalities while dealing with their infants. If parents always matched their young child's moods and feelings, the child would seldom feel tension and frustration, and there would be little motivation for taking initiative or attempting to grow toward autonomy. We certainly do not believe it is pathogenic for parents to fail their children or make mistakes regularly or to become preoccupied with matters other than the child. We believe, in fact, that it is absolutely imperative that children learn to match up with and adapt to their parents *as well as* vice versa. As-if pathology is likely to result when children are forced to adapt to their parents *instead of* the mutuality of normal mirroring. In normal development, mirroring is an interaction during which both child and parent demand some accommodation and responsiveness from the other. In as-if development, the child does most of the accommodating.

We speculate that children who later become quiet borderline individuals suffer some deficit of assertiveness and the drive toward independence. Our impression is that our patients were unusually passive as children, that they did not protest and fight overmuch against their parents' apparent discomfort with their demandingness. As children, they seemed to find conflict and its attendant tension especially aversive. Eventually, the very possibility of disagreement came to be avoided (which, in turn, produces an almost complete lack of experience with reparation as they grow up). These children learned to tone down their demands so that they experienced less and less rejection and conflict. Gradually the balance shifted away from asserting their own needs, and they became oriented to providing what the other person wanted.

In the same way that Kernberg (1975) speculated that (what we would call noisy) borderline patients suffer an excess of constitutional aggression, we suspect that quiet borderline patients suffer a constitutional lack of it. Until there is much more clinical writing on these patients, the question must remain speculative. It is an important matter, however, for it points to the child's role in the formation of as-if pathology, which in turn highlights the role of the family *interactions*. It is not solely that the parents were apparently underresponsive or that the child was unduly passive; the problem is the match between parent and child. In the case of the quiet borderline patient, relatively ungiving or unresponsive parents seem to have been matched with a child who did not fight for a more intense parental response.

When parents, for whatever reason, do not see and confirm what is there to be seen in the child, they are generally reflecting to the child their own desires and fantasies instead. Such a reflection amounts to a tacit demand by the parents that the child surrender his or her own feelings and potentials in favor of their intentions and moods. Essentially, such parents are shaping their children to feel differently from what they actually feel. Children then become uncertain whether they can be endured as they really are.

Gruen (1968) has described how this uncertainty causes identification with the parents to miscarry and become the basis for a false compliance that replaces the drive toward autonomy. Laing (1960, pp. 100–112) has argued that this set of issues becomes the embryo of a false self organization in which automatic compliance with the wishes of others takes the place of the capacity for initiative. Although we do not believe that the concept of a false self applies to quiet borderline patients (as argued in Chapter 2), in general we agree with this position: When children are forced to become pseudo-empathic reflections of the parents, they cannot complete the identification process. An endless series of transient identifications results, as children try to match up with what they see about them, effectively tuning out their own intentions.

We believe that clinicians will note the "good child" features of their quiet borderline patients. As children, these patients were especially compliant, as though the limits and structures imposed by others were no insult to their own wishes. This compliance can become obvious early in treatment, in fact; when therapists ask for information from the patient about the parents, they will be surprised to hear excessively bland and vague information in reply. It is as though these patients have gone out of their way not to note anything with which they might have been at odds. Generally, even healthy people can muster some complaints against their families. By contrast, the quiet borderline patient seldom does, an indication of the degree to which personal reactions have been jettisoned in favor of adapting to the way the parents saw things.

This remarkable compliance suggests the surrender of the child's desire to become a center of initiative. Whereas normal children must work out a steady series of compromises between their own wishes and the world's limits, the as-if individuals became a passive imprint of the attitudes of others. It is as though they lost sight of themselves altogether and came to know only how to mirror the attitudes and expectations of others toward them. As noted earlier in this chapter, they virtually lost the capacity to experience themselves directly and instead could experience themselves only as the other person's object.

Compliance becomes the foundation for feeling connected to the parents. Normal infants may feel connected and real when what is "in here" is matched "out there" in the mother's mirroring gaze. But the child who will become a quiet borderline individual finds that there is no mirroring gaze; there is only a void, and if this gap between mother and child is to be crossed, it is the child who must cross it. Thus, the absence of the mother's mirroring function is experienced by the child as a demand that he or she respond to the mother's moods and needs. When the child responds thus, there is a sense of being connected, since there is congruence or affective attunement between mother and child. While this reversal of roles inhibits children from clarifying or defining their own feelings, the feelings of others become urgent and imperative, since failure to intuit the parental mood threatens the child with unconnectedness or aloneness.

The child is in the following position. First, his or her own vaguely felt and ill-defined tensions, urges, and feelings remain amorphous and probably confusing. Second, the child feels connected and better defined when matching up with and responding to the needs and moods of the mother. Third, over time such children develop the sense that they cannot be endured as they really are, and they surrender initiative, or the determination to express their own wishes or intentions. Fourth, children in this situation become hypersensitive to how others are experiencing them; since their experience of themselves has remained vague, they have identity (albeit a transient identity) only as the other person's object. Finally, compliance with the real or fantasied expectations of others replaces autonomy and becomes the chief means of feeling connected to others.

With these considerations, we can see the miscarriage of the mirroring process and the failure of object constancy. Given the kind of mirroring that has been internalized, the as-if individual travels through life needing continually to be seen or defined by another person. That is, the as-if individual can feel real and alive only when playing out some role given by the outside world. It would be a mistake to assume that such individuals use these roles to build up an eventual identity; they have no commitment to the role and can easily exchange it for another, usually with no particular feeling about the change. The roles they play are transient identifications (with the image of themselves given by the other person) and do not make a lasting impact. Thus, there is no lasting identity, only a series of parts to act out or a series of roles suggested by others. No matter the role, quiet borderline individuals are only acting as if they were the person in the role.

THE QUIET BORDERLINE PATIENT'S ADAPTATION TO THE FAMILY

In the preceding sections, we have focused mostly on the dyadic aspects of etiology, on the role played by the mother–child relationship in establishing as-if pathology. Clinicians do not generally have the chance to observe the mother–patient dyad, however, unless they are working with infants, and most of what therapists believe about early mother–patient interactions is a series of educated guesses based on what the patient remembers from much later in life. Therapists usually have a much clearer sense of how the entire family functioned during a patient's growing-up years than of how mother and infant got on in the first years. Most patients can produce clear pictures of each family member, and with time the strengths and problems of each come clear to the therapist.

This clinical picture of the family is hardly irrelevant; the family was, after all, the context within which mother and infant dealt with one another, and such factors as the mother's relationship with the baby's father were sure to affect how she saw and reacted to the child. Winnicott (1960 p. 39n) once remarked that there is no such thing as a baby alone, that a baby always implies a mother. The same observation can be extended; mother and infant always exist in a social context, and there is no such thing as an abstracted, mother–infant dyad. Mother and infant are supported, pressured, and/or undermined by the rest of the family (or its absence). Long past infancy, the family will be an influence on the patterns of self-experience and interpersonal relatedness laid down earlier in the dyad.

In addition, later family interactions illustrate, or reflect, the internal world of the patient (and of other family members). Early in this chapter, we defined internalized self and object images as the types of interpersonal experiences the child is most likely to create or be receptive to. Thus, later interactions are, to some extent, externalizations of these internal images. The way the patient carried on with other family members across the years reveals the patient's internal world (in interaction with the private worlds of others). While the patient's inner world is presumably affected by interactions with other family members across the years, those interactions are also surely the clearest illustration available to the clinician of the self and object images created earlier.

It is therefore not necessarily a handicap that therapists usually have a better sense of a patient's familywide relationships later in life than of mother–infant dealings. The family was the context of the mother–infant relationship and therefore had a determining influence, and later family life can reveal to the clinician much of what the patient learned about self and other from the mother–infant dyad.

What is most striking about the pictures of family life given by quiet borderline patients is that the family sounds quite normal (cf. Akhtar 1992). Therapists who listen for obviously problematic or conflictual relationships in hopes of forming early impressions of how the patient came to be disturbed will be disappointed. When asked about their families, our patients have been very contented with such descriptions as, "They were the usual," or, "Dad worked, and Mother was a homemaker." Indeed, from the patient's depiction, it is usually very hard to tell how the family contributed to the patient's problems. Quiet borderline patients seem to see their families as quite average on the whole, and whatever went amiss during the growing-up years was not obviously amiss to the patient.

With most as-if patients we never hear complaints that point to patterns of family interaction that would account for the patient's severity of disturbance. Throughout lengthy treatments they describe their parents and siblings in fairly undetailed, neutral, and colorless ways. The only surprising thing is how little emotion appears to be tied up in the parents and in childhood memories. In a few cases we have (eventually) discovered alcoholism and sexual abuse in our patients' families, but even when these clearly pathogenic factors are present we have been surprised that this information was, first, presented relatively late in treatment and, second, that it was presented in a flat, matter-of-fact manner with no evident affect. In a word, our as-if patients seem quite blind to their family's influence on them, even in the minority of cases when it was flagrantly pathogenic.

> One patient stated that her family was "nothing out of the ordinary" and then added, "I got married at 19 to get out of the home." When the therapist said, "That's early," she stated blandly, "I wanted to get away." She went on to say that her

father had often criticized her clothes when she was a teenager, but she could say no more about why she left. The conflict over her clothes appeared to be all that she was aware of.

Another patient very casually mentioned that his mother was an alcoholic. He said this in the context of telling the therapist that his family life had been unpredictable, since he would never know whether his mother would be drunk when he came home from school. He said all of this in an amazingly bland manner. Another therapist had told him it was significant, and he otherwise might not have mentioned it at all.

Quiet borderline patients tend to talk about their families in flattened, nearly depersonalized, ways. They sound almost as though they were talking about someone else's family—they are that uninvested emotionally. One reason, in fact, that these families sound so normal is the bland tone in which the patient presents the family to the therapist. This tone implies a certain detachment. Patients sound as if they were outside the family watching it all from a distance, and in a sense they probably were. They seemed unable to give themselves over to spontaneity but had to stand, as it were, to the side, carefully watching the other person's reaction to them. What were they watching for? We think that they watched for cues, cues on what to do next.

What does this tell us about the parent–child relationship? We believe that the patient's apparent avoidance of spontaneity as a child (and, of course, later) reveals an absence in the family of spontaneous, joyful interactions in which people take delight in one another. Our impression is that the parents of our patients took pleasure in them when they were *performing,* not when they were being themselves without inhibition. This raises the question of why performances are preferable to spontaneous displays: The performer's actions are controlled and therefore predictable. We believe this is a key—spontaneous affect drove the parents off, while well-trained behavior produced a satisfying reaction.

A middle-aged woman told her therapist that she took on the role of entertainer in the family from a very early age. She remembered knowing by age four how to say things to make her father laugh. As she grew she took up several musical instruments so that she could play these for the family. She said in an early session that she was "always performing for others—it seems like all my life has been spent watching others looking at me." She said this matter of factly and did not seem to feel it was in any way unusual.

It is not the case that the parents were never available for the child, that the mother never tolerated willfulness, or that the father never played with the baby. We have not found the parents of our patients to have been emotionally absent altogether. Rather, it seems to have been a matter of limited capacity for emotional displays. Our patients' parents, as a rule, got their fill of open emotion pretty quickly. They were able to handle only a little spontaneity before having to withdraw. To use an oral metaphor, they fed the child a little, but never allowed the child to eat his or her fill.

In this circumstance, children learn that it is not safe to surrender to emotion. They come instead to watch the parent closely for signals about what will be acceptable and then, as it were, respond on cue. There are pluses and minuses to learning to perform on cue. On the plus side, these individuals typically do well in school and adapt to the work place (albeit without commitment). Since intimate encounters have no predefined structure, however, close and warm relationships with others are precluded.

This leads to an observation often seen in the literature, that as-if individuals frequently resemble well-trained actors. What is not widely understood is that the parents may have been doing the same thing. It is easy to form the impression that the as-if individual was an actor in a family where others were more authentic. However, we have not found this always to be the case. The fact that others in the family may also have been actors and actresses is shown by the way words were used: Words seem to have been meaningless, used to create a certain impression more than to make contact with others. A principal function of language is to allow the speaker a chance to reveal him- or herself and thereby to make contact with others. In the as-if individual's family, by contrast, words were not used in this way. Our impression is that family members may well have said the same sorts of things that every mother, father, brother, or sister says (for example, "I love you"). However, these seemingly ordinary statements were not intended to reveal anything about the speaker. Rather, they were intended to promote the semblance of normalcy, that people in the family felt the way people were supposed to feel.

When we say that the parents used language to create an appearance of normalcy, we are saying something about the way reality came to be defined in family life. In most families, the parents present and represent reality to their children, insisting that children gradually surrender their personal wishes and desires to the demands of external reality. For most children, this is a struggle, a matter of battling the parents over whose will is stronger and whose way of viewing the world will win out. In the course of this (healthy and thoroughly necessary) struggle, parents increasingly insist on a kind of submission from the child. The child must submit his or her selfish desires to the wishes of others and the limits of what the world has to offer. In the course of the submission, the child becomes a creature of reality, living in a social world rather than a private universe.

This battle of wills does not seem to take place in the family of the future as-if individual. This is not to say that the child is allowed to have his or her way; if that were the case, the child would simply become spoiled. Rather, the child's willfulness and demandingness seem to have been largely invisible to the parents. The child was neither forced to submit nor given his or her way; the parental response (if that is the right word) was to indicate that "we are supposed to act this way." The parents did not, however, take responsibility for having defined how "we are supposed to act." They refused the mantle of authority, as it were, imposing roles on the child without acknowledging that they were doing so. In normal development, the child's capacity to adapt to the larger world is the result of a long struggle with the parents, but in the as-if individual's home, adaptability was offered as the way of living.

Unfortunately, such a way of learning to adapt to the larger world leaves the child confused about responsibility. The child cannot detect personal agency or ownership in the family or in the roles he or she learns to play. It is a world in which things just seem to happen, but the patient does not know who is behind it. We do not believe that the child can come to a sense of personal intentionality in such a family. By contrast, the child is likely to be confused when confronted with any situation calling for personal choice or spontaneity, and there is a certain impersonal or generic quality to experience.

> A therapist tried to get a sense of how an as-if patient's family handled special, intimate occasions. He asked the patient what Christmas was like in her family. The patient replied, "How it was supposed to be." When the therapist asked how that was, the patient said, "You know, like you've seen on television." The therapist pressed the matter, asking, "Is that how it was?" The patient thought about it and then said, "I don't know— maybe I'm confusing it with what I saw on TV. I know we exchanged gifts and said 'thank you.'" The only genuine, spontaneous moment the therapist could find in the report came a moment after this exchange, when the patient suddenly added, "You know, I don't remember ever getting a gift I wanted to say 'thank you' for."

When the lines of authority and responsibility are so blurred, the child will, of course, not be sure how anything really happened in the family. Children of the family may know the rules about how to behave, but have not been exposed to a connection between rules and the rule makers. Earlier, we mentioned that quiet borderline patients cannot give the therapist a good sense of what went on in their families nor of how the family contributed to their problems. It is easier now to see why. The therapist who cannot determine how such an apparently normal family produced someone with severe pathology is experiencing the patient's own dilemma while growing up. The patient simply believed that "this is how it is supposed to be" and, like the therapist, could not find a way to fit in those experiences that might have suggested something was wrong.

THE CHILD AS FAMILY PROTECTOR

We have been commenting on the quiet borderline patient's blindness to family problems and difficulty describing family life. To understand this blindness more fully, we must see that there was a payoff for the child in experiencing and remembering the family as normal and untroubled. The quiet borderline individual was able to feel that he or she was a good child who helped to keep the family together by doing nothing to disrupt it. There seems to have been an attitude to the effect that, "if we just keep on functioning as though nothing could be wrong, things will stay okay." We believe that the child then fantasied being the family benefactor *through wanting nothing from the family.*

It is a short step from this fantasy to precocious ego development, or the adoption of a pseudo-mature facade. We believe that children are most likely to attempt a pseudo-mature posture if they perceive the family structure as fragile; future as-if individuals seem unsure what exactly holds the family together or what it is that would keep everyone in the home. One as-if woman explained her childhood good behavior by saying, "I didn't want to do anything to disrupt what seemed to me to be fragile." By adopting an attitude of precocious maturity, the child avoided dependency and self-assertion, which were felt to be dangerous, and assumed a stance of keeping the family together through self-sufficiency.

In effect, the child was protecting first the mother and then later the family from a dependency that was vaguely felt to be aggressive and therefore dangerous. The child was not left with any conscious sense of protecting the family, and as an adult the quiet borderline individual does not seem fully aware of having held such a status. Nonetheless, we believe there are echoes or perhaps derivatives of this protector role.

Patients can often recover childhood memories of feeling that they were important caretakers in the family, that they did something that made it better for everyone else. It appears that they often received some recognition for whatever they did that was defined as caretaking. Thus, children who adopt a pseudo-mature posture may come to feel special. The child may feel in possession of special powers to preserve the fragile family. This feeling can become a well of secret narcissism in the young child, a much needed source of pride and valuation. Needless to say, this circumstance makes it even less likely that the child will return to the uncertainties of normal dependency on the parents.

In place of the insecurities of dependency, these children become important caretakers in the family and receive recognition for it. They may have some sense that their situation is inauthentic, but such an awareness is vague at best. The narcissistic rewards can be satisfying and will often drown out any feeling of ingenuineness on the child's part. Consequently, once the fantasy of helping the family in a special way through self-sufficiency is aroused and precocious ego development is begun, the child is locked in place. Change would mean giving up a place in the family, since the family has not left many other options for feeling valuable and connected.

> One patient remembered being praised for not bothering anyone; he vividly recalled being told, "You can be helpful by staying out of Mother's hair." This feedback unfortunately complemented his already too great fear of his own neediness and solidified his growing pseudo-maturity.
>
> Another patient felt that "something bad would happen" if she ever demanded her own way. She felt that her parents were somehow stretched too thin by health problems she had suffered as a young child and that she might lose them forever if she placed any further demands on them. She became a miniature adult, first in the family and later in the school and community. In the process, she so successfully jettisoned her own needs and

wants that she was almost completely unable as an adult to recognize what she was feeling except in the most extreme situations. Even when she knew what she felt or wanted, she could seldom say it aloud without massive guilt.

A 25-year-old woman told her therapist how she took care of her father from an early age. Her mother had died when the patient was 6 years old. From that time the patient had essentially been a surrogate wife for her father. With the exception of sexual relations, the child served all the functions of a spouse, even dressing up and accompanying the father to professional meetings, dinners, and parties. The father was, in fact, quite dependent on his daughter (when she told him that her graduate course of study would entail a year of work in another city, he said he would quit his job and move with her). The patient had received many rewards for this role reversal and had never really questioned its appropriateness. She seemed to feel proud of this role and was offended when it was even slightly questioned.

Another secret source of narcissism that is worth noting is that the quiet borderline patient very seldom heard "no" from the parents. We have already noted that the parental style did not typically include challenging the child's willfulness or independence. This normal willfulness was invisible to the parents and therefore not responded to. As a result, the child did not have the experience of being intruded upon and limited by outside authority. By contrast, what reactions the child was able to draw were confirming reactions (when the parents responded positively to the child's seeming maturity). The parents' confirming reactions led the child to feel safe and special as long as he or she played out a pseudo-adult stance. Later in life, as-if individuals can have difficulty responding to criticism. They seem unprepared for the experience, as though they had not thought such a thing possible as long as they clung to their pseudo-mature role. The child has become narcissistically invested in being accomplished, perfect, or competent beyond reproach. In turn, there is what might be termed a narcissistic payoff: As long as the child feels proud of the special role played in the family (and of the later variations on the theme in school and the work place), he or she will not be able to see the ingenuineness of the role and will feel safe from criticism or rebuff.

With this precipitous move from needy child to family protector, normal development has been stood on its head. Instead of attaining object constancy and the consequent confidence to experiment with independence and initiative, these children feel that they must be available to mirror and meet the expectations and needs of the family. What the children inevitably mirror is a false independence, the appearance of not needing anything emotionally from the family or of being surprisingly mature. In fact, of course, this seeming independence is a form of pathological dependency, since these children cannot feel real apart from the defining gaze of another person or the roles given by other people. Such individuals cannot generally be on their own, and they become uneasy when they lose the relationships through which they find roles to perform. In general these individuals continue to play the parts learned at home—not allowing themselves to show need of or dependency on another person, matching up compliantly with the mores and lifestyles of those they are with, and seldom spending any time without some relationship by which they define themselves.

Part II

CLINICAL APPROACHES TO AS-IF PATHOLOGY

INTRODUCTION

This is the clinical section of this work. Given that this is the first attempt anyone has made to set forth a clinical stance with as-if patients, we have not tried to be exhaustive. Rather, we have tried to target those things that most caught our attention and, in particular, those elements of treatment that were problems for us.

We start with an attempt to outline a general treatment approach. That approach may be summarized as the therapist's efforts to awaken in the patient a desire to be taken seriously. We then turn to three of the defining characteristics of the as-if patient (as presented in Chapter 1)—the appearance of normalcy, a history of precocious ego development, and the virtual absence of a sense of identity. We believe that each of these characteristics will appear in the as-if patient's treatment and that the therapist ought to be prepared to wrestle with them.

A transcript of an actual therapy session is appended to each of the last three chapters in this section, along with commentary. The sessions are far from perfect and were not chosen for this book because of their craftsmanship. Rather, they are here to illustrate themes and problems that are certain to arise in the treatment of these patients. We believe it can be useful to have actual illustrations of the phenomena we are trying to describe. We have included sessions in their entirety, or nearly so, realizing that this can strain the reader's patience. However, therapy sessions are seldom exciting, certainly not with this patient group. It is better, we think, to show the whole session rather than to hit the highlights and thereby present a false picture of what sessions are like with as-if patients.

4

General Treatment Approach

INTRODUCTION

To our knowledge, no one has proposed a treatment approach specific to the as-if patient. In this chapter, we want to trace the outlines of such an approach, elaborating the picture in the following four chapters. At the outset, we ought to say that what we offer here is more general than we might wish. Given the variability of these individuals, it is not possible to state a series of rules for therapy that will hold for all quiet borderline patients. There is no approach that can be mastered in a "how to do it" sort of way, and readers ought not approach this chapter looking for a sequence of tasks to be accomplished as a kind of preset treatment plan. What we hope to do in the pages that follow is to establish a conceptual context in which therapists can think through treatment issues.

It is easier to say how therapists ought not proceed than to say how they should. For instance, there is no role for problem-solving approaches with as-if patients. The reasons for this ought to be fairly obvious, that these patients seldom have a well-defined problem. If they do, it is almost certain to be something someone else told them was a problem, not the product of their own observation. This is hardly surprising: As-if patients have as-if problems. If they feel that their therapist expects a circumscribed issue to be the focus of treatment, quiet borderline patients will try to comply, but in this case no therapy is going on—the patient is simply complying with what he or she believes are the therapist's expectations.

Time-limited or brief psychotherapy is similarly impossible. A brief treatment makes sense in either of two situations. First, patients may use brief therapies when they are relatively intact psychologically and chiefly need help in marshalling their already established resources against a fairly well-defined problem. Second, patients who are psychologically primitive or unstable may benefit from a time-limited approach, since the limitations of brief therapy work against regression and dependency, thereby supporting the patient's fragile adaptive capacities. Neither of these two situations seems to apply to the quiet borderline patient, however. They are neither intact psychologically nor prone to regression.

In addition, one particular characteristic of the quiet borderline patient argues against brief and time-limited approaches, namely, that the as-if patient has no firm time sense. Brief and time-limited approaches assume that the patient is aware of and influenced by the limited time available; this is a motivation to the higher functioning patient and a reassurance to the primitive patient. As-if patients, however, tend to live in what might be termed a timeless world (cf. Nayman 1991). Their experience is not entirely linear; they lack a sense of how their lives have unfolded, flowed, or moved from one stage or set of events to another. Therapists may be surprised at the way these patients report events with no good sense of the connection between them. Even when life events are reported sequentially, it is usually clear that the patient lacks a feeling for how the present flowed from or was discontinuous with the past. Time sense and identity are intimately connected; the quiet borderline patient's lack of firm identity inhibits the capacity to experience continuity and, hence, the ability to appreciate the significance of limited time.

A corollary to these comments about the quiet borderline patient's time sense is that the therapist ought not be hurried. It will not come as news to practicing clinicians that there is ever-increasing pressure from third-party payers to work fast. In a previous work (Cohen and Sherwood 1991), we noted that Western society's collective time sense is increasingly dominated by a sense of instancy. Clinicians may be hard pressed to work in this culture and in our present health care climate without feeling considerable pressure to get something done sooner rather than later. There is, however, no point in beginning to address the problems of the as-if patient and at the same time thinking in terms of a few months of work. These are cases that last years if they go well; a treatment that is deliberately short has simply wasted the patient's time (and the third-party carrier's money).

GETTING STARTED: THE QUESTION OF HOW ACTIVE TO BE

Those familiar with our work (Cohen and Sherwood 1989, 1991) on borderline patients may remember the phrase *standing still*. This phrase was our attempt to capture the therapist's capacity to endure the tension and intense affect produced by many borderline patients in the first phases of treatment. We have argued that therapists ought not to try to solve the borderline patient's problems, engender insight, calm anxieties, or do anything else to reduce the tension level. By contrast, we proposed that therapists should try to weather the storm and that this was the most important early task of therapy. We used the term standing still to describe the therapist's calm and benign inactivity in the face of the patient's demands to "do something to make me feel better."

The approach of standing still was designed chiefly for noisy borderline patients. It is not entirely applicable to quiet borderline cases; with this latter group therapists will have to be more active. The therapist's aim with noisy patients is to communicate that the world can withstand their anger and distress without becoming as troubled as the patient. With as-if individuals, however, the therapist's task is to show that the world can bring them to life.

There is one aspect of standing still that is nonetheless quite applicable to the quiet borderline patient: The therapist ought not try to accomplish anything in the early stages of treatment. The time pressures we noted earlier will quietly influence the therapist to try to "get something done" as soon as possible. In addition, these patients are quite good at inducing others to provide a role to play or a scenario to act out. Thus, they will surely invite the therapist to give clues on what kind of work the therapist considers important. If, for example, the therapist hints that the maternal relationship might be crucial, the as-if patient may produce seemingly important material on that subject. The therapist may then feel tempted to mine this apparently rich vein, trying to develop the material. From our point of view, of course, such work is folly. The therapist is simply helping the patient continue the as-if pattern in the therapy session, and the resulting work is as-if work.

The therapist ought not, therefore, try to make progress with the patient. The only important thing to be accomplished in the early months of treatment is to try to produce a relationship with some genuineness to it. No meaningful work is possible until that is done, and it is likely that the better part of a year will be spent in the effort. A kind of discipline and self control will be necessary for the therapist, who must resist the temptation to be "therapeutic" early on, remembering that the patient is essentially acting like a patient, not being a patient.

The best approach for the first few sessions is to let the patient talk. It is not likely that a therapist will determine that a new patient is an as-if individual until several sessions have passed. The therapist will probably start the treatment with a different diagnosis and change it only as the original impression fails to match up with how the case unfolds. Even after three or four sessions the diagnosis is likely to be tentative, and therapists are more likely to be in the process of wondering if the patient is a quiet borderline individual than to have firmly concluded it.

What usually makes the therapist begin to consider the as-if category is a kind of hollowness to the patient's verbal productions. More particularly, the patient's verbalizations are likely to be affectively flat and lacking in development. By affectively flat, we mean that the patient will seem relatively uninvested even in the dramatic events he or she reports; there is no emotional aliveness behind the words. It is as though these patients do not know which events should draw an emotional response from them, and they need someone else to tell them when to be upset, joyous, or agitated. In addition, the content of the patient's productions tends not to develop over sessions. The therapist may think that the patient is staying close to the surface and is sure to deepen the material soon. Over several sessions, however, the therapist finds that the patient has not deepened or developed the material at all but is still saying pretty much the same things, even after comments from the therapist that were designed to help the process.

The therapist may initially conclude that the patient is resisting treatment and that this explains the hollowness of the material. Such defenses as intellectualization, displacement, and splitting can siphon off painful affect and leave any patient's productions sounding arid and emotionally empty. When therapists confront this avoidance of difficult themes or feelings, most patients become more real—affect becomes more congruent with content, and the patient seems interpersonally more present. Usually the patient is anxious or visibly upset as well. It is a different matter with quiet borderline patients. They seem nonplussed when the therapist confronts them with issues that appear to be painful or conflicted, and overall there is no appreciable change in how they present themselves. The as-if patient remains as hollow after the confrontation of "resistance" as before.

The reason that as-if individuals do not change in response to the therapist's confrontation is that their hollowness is not due to defenses or to what might be termed resistance. The very word resistance implies tension with the inner or outer world, and tension in turn implies opposition and struggle. The quiet borderline individual is not opposing or struggling with self or world, however. These individuals are plastic, automatically conforming or adapting—the very opposite of struggle or conflict. Their hollowness stems from just this trait: They are not hollow because they resist unwanted truths but because they resist virtually nothing.

The capacity to resist presupposes some measure of identity. Resistance is built on the need to fend off wishes, urges, and fantasies that are at odds with who we think ourselves to be. In turn, this assumes some continuity of self experience over time; identity is built on such continuity. Yet the quiet borderline individual is born anew with every situation and scenario. There is no abiding core of sameness that continues across time and situations, only the role that is being played out at the present moment. Hence it is problematic to refer to an identity; there is a series of identities depending on circumstance, but each is shed as new situations come up. Consequently, there is no firm basis for resistance.

Therapists who observe that their patient's productions are hollow and that the hollowness remains even after interventions that were designed to bring about more congruent affect and a deepening of the material, should begin to consider an as-if diagnosis. Most experienced clinicians will also consider the possibility of schizophrenia under those circumstances. A differential diagnosis can be made on the basis of the patient's preference to be alone versus being with people. Schizophrenics will not characteristically seek out other people, but the quiet borderline individual will. While the quiet borderline patient does not grow deeply attached or committed to others, he or she does need to be with others in order to feel defined and alive. It is rare to find such a person who stays out of a relationship for any length of time.

Even after therapists conclude that their patient is an as-if individual, it is still best to work slowly. It is true that most of what the patient says remains hollow, but this is not something that will change quickly. There is therefore no need to comment on it. Therapists should be willing to endure material that seems unimportant and insignificant for quite a long time. The content of the patient's productions will not be especially important until some rudimentary identity begins to form. Until then, the only question is what sort of relationship the patient can tolerate. When therapy begins, these patients will not know that another person can actually hear what they say or might even want to hear what they say. They grew up with the sense that words did not mean anything, and it is not surprising that they can flood the therapist with meaningless words. Therapists should tolerate this and not try to introduce more substance into the relationship than the patient can respond to.

Quiet borderline patients will behave in the therapist's office much as they do anywhere else: They will search out a role to play. This means that they are *reacting* to the world, or in this case, the therapist. The therapeutic task is to try to bring about some *interaction* instead. As long as the therapist is silent, there is the risk that as-if patients are simply talking to themselves, responding to the few clues the therapeutic setting provides, and playing out the role of psychotherapy patient. Thus, a silent therapist runs the risk that quite a bit of time can pass and nothing will change. This is the problem Deutsch (1942) pointed out, that treatment can seem to be going well for a long time while in fact there is no emotional investment in the process or emotional aliveness to the material.

Paradoxically, an active therapist runs exactly the same risk. Given the patient's ability to act out roles, an active therapist may simply give the patient more clues on what is expected, more material from which to deduce a role. There is no reason to believe that Deutsch's cases would have turned out differently if only she had been more talkative in sessions. Nonetheless, we believe there are better reasons for being more active with as-if cases than for strictly maintaining the disciplined reserve of standing still that we have proposed with other borderline patients. While therapeutic reserve and activity alike hold the danger that the patient will find roles to play out in sessions, we believe there are better prospects for change if the therapist is more active. There is a further consideration against rigorous and disciplined silence with these patients that should be mentioned here. In Chapter 1, we observed that many quiet borderline patients cannot tolerate silence, since it does not offer the cues needed to know what role to play.

> One quiet borderline patient talked steadily for the first three sessions. The material was important in content but was delivered in a rote, mechanical way. At the start of the fourth session, the patient asked the therapist what else he wanted to know. The therapist said, "You can talk about whatever you'd like, or we can sit quietly together." With this the patient's entire manner changed. Her face contorted, and her body tensed up. She grabbed the arms of her chair tightly and tears welled up. She began to cry and said, "I don't know what more you want from me!" The therapist kept silent. The patient, in evident distress, began to describe sneaking into her brother's room at night when she was a teenager. He was a successful athlete, and she would masturbate with his sports trophies, fantasying that she had a penis "bigger than my brother's." She said that she would reach orgasm and then throw the trophy on the floor in disgust, feeling "horrendous guilt." She would then wipe off the trophy and replace it, often picking up and hugging another one, comforting herself with thoughts of "my wonderful brother." After relating this story, the patient asked, "Is this the kind of self-disclosure you want?" In this case, the therapist's silence had left the patient feeling too alone and at sea. Accordingly, she tried to guess what would please the therapist and prompt him to become more interactive. In the process she produced important material but long before it could be dealt with meaningfully. The material was more intimate than the therapeutic relationship, and the therapist had to ease away from the material into something more neutral, returning to it months later, after a

more secure attachment existed between patient and therapist. (A fuller discussion of this case is offered in Cohen and Sherwood 1991, pp. 180–182).

This is not the case with every quiet borderline patient; many who have been in treatment before will be happy with the therapist's silence and will simply play out whatever role they learned from their first therapist. Many as-if patients, however, will become uneasy and agitated with silence early in treatment and will probably not be able to stay with treatment. In spite of the fact that these individuals are only pseudo-related, they nonetheless need the other person's responses. They do not handle aloneness well, and they may feel alone with a largely silent therapist. As treatment goes on, the therapist should try to return to silence as the basic intervention; in the first months and possibly the first year, however, rigorous silence is probably a mistake.

MOVING FROM DIAGNOSIS TO THERAPY

The question, of course, is what sort of activity will be helpful. Given our argument in the preceding chapter, it might appear that we would propose a Kohutian approach at this point, endorsing a consistently empathic, mirroring stance. The reasoning behind such a proposal would run as follows. Borderline dynamics—quiet or otherwise—stem from the failure of object constancy. Failed constancy, in turn, seems related to a breakdown in the mirroring process during the early years. The breakdown in mirroring is essentially that interactions with caretakers failed to confirm and define the child's feelings and other aspects of the inner life. This failure left the child overly dependent on others in order to feel alive and real. Thus, according to this line of reasoning, the task of therapy would be to resume the miscarried mirroring process, leading the patient eventually to experience the therapist as a constant object.

We do not endorse this argument, however. We have both

practical and theoretical objections. Practically, we believe that many therapists confuse empathy with being warm and sympathetic. Thus, a number of therapists who hope to be empathic wind up simply being nice instead, and we doubt that any good can come of such a situation. We do not believe that most patients will change simply because someone has been relentlessly nice to them. In addition, empathic responses tend to create the illusion of closeness where there has been neither the time nor shared experience necessary for genuine closeness. With as-if patients, such a circumstance is especially countertherapeutic, since the as-if patient will not be able to distinguish the illusion of relatedness from the real thing. Thus, on practical grounds alone, we are not optimistic that empathic mirroring is the best approach.

We also have theoretical objections. We do not believe it is possible to view pathology as though the patient had simply stopped developing at some point and needs only to resume. A great deal has come between the developmental failure and the patient's arrival for an appointment. The therapist is not treating an arrest in development but the many and complex consequences of that arrest. It is not possible to access the patient as though he or she were still in the early years of life, yearning for the satisfaction and excitement of being known and held in the loving gaze of the other. Over the years the patient has made many decisions on what to make of the world and how to behave in it, and these decisions are what confront the therapist when the patient sits down in the office. The therapist must meet the patient where he or she lives, not where he or she stopped living several decades earlier. Thus, we do not believe that empathic mirroring is the proper treatment approach to as-if patients.

The task of therapy is to create a relationship through which the as-if patient can discover his or her integrity, that is, a relationship through which patients can both feel themselves to be the authors of their actions and find the ability to resist whatever is inconsistent with their preferences and values. The therapist's only tool for accomplishing this task is the relationship with the patient. The patient will immediately try to define the therapeutic relationship like every other relationship, as a matter of acting parts given by the other person. The therapist must interfere with the patient's tendency to define the therapeutic relationship in such a manner.

When we say that the therapist's only tool is the relationship with the patient, we mean to downplay the significance of what the patient has to say. As we have already noted, the content of the as-if patient's productions is relatively unimportant in the early months of treatment. Since the type of relationship the patient is trying to create is the proper focus of the early months, the therapist must find ways to spotlight the patient's interpersonal intentions, or, more accurately, the way the patient is not being *inter*personal at all.

The therapist is looking for genuineness in the patient, or in the way the patient deals with the therapist. In this task, therapists must rely on their personal criteria for what constitutes genuineness. Most people have some sense of what is genuine for them, but there is probably no such thing as a universally genuine relationship or a universally genuine personal manner. Each person is genuine in his or her own way, and we must suspend formulae in this area—otherwise, we run the risk of telling others how *they* should be genuine, which is, of course, a contradiction. Perhaps it is easiest to decide whether the other person is letting us be genuine; it is usually less clear how genuine the other person is.

While there are no formulae for these issues, there are some generalizations that can be made about what defines genuineness in a relationship. A relationship is more likely to be genuine if a range of emotion can find free expression within it. Similarly, when we do not need the other person to change, but are willing to experience (although not necessarily accept) others as they are, there is a greater chance for genuineness. These conditions are necessary in therapy. It is important that there be no contrived, one-up or one-down stance on the part of therapist; the difference in status between therapist and patient does not dictate what happens in the therapy hour or what emotion gets expressed. The therapist tries to create a setting in which what is most appropriate at any given moment is free to appear. The therapist does not demand change as a precondition for taking the patient seriously. These are some of the factors that make genuineness a possibility in therapy.

When working with as-if patients, however, therapists will eventually become aware that nothing genuine is happening. This will not, as a rule, be apparent in the first sessions. Initially, therapists may feel that the patient is fairly open and cooperative. As-if patients usually manage to communicate that they are receptive to the other person's demands and virtually invite the other to make some demand of them. There is no reciprocity, though; the quiet borderline patient has nothing to demand of the therapist. What this means is that the relationship will be completely one-sided and, hence, ingenuine. There can be no honesty or true involvement when one person is unwilling to demand being taken seriously by the other.

The therapist can therefore start the treatment by trying to answer this question: What does it mean to live like that, to be available for others but seldom or never make a demand for oneself? The answers to this question should guide interventions. The therapist's aim is to get in the way of the patient's pseudo-relatedness during the therapy hour, to make some genuineness possible during the session. The patient is trying to be invisible as a person and to replace actual involvement with passive compliance. The therapist can therefore begin to work by doing the one thing that will interfere with the patient's attempt at invisibility: taking the patient seriously.

TAKING THE PATIENT SERIOUSLY

At the outset of treatment, the patient fears being taken seriously. The patient hopes, instead, that his or her *act* will be taken seriously, supported, and perhaps even enhanced by therapy. These patients do not want to be separated from their acts, and when the therapist tries to focus on the person behind the act, it creates problems. When their act is not being accepted, these patients feel the risk of not knowing what is expected. As-if individuals hope to hide their lack of genuine involvement behind a facade of cooperation, hoping also to remain invisible. The therapist must stay aware of what lies behind the facade, a fear of being seen. If the therapist works long enough and well enough with the patient, a deep hope of being seen (and known) may also be discovered, but at the outset of treatment, the patient fears being seen and therefore fears being taken seriously.

The as-if patient will not understand this issue, since he or she gave up hope of being taken seriously long ago. The as-if patient does not feel capable of holding the attention of the other person or of having meaning for another person in any posture except that of actor or actress. Thus, for the as-if individual, the idea of being oneself is roughly equivalent to the idea of being left alone and directionless. It has been a very long time indeed since the as-if patient asked to be taken seriously, and it was not a fortunate experience then. When the therapist wants to focus on the issue, therefore, the patient will not welcome it. Nevertheless, the therapist must—fairly early and fairly gently—raise the question of whether the patient can imagine being taken seriously.

There is no cookbook of ways to raise this question, no set of strategies to be used in every situation. A good deal of trial and error will (unfortunately) be required of every clinician to learn what might work. No matter what particular interventions are used, therapists are trying to interrupt the way the patient experiences the situation in order to suggest that there are other ways to be with people. The patient is locked into a pattern of being an extension of his or her situation and of having little left over in terms of spontaneity or initiative. The therapist wants to challenge the pattern and in the process imply that the patient can be accepted without having to meet the therapist's expectations.

In a sense, the therapist is proposing freedom to the patient. Therapy must become a setting in which the patient can hope to be accepted in a wide variety of ways, where the therapist's attention to the patient is both reliable and also free of the contingencies the patient has come to expect. Consequently, the therapist starts by being alert for signs that the patient feels obliged to meet certain expectations he or she imagines the therapist has. If the therapist observes that the patient appears to be playing a preset role (which is to say that the patient is trying to meet what he or she imagines are the therapist's expectations), then the therapist is seeing evidence that the patient does not hope to be taken seriously. Hence, the patient has not, strictly speaking, shown up for the session; rather, the patient playing a role has shown up.

In this situation, the therapist may wish to focus on the patient's manner of being with him or her. It may be possible to do this simply by saying something to the effect, "I wonder whether you want me to take you seriously." The therapist should not be surprised when the patient replies that he or she does not know, which is very likely true. Most as-if patients will be confused by the subject of being taken seriously and will try to elicit guidelines on what they are being asked to do. Of course, to the extent that anything is being asked of them, it is that they stop defining themselves by what others want them to do. Thus, the therapist ought not try to define the situation for the patient; it is better for the patient to struggle with the issue, and the therapist's interventions should simply aim at keeping the theme alive. Questioning whether there are people who take the patient seriously and whether the patient knows when he or she is taken seriously can be useful in doing this.

We should emphasize, however, that the patient truly cannot respond to these questions in any depth and possibly cannot even fathom them. Therapists may be tempted to conclude that the patient is resisting when questions are met with puzzlement and evident confusion. We do not believe the problem is resistance, however. Rather, we believe that quiet borderline patients cannot comprehend the possibility of *wanting something for themselves*. Wanting is a problem for borderline patients in general (cf. Cohen and Sherwood 1991). Noisy borderline patients try to cover over the fact that they want something from others, using weakness and anger to coerce others into providing what they cannot allow themselves to want and ask for in a more open, honest manner. By contrast, quiet borderline patients cannot even imagine wanting something from others.

The experience of wanting presupposes someone to hear and acknowledge our wants—regardless of whether the wants are satisfied. This is what as-if patients cannot imagine, that others could see and confirm their wants. It is not that these patients feel deprived; deprivation presupposes feeling that others could meet one's needs but have failed to do so. By contrast, quiet borderline individuals simply do not have the sense that any of their wants will be visible to anyone. Consequently, their wants become invisible to them as well. As-if patients try to turn this liability into a virtue: They present themselves as nondemanding and as willing to take on the wants of the other. In the course of normal living, this trait makes them attractive; people usually find it narcissistically gratifying when someone seems so receptive to their wishes. It is natural for people to assume that as-if individuals could make demands if they wished but that they are willing to defer for now. It can be a shock to learn after a time that as-if individuals make no demands on others because they cannot do so. Eventually, the very trait that made the as-if individual seem attractive can destroy the relationship: When others notice that the as-if individual never reveals his or her own wants and demands, they may feel unsatisfied at this lack of mutuality and end the relationship. (It is worth noting that a narcissistic person may never notice this and may therefore never grow dissatisfied at the lack of sharing.) Our point here is that since as-if patients cannot allow the experience of wanting something for themselves, they cannot really grasp the issue of wanting to be taken seriously.

If the therapist does not try to take the patient seriously, it means that the therapy hour goes much as the rest of the patient's life has—therapy becomes just another event in which nothing that passes leads to reflection or meaningful action. Such sessions mean that the two people in the office walk away with no greater knowledge of themselves or the other than before they sat down together. The therapist tries to change this circumstance; since the patient does not welcome the change, it is not likely to occur quickly. The therapist should not, therefore, try prematurely to reach closure on this issue. It will be many months at best before quiet borderline patients can even imagine being taken seriously, and the therapist will see little progress for a long while.

This very slow movement is due to something we noted earlier, that as-if patients fear being seen, or known. More particularly, they fear having their unconnectedness seen. These individuals are physically present, but that is the only sense in which they are present as themselves. Beyond that, they are present as the other person's object, or as an extension of the other. Just as the quiet borderline patient is willing to be an object for other people, he or she is willing to be the therapist's object. However, being the other person's object is not the same thing as being genuinely connected to that person.

What is missing is the willingness to be a subject. Subjectivity is the ability to create a personal world, to define one's space and time and invest these with private meanings. In the process, other persons become our objects. Given the nature of subjectivity, we do not only come to know other persons—we may be said to create them as well, seeing them through the prism of our private meanings and intentions. Genuine connectedness implies two subjects, each willing to risk being the other's object but also willing to define and create the other through subjectivity. It is here that the quiet borderline patient remains unconnected. These individuals can fill only half of what is needed: They can be the other's object, but they lose all sense of who they are when it is their subjectivity that is required.

One therapist found himself unusually bored and sleepy during sessions with a patient he had originally felt positively about.

The patient was willing to please and to do whatever the therapist wanted, but this passive compliance meant that the therapist was left to define sessions. The patient even had trouble talking until she tried to find what the therapist wanted her to talk about, leading usually to strained and tedious exchanges that went nowhere. The therapist came to dread appointments and felt almost as though he were being called upon to carry the patient physically. He began to see the roots of his feelings when the patient reported that her boyfriend had broken up with her, accusing her of being unable to "pull her weight." The boyfriend told the patient that he had originally liked her because she was always willing to do what he wanted to do and to listen to him. He said, however, that the woman seemed to need nothing from him and that he felt the woman did not even know him. The therapist came to believe that his boredom with the case reflected the patient's having placed no demands on him. He had experienced this as a narcissistic injury (since it implied that he was not needed) and had withdrawn behind his sleepiness.

When we take other persons seriously, we become willing to consider the way *they* have created or defined the world, including the way we ourselves are defined in their world. We invite them to create us in their imaginations, out of their perceptions and also out of their fantasies and needs. We then learn whether we can be the person they imagine us to be versus whether they have seriously mistaken us (this is the essence of transference). As-if individuals are not at all happy with this invitation to be subjects, however. Not wishing to create a private world of personal meanings and intentions, they do not know what to do with this situation.

As-if patients are therefore unconnected when invited to be taken seriously. It is this that they fear will be seen, their unconnectedness, that they are not truly there but are there only as an extension of the therapist's world. The as-if patient is, in a sense, purely the therapist's creation or at the very least is trying to be. The therapist, however, is unwilling to tolerate this situation. By raising the question of whether the patient can imagine being taken seriously, the therapist has exposed the patient, as it were. This is not comfortable for the patient— not because he or she is embarrassed at the exposure, but because the patient truly does not know how to respond. As-if patients cannot suddenly stop being someone else's object and reclaim their abandoned subjectivity. They will, therefore, scramble to regain their accustomed position as the other's object, wanting to know what the therapist wants them to do or say.

Watching this process in the therapy session, it is easy to see how these patients can have histories of sexual promiscuity, become involved in deviant activities, or suddenly find themselves in situations they are hard pressed to explain. These patients are not making choices; they merely take on whatever complementary role needs to be assumed. They do not, then, "decide" to go to bed with their date, use drugs, or do anything else that they do. They simply assume the part created for them by the other person and seldom know how their actions came about.

> One quiet borderline patient reported on her weekend by saying, "I had this blind date and then suddenly we were in bed." At first the therapist thought that they had gone to bed almost immediately upon meeting. Upon (slow and tortuous) inquiry, however, he found that six hours had passed between meeting and going to bed. The patient had no clear idea what led up to the sexual encounter or how she made the decision to have sex with the man. She did not seem to be aware either what he had done to suggest sex or how he led her to it. She knew what had occurred but was at a loss to say how it had come about or to account for her decision in any way. When the therapist asked what kind of person her date had been, the patient could not even answer that, much less connect it to her decision to have sex with the man. She answered innocently, "Do you mean was he nice?" This was the extent of her awareness of her own perceptions and choices.

Earlier we suggested that therapists may wish to focus on the patient's manner of being with them when they see the patient playing a preset role during sessions. We suggested that one way to do this was to raise the question of whether the patient could imagine being taken seriously. The therapist may also ask what patients expect from the therapist. Quiet borderline patients will probably try to avoid the question, either answering with something they have read or heard elsewhere or saying that they do not know what to expect. Therapists can press the matter, asking what patients hope will happen in therapy and how they want the therapist to treat them.

We would not ask such questions of most patients, but we believe they are useful with quiet borderline cases. With many types of patients, these questions could serve to mask narcissistic acting-in on the part of the therapist ("let's talk about me for a while and how you see me") or might seem to legitimize transference distortions, but they serve a different function with as-if patients. They are ways to make the demand that the patient take the role of subject, quitting for a time the more comfortable position of being the therapist's object. They are, therefore, invitations to define the therapist and assume the position of someone making choices. This is the general purpose of interventions that focus on the patient's manner of being with the therapist, and any intervention that emphasizes the patient's subjectivity may be helpful.

What will not be helpful is pushing the issue very hard. The matter should be raised and defined but not dwelt on at first. As we suggested earlier, the therapist is trying to create tension between the patient's as-if style and the therapist's desire for genuineness. The therapist should not push tension very far in the first months of treatment, however. The idea is to create tension and then back off. Quiet borderline patients cannot really even comprehend the subject at first, much less change in the desired direction. The therapist is trying to plant a seed, as it were; it will take time for something to grow.

Genuineness is the sort of theme that should be brought up across many sessions and not something to be pressed very long in any single session. The patient is placed in an uncomfortable position and can be driven from therapy. It may seem that all the therapist is asking is something on the order of "be yourself"; we believe, however, that it is not an exaggeration to say that there is virtually no self for the patient to be. Except as the therapist's (or someone else's) object, the patient lacks coherence.

> The following sequence from an as-if patient's sixth month of treatment illustrates our point. The patient has just said that she felt "terrible" after the last appointment; she had been bothered by the therapist's silence.
>
> **PT:** I know what you wanted me to do, but I just couldn't.
>
> **TH:** What did you think I wanted?
>
> **PT:** You said I could say whatever was on my mind or that we could sit quietly together. But I couldn't do it. I wanted to know what you expected.
>
> **TH:** What happens to you when I don't define you and tell you what to do?
>
> **PT:** It's not that I don't exist, but I'm spread out all over the place, and I don't know which way to go. If I don't have a hint of which way I'm supposed to go, I'll go the wrong way.
>
> **TH:** That makes me a kind of judge, and you're like a prisoner pleading her case?
>
> **PT:** I don't like not knowing . . . anything! I've always had to be that way, acted the way I was supposed to act, never causing anybody any distress. Either . . . you know, kids are supposed to be seen and not heard, but I wasn't supposed to be either. So I try to make sure I know what somebody wants. Then I have the option of doing it or not doing it . . . (She falls silent.)

TH: I think this is important. I invite you to explore it further.

PT: If you're in a crowd, nobody notices you. But if it's one on one, it's obvious that either you participate or you don't. When I was growing up I was expected to act like a twenty-year-old. And I got . . . I didn't get noticed as much for doing what I was supposed to do, because nobody notices you until you do something wrong. So I could just . . . fade into the woodwork. I never like being the center of attention.

This woman is describing how very hard it is for her to function as a center of autonomy, feeling, and initiative. It took her six months to be able to say even this much, and she was still months away from actually saying aloud anything that she privately thought.

RESISTING THE PATIENT'S COMPLIANCE

By now it should be clear that the therapist is looking for moments of honesty, or moments in sessions when honesty is at least briefly a possibility. We do not expect patients to be able to do this on their own initiative; quiet borderline patients will reach for compliance rather than honesty. It would be better if these patients were able to resist the therapist; as we have noted, resistance implies at least a rudimentary identity and is the foundation for further self–other differentiation. Lacking a core of identity, as-if patients also lack the capacity for meaningful resistance. It is therefore up to the therapist to provide the resistance out of which the patient's identity may be created.

The therapist should try to interact with the patient in ways that offer resistance to the patient's characteristic compliance. For example, the therapist may ask whether the patient would like to have something different during sessions from what happens with people outside of sessions. The patient is very likely to misunderstand this idea. Certainly the as-if patient will not normally assume that interactions are even possible without the other person's providing cues and the patient's offering compliance.

> One therapist asked his patient, a 25-year-old office manager for a small company, whether she wanted to have something different happen in sessions from what usually happened to her outside sessions. The patient, who had been quite promiscuous, immediately assumed that he was proposing a sexual encounter and exclaimed, "You can get in trouble for that!" The therapist replied, "I'm not talking about sex; you do that outside of here already" and repeated his question. The interaction illustrates how hard it is for quiet borderline patients even to imagine a different type of relationship. This patient had immediately fallen back on the only role she knew to play with men. After the therapist's reply, the patient fell silent and seemed confused about what the therapist could possibly be offering.

When the patient becomes confused, the therapist has the chance to develop the idea. For instance, the therapist may propose that in sessions the patient could consider saying something only if he or she truly meant it, noting that in daily life people sometimes say things that they do not fully mean. The therapist can follow up by interrupting from time to time, asking whether the patient in fact means what he or she is saying. The therapist can point out cues that lead to doubts about the patient's honesty—for example, that the patient has scanned the therapist's face carefully while talking, as though the patient were an actor "playing to the crowd."

These sorts of comments are important, for they offer an expanded dimension to the patient, namely, subjectivity. The therapist is proposing something about the patient's intentions, and this is radically different for the patient, who has not so far been able to glimpse his or her "inside" or private self. Suddenly, there is a prospect of seeing in the therapist's response something hitherto invisible (i.e., subjectivity). By grasping the cues the therapist uses to catch sight of this inner self, the patient may start to use the therapist as a mirror; that is, the patient may start to monitor his or her behavior, watching for some of the same cues and reaching conclusions about underlying feelings and intentions that were previously invisible. This is in contrast to how the patient has used the therapist previously. While it is true that the patient has already looked to the therapist for cues on how to behave, this was for the purpose of becoming an extension of the therapist, or continuing the pseudo-mirroring he or she had begun in childhood. Now for the first time the patient may actually catch a glimpse of him- or herself apart from the therapist, that is, using the therapist as a true mirror.

The therapist may also resist the as-if individual's characteristic compliance through focusing on the patient's body. We believe that the capacity for integrity and honesty is grounded in our bodies, in the irreducible fact that we are corporeal. There is a reality to physical existence that defies our capacity for fantasy and illusion; the language of the body will eventually prove louder than the language of abstraction. As-if patients are essentially trying to avoid the boundedness of physical existence. These individuals are, after all, trying to be extensions of others, which is to say that they are trying to avoid being separate persons. Their passivity and compliance serve this aim, to define themselves as another's object, not as independent subjects. A therapeutic focus on the patient's body calls the patient back to him- or herself and separates the patient from the therapist psychologically.

This is not to say that quiet borderline patients are necessarily oblivious to their bodies until the therapist focuses on this aspect of existence. Far from being oblivious, these individuals can be quite aware of the impact of their physical manner and appearance on others, including the impact on the therapist. Yet their awareness of their bodies is from a psychological distance; as-if individuals see their bodies as they imagine others are seeing them. We might say that they *have their bodies* but not that they *are their bodies*. The therapist's aim is to change this, to make patients experience their bodies from the inside, as it were, rather than from an objective point of view.

Therefore the therapist may refer patients back to the cues that can be taken from their bodies. The therapist should observe how patients sit, what they do with their feet and hands, and how tense or relaxed they seem in their posture. These may be the basis for comments on what the patient seems to be feeling.

> One therapist asked an as-if patient, "Are you as tense as your body looks to me?" The patient replied, "How tense do I look?" The therapist said that the patient had been kicking her foot back and forth rapidly and was sitting in a rigid, tight posture. The patient reflected for a moment and said that she guessed she was in fact feeling tense that day. In this case, the therapist had used a focus on the patient's body to help the patient identify a subjective state.

Other ways to focus on the patient's body include watching for discrepancies between what the patient says and his or her facial expressions. A patient who says that he or she is sad while looking relaxed and pleasant, for instance, offers the therapist the chance to comment on the mixed message. The therapist may ask, for example, "Which do you want me to take seriously—what you're saying or what your body is saying?" The therapist may also ask the patient to put into words what the body seems to be saying; the therapist is suggesting, as it were, "I already know that your body is speaking the truth, and this is your chance to speak truthfully as well." Again, the intent is to offer a glimpse of the patient's potential for an inner world, or what we have earlier called subjectivity.

The therapist must communicate that he or she is not focusing on the body for his or her personal gratification or enhancement. Rather, the therapist wants to convey that the patient is "in" a body that is capable of communicating with others. The therapist is intent on showing that he or she is paying attention to the patient's communications. All of this is in contrast to how as-if patients experienced their bodies while growing up, when their bodies—like the rest of them—seemed to be there for the sake of the other person. The therapist is trying to point to the question of who owns the patient's body. It was the patient's experience growing up that there was nothing purely private in life and therefore that the body was to be experienced from the standpoint of the other, not from a personal, subjective position.

Such a theme is certainly not something that will be laid to rest in one or two sessions. The matter of who owns the patient's body (like the larger question of becoming a subject) will persist for many months. At first, the patient will very likely assume that the therapist has some sexual interest when there is any focus on the body. Patients who have been promiscuous will usually be aware of what impact they have sexually, including the impact on the therapist. It will not be an easy task to communicate that this is not the therapist's focus as well, that the therapist is trying to see the whole patient, not just a part. The therapist's message is that the body is part of who the patient is and how the patient relates and communicates; the body is more than sexual, because the patient is more than the therapist's object.

Finally, let us highlight one more way that the therapist can begin to offer resistance to the patient's characteristic compliance: It may be useful to ask what has led the patient to seek out therapy at this particular time. Presumably something has taken place in the patient's life that has prompted at least the idea of a change. In itself, the idea of change is not enough to cause the patient to become different upon entering the consulting room. The patient will quickly revert to form, trying to become an extension of the therapist, hoping perhaps that it will be better than being an extension of someone else. By paying close attention to the experiences that led the patient to come to therapy at this time, the therapist may help the patient recover some sense of dissatisfaction with his or her life. If this happens, the therapist is in a better position to point out that the patient appears to be dealing with the session pretty much as he or she deals with life in general. The question may then be raised whether this is not something the patient had wanted to change. While this is a strategy that could be used with any patient, we believe it is especially useful with as-if patients. They have trouble letting themselves be aware of their own dissatisfactions and complaints, since they avoid whatever might put them in conflict with the environment. This line of questioning by the therapist helps the patient recall what events led to thoughts of change and in the process tends to legitimize feelings of dissatisfaction the patient would otherwise be tempted to avoid.

In this chapter we have traced basic elements of a treatment approach to the quiet borderline patient. Much of what we have said has been negative, that the therapist should avoid time-limited and problem-solving approaches and that the sorts of approaches commonly associated with Kohut's thinking seem unlikely to succeed. It is harder to propose specific strategies and interventions. The therapist is trying to show that the world can bring the patient to life; needless to say, there is no single set of interventions guaranteed to bring such a thing about.

Our approach emphasizes the relative unimportance of the patient's words and the overarching importance of what type of relationship the patient is trying to create with the therapist. The therapist should watch for evidence that the patient is avoiding subjectivity and instead seeks simply to be an extension of the therapist. This leads to the question of whether the patient is capable of genuineness in a relationship, which in turn is the question of whether the patient can want to be taken seriously.

The approach we have outlined is essentially designed to bring this issue home to the patient. The therapist seeks to take the patient seriously and force him or her out of simply being the therapist's object. To accomplish this, the therapist overtly raises the question of whether the patient wants to be taken seriously or can even imagine such a thing. The therapist's strategy is to raise the question in order to produce some tension with the patient's normal way of living. The therapist does not press the matter, however, working slowly instead of seeking premature closure.

The patient can be counted on to respond with compliance to whatever he or she believes the therapist wants. The therapeutic stance is to resist the patient's passive compliance and pseudo-relatedness. The therapist does this by raising the question of whether the therapeutic interaction can become different from others in the patient's life, by focusing on the patient's body as the patient's most honest way of communicating, and by reminding the patient what led him or her to seek treatment at this time. All these interventions are designed to produce moments of honesty and, eventually, genuineness on the part of the patient.

5

The Appearance of
Normalcy

INTRODUCTION

In this chapter we are primarily concerned with the first three or four sessions. We must admit that we cannot recognize as-if pathology in the first session, sometimes not in the first several sessions. It would be strange, in fact, if it were otherwise. Therapists go into initial sessions with certain silent assumptions, that the person who comes to see them is seeking something and hopes (or wants to hope) that the encounter with the therapist will somehow change matters. These are reasonable assumptions for the therapist to have at the outset of treatment, and the new patient will be seen in their light. Unhappily, such assumptions cloud the therapist's ability to see the as-if patient accurately. As-if patients do not enter therapy as seekers but want primarily to respond to what others seek from them.

In some ways, quiet borderline patients will initially sound much like anyone else. They will tell their story to the therapist, and there are usually no warning signs that it is an as-if story or that the patient's problems are as-if problems. The therapist's first clue that matters are not what they seem will probably occur near the end of the first session, when the therapist finds that he or she is still not sure why the patient is there. Therapists will notice an unaccountable discrepancy—the patient seems to be relating information about a problem or concern, but somehow it has all remained so vague and hard to get hold of that the therapist is not sure how to summarize it. It is as though the patient has produced an illusion: There was the appearance of giving out important information, but nothing has actually been communicated.

In this situation, therapists may find that most of what they believe about the patient's problems is the result of their own interpretation, not the result of what the patient has said. In effect, the patient has provided a very general outline and induced the therapist to fill in the details. Unless they are very careful, therapists will jump to small conclusions here and there about what ails the patient, only to realize later that these conclusions did not come from what the patient said but from their own desire to discover meaning and reach closure. Therapists are trained to find meaning in events; it can be hard for them to tolerate incomplete and seemingly meaningless sequences, and it is tempting to impose their own conclusions instead. The patient's vagueness is a quiet invitation for the therapist to create a plausible fiction for the patient to live out with the therapist.

> One patient came for treatment, saying only, "I'm turning 40" when the therapist asked about presenting problems. The patient seemed to believe that the therapist would then pick up the theme and develop it and said nothing more. The therapist did not think that he had anything worth saying at that point, and so he waited. The patient responded to the therapist's silence by saying, "I don't like that." The therapist noted the communication and waited some more, still feeling that there was nothing worth saying and not knowing what, if anything, the woman expected him to do about her turning 40. Over several sessions it became clear that the patient was affectively vacant and could neither recognize nor verbalize what she felt or wanted beyond

vague, halting statements such as her presenting complaint. She typically let others develop her feelings and attitudes for her, as it were. It would have been easy for the therapist to pepper the woman with questions about the significance of turning forty; each question would surely have implied the therapist's own assumptions and would have hinted what he was prepared to believe about the woman. The patient would probably have gone along with this approach, and the two would have crafted a script for her to live out during sessions. However, the patient herself would have been completely lost to sight, and the "problems" worked on in sessions would have had nothing to do with the patient.

There is, therefore, the problem of what brings the patient to treatment. This is actually the problem of how to realize that the patient seldom knows why he or she has come. The therapist has started the treatment with the (understandable but mistaken) assumption that the patient has some idea, and the first step to a proper diagnosis is for the therapist to correct this assumption. After one or more sessions, the therapist will begin to think, "I still don't know why you're here"; a step toward diagnosis will be taken when the therapist realizes that this puzzlement parallels the patient's state of mind: The patient cannot tell the therapist why he or she has come because the patient cannot imagine what could be hoped for or how things could be different. All the patient knows is to carry on as usual. The therapist's puzzlement, therefore, reveals the patient's inability to make demands on the therapist or to imagine alternatives.

The reason the as-if patient's first session(s) can leave the therapist in the dark is that the patient does not know how to be *abnormal*. Human beings tend to look normal to the extent that they are in touch with the social world and can respond to it. When people forget or ignore the rules that govern public behavior, they appear eccentric, strange, or abnormal. In the therapist's office, patients have the freedom to let loose of the restrictions that normally govern their speech and behavior, exploring and expressing possibilities that would be deviant in another setting. To accomplish something in treatment, patients must be willing to bring their problems into the office and, in effect, be abnormal for the duration of a session. Even in the first session, most patients will find themselves saying things that would be quite out of place with the other people in their lives. The therapist is used to this and thinks little of it—unless it fails to occur.

As-if patients tend to speak and act in the therapist's office much as they do outside the office; they are still responding as they would to the social world in general. In contrast to most patients, who gradually show their private selves to the therapist, as-if patients remain their public selves, trying to be acutely aware of what the other (in this case the therapist) expects. Thus, even when as-if patients describe problems to the therapist, there is a reserve and lack of ownership, as though they were discussing someone else's problems. Even if the content is intimate, the manner is general and public.

The therapist is not likely to hear anything from as-if patients in the first few sessions that would awaken concern or alarm. There is no sense of crisis unless the patient feels that this is expected. As-if patients seem unhurried, relatively untroubled, and even content. They do not seem concerned about the future, nor does one hear guilt and regret over the past. There is little variation in the intensity of affect, nothing high or low really (this too-flat affective picture was probably one reason Deutsch was willing to consider a schizophrenic basis for as-if pathology). All this blends together to give the appearance of normalcy to these individuals, even in the therapist's office. Paradoxically, this is in itself quite abnormal. It is, therefore, an ironic fact that the therapist may first suspect how ill these individuals are after noting how normal they have managed to look for several sessions.

FIRST IMPRESSIONS

Most treatments start with some statement from the patient about why he or she has come. As already noted, this is something that is likely to remain unsettled by the end of the first session; the actual encounter with the patient tells the therapist relatively little. The therapist will very rarely hear a specific question in the first session with a quiet borderline patient, and it will not be at all clear what the patient thought would happen in the session or wanted to happen. Curiously, these patients do not seem to have doubts about whether therapy can be helpful (this is not to say that they have a clear idea what would or would not be useful). Quiet borderline patients usually take for granted that whatever the therapist says or does is the right thing, which is part of their overall pattern of not doubting the other or knowing how to make demands of the other. It will not be clear to the therapist that the patient knows why they have gotten together or why they will come back together for another session.

The therapist will probably note a kind of amiability to these patients. They often try immediately to create a friendly atmosphere, as though they were trying to be nonthreatening to the therapist. In this respect, they can appear hysteroid at first. They seem to want the therapist to be comfortable, not to say or do anything that will make the therapist feel bad. Possibly for this reason, therapists may notice at the session's end that they have not been especially confrontive or hard-nosed during the first session. Therapists who find that they have felt more comfortable and been less confrontive with a new patient than is usual for them may begin to wonder whether this was the patient's intent. If the pattern persists, they would do well to look for other signs of an as-if adaptation.

The as-if patient's amiability can help the therapist distinguish this type of pathology from schizoid conditions. As-if individuals are not detached, as one would expect of schizoid individuals. It is true that the as-if patient's friendliness and sensitivity are not genuine and represent an invitation to a pseudo-relationship, but it is also true that schizoid individuals seldom make such an effort. The therapist will eventually decide that the as-if patient is shallow and vacuous; at first, however, there is likely to be the appearance of involvement, in contrast to the initially arid, reserved manner of most schizoid individuals.

The quiet borderline patient's amiability is part of his or her overall ability to fit in socially outside of treatment. It is part of what contributes to the appearance of normalcy in these individuals. They are able to fit in on the job, in school, and in other social settings because they seldom create conflict with others. Indeed, they tend not to be aware of conflict, much less cause it. In an intimate relationship, this is abnormal; human beings inevitably clash with one another from time to time if they are intimately involved. Thus, in an intimate relationship, it will become gradually obvious that something is amiss if one person is unable to make demands or do anything else that might create tension. On the job or in other less intimate settings, however, an individual who fails to see and never creates conflict may fit in quite well. They may not only appear normal but they may even appear superbly well adjusted.

As-if individuals tend to have problems on the job or in social settings only when they are caught between two other people in conflict and are asked to take a side. Again, in this situation they can appear hysteroid. Hysterics are notorious for mishandling conflict in three-person interactions; while they may actually generate tension in two-person interactions (usually in the interest of producing more closeness, however), they avoid assuming responsibility for taking a position in three-party settings. The hysteric's discomfort in triadic relationships reflects the oedipal dynamics that underlie this pathology and ought not be confused with the quiet borderline patient's dilemma. The quiet borderline individual would feel uneasy with conflict in both two- and three-person interactions, and there is nothing oedipal about it. Having to choose a side means having to be a subject, to define the situation out of one's own private intentions and meanings. The quiet borderline individual seeks to be the other's object, however, and therefore cannot choose sides. These individuals are usually paralyzed when they are caught between two other people in conflict; they tend to act as though there were no conflict, or they agree with whomever they are with at the time. In these settings they can look quite bad to others, since they may seem to be lying or manipulating when in fact they are only continuing their pattern of being whoever the other person wishes them to be.

> One quiet borderline patient came for marital therapy after her husband showed signs of dissatisfaction with their relationship. In their first appointment with one therapist, the husband and the therapist began an especially heated argument. As the patient remembered it several years later, the exchange was so intense that she felt her husband and the therapist would come to blows before the session ended. The patient found herself unable to say or do anything, although she felt terribly uncomfortable and agitated. She began picking the leaves off a large plant in the therapist's office in her agitation. By session's end she had stripped the plant of all the leaves on one side. The therapist had apparently been so lost in the argument with her husband that he never noticed. At session's end, the patient found herself very pleasantly saying good-bye to the therapist as if nothing upsetting had occurred.
>
> Another as-if patient was increasingly upset by severe conflict in the home between her son and her husband, the boy's stepfather. The woman could not bring herself to say or do anything about the increasingly bitter struggles between the two even though she felt torn and upset. She sided with whichever person she was with at the time and tried to withdraw physically during arguments. The woman was genuinely troubled by the ongoing conflict. Her eventual solution was to try to arrange individual therapy for herself, her son, and her husband. She was trying to turn a three-party problem into a series of two-person interactions. Not surprisingly, in her own therapy she could not define what she wanted to work on; she could only say how much she wanted her husband and son to get along.

The quiet borderline patient's dilemma when trapped between two people in conflict reveals the abnormal nature of what at first appears to be normalcy. As we noted earlier, truly normal people have the capacity to be deviant. They find some situations to be an affront to their integrity, and they rebel. It is therefore a part of having integrity to be capable of producing tension, behaving angrily, and being willing to make others unhappy. When therapists notice that a patient is not capable of these normal instances of protest and rebellion, they should probe for what might be termed automatic normalcy on the part of the patient. The question to be answered is whether a patient is willing under any circumstances to defy the norm laid down by the other. The less individuals are willing to do this the less healthy they are, even though they will look quite normal in most settings.

It can be useful for therapists to adopt an interpersonal orientation when trying to think through whether a new patient shows as-if pathology. The central question in such an orientation is: What role is the patient trying to make the therapist play? Most patients will have some preference about how the therapist interacts with them, and they will eventually, if not immediately, try to engage in very much the same patterns of interaction that characterize their out-of-session behavior. If they are most comfortable with sadomasochistic relationships, for instance, they will try to create exchanges with the therapist that are colored by anger, tension, and abuse. For another example, if they are used to experiencing themselves as righteous and indignant rebels against unjust authority, they will seek to define the therapist as someone who wants to control and dominate them, trying to elicit an interaction that supports this expectation and, consequently, their experience of themselves. No matter the type of interaction the patient is comfortable with, some role is implied for the therapist, and much can be learned about the patient through trying to determine what role is being assigned.

The striking thing about quiet borderline patients from an interpersonal point of view is that they are not apparently trying to maneuver the therapist into a role. They appear to have no particular expectations; if they do, these expectations are far from obvious. As-if patients do not seem to have preset ideas about what would constitute a good session or about what would be a proper goal for their work in therapy. Therapists who watch for an indication of what role the patient expects them to play may find that they have spent the entire session waiting in vain. Commenting on this phenomenon, one therapist said, "At the end of the session it's like having stared at the sky all day waiting for the sun to come out."

To the extent that the therapist is asked to play a role, it is that he or she set the tone of the session and provide its energy. In listening to the as-if patient's story, the therapist may notice that there are not the usual emotional ups and downs. The patient may be talking about seemingly meaningful and important material, but there is nonetheless nothing especially exciting or saddening about it. It is as though the therapist were supposed to provide the emotion and energy to go with the material. The patient may report events that would seem to call for strong affect, and in fact the therapist may even feel called on for some response but not be at all sure what the response ought to be. Therapists may over and over have the experience of simply not being able to tell what the patient's reaction to an event has been, or even if there has been a reaction.

> In the first session, one patient reported that her mother had died two months earlier. The therapist could not tell what impact this had on the patient and was at a loss how (or whether) to respond. He asked, "Do you miss her?" The patient said, "I think about her sometimes." The therapist did not feel that he knew much more than before he asked, and so he repeated his question. The patient answered along the same lines, and the therapist asked the question for a third time. The patient's third response was, "I'd like her to be around sometimes." This was as close as the patient came to showing some reaction to her mother's death. The therapist was struck that the subject opened up nothing emotionally and produced no basis for a more intimate exchange with the patient. The subject seemed to have no importance for the patient, nor was there any interpersonal significance for the patient in telling the story to the therapist.

Quiet borderline patients tend to be fairly smooth and unruffled in their first sessions. It does not appear to be hard for the patient to be with the therapist, and there is usually no sign of anxiety or unease. The patient's presentation tends to be fairly even; there is little halting or hesitancy. The most frequent exception to this occurs when the patient wants cues from the therapist on how he or she is doing and in the process grows uncomfortable if these cues are not forthcoming. For the most part, however, these individuals seem comfortable and offer the appearance of normalcy. To the extent that there are deviations in any of this, the patient is probably not an as-if individual.

MOVING TOWARD DIAGNOSIS

There are several indications of as-if pathology that can be seen in the first three or four sessions, and it is useful to look for them. The patient's appearance is one of relative normalcy, and the therapist needs some way to see what lies behind the appearance, ways to tease out pathology that hides behind a seemingly adaptive exterior. Our experience suggests that each of the six indications we discuss will likely be visible in the first four sessions.

The Absence of Affective Variability

In the previous chapter, we suggested that therapists may begin to move toward an as-if diagnosis when they note a kind of persistent hollowness to the patient's productions—there is no affective vitality to the patient's words. The therapist should try to determine whether there is a range of affect as the patient talks and whether any of the therapist's interventions deepen the patient's affect. It is not enough simply to listen for words that suggest a range of emotion; the question is whether the patient communicates affect that is consistent with his or her language. Even if the patient's language suggests a wide array of emotions, the as-if patient tends to talk in an even, slightly stiff or stilted tone.

What is missing is spontaneity. Our words come to life when we intend to summon up our private world in order to reveal it to another person. There is a kind of creativity to this, an energy that is contagious and enlivening when people do it especially well—hence the impact of a good poem or the deep excitement we feel from long, intimate conversations in the early days of love. The energy, contagion, and enlivening come from our sense that there is no distance between the speaker and his or her words. The speaker is in some sense spontaneously in the words that are being used.

This is not at all the case with the as-if patient, for whom words seem merely to fill up time or cover over interpersonal gaps. Even when the content seems intimate and laden with emotion, the impact on the hearer is much as though it were cocktail-party conversation. It is as though the patient grew up in a world where words were relied on to structure situations but not to reveal anything personal. Consequently, the patient's words have little to do with actual affect; even if the patient says, "I was angry," the therapist will not have a sense that it was so, only that the patient knows that he or she should have been angry or will be expected by the therapist to have been angry.

Consequently, there is no range of affect as the patient talks, even as the patient talks about important matters. Therapists may even find that they originally thought there was a range of emotion but that they were the ones providing it. They may discover that they made a series of assumptions about what the patient felt but that these were largely the therapist's projections.

The Patient's Response to Personal Questions

There doesn't seem to be anything especially private about these patients. It is difficult to violate their integrity with a question that is too personal or pointed in the first few sessions. Our rule of thumb is that patients who seem flustered or embarrassed by a question in the first sessions or who say that they would prefer to wait for a time before getting into a personal subject are probably not quiet borderline patients. We have never seen a quiet borderline patient seem embarrassed at a question early in treatment.

This is not a surprising trait. We have described as-if patients as passive and plastic. They are inclined to take the other person's word for what is or is not allowed in a situation, and in therapy they accept the therapist's questions and interventions as normal, as what ought to be asked. They lack a sense of privacy with which to oppose the therapist's questions, and so no question feels too personal. Indeed, as-if patients often produce material that is too personal too early (although even overly personal material will be produced in an affectively vacant way). While the patient seems to feel comfortable, the therapist may be the one feeling vaguely uneasy at intimate details disclosed too quickly (for example, the patient mentioned in Chapter 4, pp. 100–101).

The Discovery of Widely Discrepant Life-styles

A further consequence of the patient's plasticity is the assumption of whatever life-style is endorsed by the person the patient is with. Therapists may find that their as-if patients have done (and continue to do) things that seem utterly incompatible, yet with no sense of tension or conflict. It is as though the patient has simply taken on the values of the other person, and it does not especially matter what those values are.

> One staid, conservative, middle-class woman was quite sexually promiscuous and used drugs right up to the time when she met her current husband. Curiously, it did not seem at all difficult for her suddenly to become much more conservative in her behavior upon learning her husband-to-be's preference. For another example, an earnest and respected member of an Alcoholics Anonymous chapter had taken part in a Satanic cult in which he was involved with animal and infant sacrifices. Neither of these individuals seemed bothered by what they had

done or felt any strong conflict with how they lived in the present. They accounted for their actions by saying simply that everyone they hung around with behaved like that. They showed no signs of guilt or remorse, and there was no evidence that they found anything jarring about the contrasting periods of their lives.

This phenomenon might be understood as a matter of defective superego formation, which is how Deutsch saw her patients' sexual promiscuity. As we noted in Chapter 1, however, this problem is better understood as an identity-related problem. There must be some sense of continuity with self before the past can feel at odds with the present. The quiet borderline patient does not feel continuous; it is as though the person is re-created anew in every situation, simply taking on the dimensions of the present situation and casting off whatever came before. In other words, the patient's identity is situation specific and, consequently, time limited. There being no continuous sense of self, there is nothing jarring about a change in life-styles, values, and loyalties.

The therapist should therefore pay attention to periods in the patient's life when the style of behavior seemed quite different from the present. What the therapist will want to know is whether the patient feels uneasy with the difference. Many therapy patients have had a "wild period" in their lives and feel uneasy about what they once did or feel that at least they would not be able to do the same things now. However, in contrast to most individuals, as-if patients will not feel tension between the present and past (unless they sense that the therapist expects them to), and one readily gets the idea that they could return to that earlier style of behavior again if circumstances led them to do so.

The Patient's Response to Confrontational Statements

Generally, in the first few sessions with most patients, the therapist has occasion to make a remark that is at least mildly confrontational. With most patients the result is a certain degree of tension and discomfort. The as-if patient's response is, in our experience, unique; these individuals seem dumbfounded, as though they do not know what to do with the situation. It is not clear that they experience the confrontation as tension producing. In any event, they do not seem tense or upset and may even ask for clarification, as though they were trying to decipher how they should react.

We believe that this is a function of how quiet borderline patients handle conflict in general. They usually do not see it, simply splitting off events that would, if held in mind at the same time, produce conflict or tension. In Chapter 3, we observed that as-if patients seem unable to recognize or describe to the therapist family conflicts as they grew up. We speculated that these patients had learned never to surrender to spontaneous emotion but learned instead to stand at an emotional distance, watching and editing what they felt and did. If this is so, then the emotions most likely to be filtered out would be those that indicated interpersonal tensions. There was no point in the patient's becoming conscious of such emotions, since the patient, as a child, was looking for cues on what was expected, and these emotions would, if anything, obscure them. Thus, the as-if patient's tendency is automatically to ignore interpersonal tensions except insofar as these provide cues on roles to play.

> In the fourth session with a patient who was showing quiet borderline traits, the therapist said, "You really don't know who you are." The patient looked confused; she stared at the floor, then at her hands, then at the chair she was sitting in, and finally asked the therapist what he meant. It turned out that she did not wonder so much at the content of the therapist's remark as its interpersonal intent. She could not imagine how she was supposed to react or what the therapist wanted from her.

Countertransference Patterns

There are two countertransference patterns that may appear early in treatment as a reaction to as-if pathology. First, the therapist may feel bored and sleepy. This reaction is not likely to occur in the first session but may be noticeable during the second session and afterwards. When the case is new, the therapist is invested in trying to understand the patient, and this clinical curiosity keeps the therapist involved. Eventually, the therapist loses whatever drive comes from the desire to understand the patient, however, and initial curiosity is replaced with difficulty feeling connected. The therapist's boredom is probably based on a sense of being in the room alone and also may reflect the lack of affective vitality in the patient's productions.

The second countertransference pattern is more difficult to describe. The therapist finds that there are no reliable cues on whether he or she is having a mutually understood dialogue versus imputing idiosyncratic meaning to the patient's comments. It is as though the patient were functioning as a Rorschach card or some other ambiguous stimulus, offering the therapist the chance at times to understand the patient and at other times the chance to project extensively, with no way to know the difference.

> One somewhat paranoid therapist found himself wondering if a new patient was trying to fool him. During the second session, the patient was talking about her father and seemed to be covering important ground, although she talked in an uninvolved, mechanical way. The therapist unaccountably found himself wondering if the patient was trying to see if he could tell when she was genuinely involved in the session versus when she was just going through the motions. As the session went on, he began to think that she might be secretly comparing him with her first therapist, trying to see which therapist was sharper. Throughout the session, the patient apparently did nothing to awaken such paranoid fantasies. Indeed, the patient seemed quite content with the session and did not seem to have any questions about the way it went.

The important feature of this countertransferential reaction is that the therapist's response has nothing to do with the verbal content of the session. The therapist is instead reacting to the patient's unspoken plasticity. The patient's manner is communicating to the therapist "I am not committed to what I am saying." The very ambiguity of the situation then calls up the therapist's personal tendencies, much as a projective test might.

The Question of Another Session

During the first few sessions with most new patients, there is generally some question about further appointments. This is the time during treatment when most patients are trying to determine whether therapy will be of help, and therapists are trying to decide whether they want to work with the case. It is the time before patient and therapist have settled into some agreed-upon program with a set appointment time and the expectation of further sessions. Thus, at the end of the first sessions there is generally some uncertainty about whether the patient will be returning.

With the as-if patient, however, whatever uncertainty exists is only on the part of the therapist. We do not find quiet borderline patients to have questions about coming back for another appointment. Their manner of responding to the therapist's question, "Do you want another appointment?" is generally one of surprise. It is clear by their response that it had not crossed their minds not to return. The only exception to this we have found occurred when a patient was upset at the therapist's (possibly too) rigorous silence and elected not to return (see Chapter 1, p. 17) after only a few sessions. Apart from this unusual situation, as-if patients seem to assume that the session has gone as it should and that they are of course returning. It may help a therapist rule out as-if pathology if a new patient seems hesitant about returning for a second appointment.

FINAL CONSIDERATIONS ON THE APPEARANCE OF NORMALCY

Our impression is that most quiet borderline patients come to therapy at someone else's suggestion. Even so, these individuals seldom look very disturbed, even to those who refer them. Friends who refer these patients usually do not see them as being in danger of emotional collapse and generally think the patient is in need of help with some fairly circumscribed, reality-level problem. Others making referrals are often looking for help themselves; involved with the patient in some way, they are unhappy with the relationship and hope that the therapist can do something about it. Thus, the referral may not say as much about the patient as about the person referring the patient.

> One man wanted to break up with a woman he had had an affair with for several months. He felt guilty about this, although the woman was not very upset. He insisted that she come for therapy, and she did, although she could not quite say why. It appeared to the therapist that the woman would not have thought of coming on her own and that her ex-lover referred her in hopes of feeling less guilty.
>
> A husband pressured his wife to come to treatment after she had an affair. Although he was actually the one upset, the wife said that she was willing to come, adding only the proviso that he had to pay the bill. The therapist learned that the patient had had the affair because "it was a chance to be with someone interesting." She added that she was willing to be in therapy because it was "another chance to be with someone interesting." The woman really had no other concerns or complaints and was there because of her husband's upset over her affair.

The appearance of normalcy in as-if patients is actually the absence of flagrant pathology. If therapists will canvass their caseloads, they will find that other patients in their practice seem different from the quiet borderline patient. Most patients are clearly in need of the help they ask for or show some behavior that indirectly implies a need for help. By contrast, quiet borderline patients do not seem to behave very deviantly or eccentrically (at least not compared to those they are with) and appear relatively unburdened. They seem almost to be searching for a problem when they talk to the therapist, trying to find something that might explain why they are there.

One patient complained of "problems eating and drinking" in the first session but was unable to develop the theme. These supposed complaints never came up again. Another said that drinking was a problem, but the therapist could not find any marked difficulty in that area. When he said as much, the patient seemed uncommitted to the complaint and willingly gave it up. Finally, one patient came for treatment because of having to take work home every night. She wondered if "I will ever get a weekend to myself."

Before leaving this topic, we want to turn briefly to the question of ethnicity and the as-if patient. When we look at the issue of what types of relationships as-if patients have with family members, we find a kind of impersonality to the emotional life with a tendency toward rather little public expression of affect. That is, there is what might be termed a certain WASPishness to family interactions. Of course, the dynamics are not at all the same: In the classic WASP family, affect is being stifled and overcontrolled, while the as-if patient has grown up in a world of pseudo-affect. Yet WASP and as-if families may look the same, or, rather, the as-if family is something of a caricature of the WASP culture. This raises the question of whether as-if patients could come from ethnic groups in which a high degree of expressed emotion is accepted and in fact encouraged.

The idea behind the as-if adaptation is to avoid differences between people. By contrast, a highly emotional style of family interaction reflects an acceptance of any tension that family members might create, and in fact relatedness is often measured in terms of the intensity of emotional interchange. Where there is freedom to express a range of emotions, an arena is created for the unique characteristics of the individual to emerge. In contrast, where the range is limited, the emphasis is more likely to be on maintaining a semblance of harmony. Furthermore, there is little tolerance for overt differentiation. In such an atmosphere, conflict will be ignored or dismissed, which contributes to the problem of maintaining self continuity and failure to learn about reconciliation. It is difficult to imagine a quiet borderline patient feeling comfortable with any style that highlights—even briefly—the ways people are separate and different. For this reason, we are inclined to believe that quiet borderline patients are less likely to come from those ethnic groups that tolerate or encourage a high degree of emotionality in family exchanges.

In this chapter, we have addressed the ways the quiet borderline patient is initially likely to appear normal or at least untroubled to the therapist. These patients will not know why they have come for therapy and will present themselves in amiable, cooperative ways. During the first three or four sessions, therapists may observe several traits that suggest an as-if diagnosis. These include: the absence of affective variability in the patient; little sense of privacy; a history of widely discrepant life-styles with no sense of tension between them; nondefensive responses to confrontations; and an assumption on the patient's part that there will be further sessions, no matter how poorly the therapist thought the first session went. Therapists may also notice increasing boredom after the first or second session and confusion over whether they are understanding the patient or merely "filling in the blanks." These characteristics in patients who seem relatively normal should raise the question of an as-if diagnosis.

TRANSCRIPT: AS-IF TRAITS IN THE FIRST SESSION

This is the first interview with Dick, a 32-year-old man who has come to a training clinic, asking for therapy. Dick's wife is in treatment at the same clinic, and he has come at her urging. Dick is an engineer in a supervisory job; he is in his second marriage, and he has no children. Dick's manner of presenting himself is the focus of study here. By the end of the session it is not, of course, clear whether Dick is an as-if patient. However, he shows most of the signs that would alert a therapist that an as-if diagnosis should be considered. We want to note that the interviewer is a second-year graduate student, and this is one of her first appointments. As with anyone who is just learning, she makes many mistakes, which is to be expected; hence, except as they bear on diagnosis, her errors will not be commented on.

Dick seems to be in no distress and comes across as quite untroubled throughout the interview. His manner is casual and affiliative for the most part, and he never shows strong affect. Several times in the course of the interview, Dick notices that the therapist expects him to show some sort of problem; he tries very hard to comply whenever he sees this, even though his efforts are obviously forced. Initially, Dick seems to interact with the therapist much as he might with women in daily life, but he seems willing to change to whatever role the therapist expects.

About one third of this transcript has been deleted due to excessively banal content. This is not to say that what remains is exciting; in fact, the sheer mundaneness of the session illustrates what might be expected of an as-if patient in the first months. The transcript begins just as Dick and the therapist sit down. Dick has made a slightly flirtatious comment that was not captured on the tape. The therapist is replying to that comment as the session opens.

TH: Was that meant for me?

PT: (laughing loudly) No. If we were dating, and we were sitting like this, it might be a little uncomfortable, but . . . I don't like to be interrogated.

TH: Do you feel like I'm interrogating you?

PT: No, I don't. I, I guess that's another part of the dating ritual. You have to find out about the other person, and I may have to find out about you. (talking in a way that suggests humor and familiarity) I don't look at that as interrogation; it's just getting to know someone else, how the other person approaches it.

TH: What was your experience of that with Sherry [his wife] during the getting-to-know-each-other phase?

PT: It was a little difficult because she was, when we first met, she was still married. Our relationship was just a working relationship. I had thoughts . . . I think she had been married for about three years. And um, I think she and her husband were having some problems at that time, but, um, you know there wasn't anything that I was aware of. So, we got to know each other just on a friendly, uh, professional relationship. (pause) So there was a group of, of about eight of us, it may not have been that many, but I'd say there was about six or eight of us, all about close together in age—Sherry was probably the youngest. I don't think I was the oldest. We all hung around together—we all worked for the same company.

TH: Um, hmm.

PT: And we all played together some, and her, her husband, George, was at some of those events. So, we knew a lot about each other before we really started dating, so we really didn't have to go through that.

TH: Good.

PT: Yeah, I think that's good.

TH: That can be much more comfortable than the interrogation route.

PT: Yeah, yeah, some people I dated we went through the: Are you married, have you been married, do you have children?

TH: Is that what it's like?

PT: Where'd you go to school?
(This is the second time Dick has shown an interest in

talking about the therapist instead of himself. He earlier made the comment, "I might have to find out about you." As we noted earlier, some as-if patients prefer to talk about the therapist. However, Dick may simply be showing a certain narcissistic flirtatiousness and the hope that he can avoid focusing on himself. In any event, it is clear fairly early that Dick is not inclined to look inside himself.)

TH: Would you fill this out?

PT: Yeah, here's a questionnaire; fill it out, and maybe I'll see you again. It was never that bad. But there are some very curious people, and I ran into a few of them. That's the way they were with everybody, not just me.

TH: Would you describe yourself as a private person?

PT: (suddenly serious in a slightly dramatic way) Yeah, yeah. I like, I like to keep my things personal.
(Is Dick conforming to what he believes the therapist expects? This question should occur to the therapist, since it is already obvious that there is little that is "personal" to Dick. However, it is also quite possible that he is essentially narcissistic and is trying to impress the therapist, since he is interacting with her as he would with a date.)

TH: Was it hard for you, coming to therapy?

PT: No, uh, I think five or six years ago it would have been. I, I kind of scoffed at it, but uh, I thought most people could work things out for themselves if they were having problems, if they thought they were having problems. And I had several girlfriends that were in therapy or started going to therapy, after I knew them—not because of me! (laughing) But, and, and they thought it was a really beneficial thing for them. I think I've matured a lot in the last three or four years, and there are lots of ways to get to where we want to be. And, um, I went through, I thought I maybe had some physical problems, maybe diabetes or a brain tumor. Those are very fatalistic thoughts but, um, getting, not being at one hundred percent I thought I should get some tests. And, um, there's nothing really physically wrong with me.

TH: You had some tests?

PT: Yeah, yeah, I had some tests. I had the glucose test, and I had some X-rays. I, I convinced my doctor to let me have a brain scan, and I was, I was afraid that the aneurism my dad had could have been hereditary.

TH: Um, when was it you had the tests?

PT: That was probably about '87, '86, '87, somewhere in that time frame. So . . .

TH: Everything was . . .

PT: Yeah, everything was, there was nothing wrong, so maybe I have mental problems I've suppressed, and . . .

TH: Did somebody suggest that to you?

PT: No, maybe I'm neurotic or I've got, uh, I've got a uh, some phobias. I'm not a hypochondriac, I don't think. Well, for a while I was going to the doctor about every little thing, and I thought, maybe I'm a hypochondriac, thinking things are wrong with me. But I don't think that's the case. There's nothing physical wrong, so maybe I've got some emotional disturbances. And an evaluation could help me—huh?

(Dick's revelation that he suffered a hypochondriacal period may be a factor against an as-if diagnosis. Quiet borderline patients have an odd relationship to their bodies; they are not disembodied as, for example, schizoid patients, but neither are they embodied in a

normal way. It is possible that an as-if patient might suffer some crisis in his or her relationship to the body and, experiencing it more as a possession than a part of the self, develop hypochondriacal concerns. However, a more likely possibility is that Dick is narcissistic and overly focused on all aspects of himself, or that he is moderately hysteroid.)

TH: (interrupting) Do you worry about things?

PT: Do I worry about things? Yeah, sometimes.

TH: What do you worry about?

PT: Oh, global warming and, uh, teasing you. Actually the temperature of the earth is decreasing rather than increasing, so . . .

TH: So you don't have to worry about that?

PT: Yeah, that was a great relief. (both laugh) I don't know, I worry, I worry about paying my bills, even if it's a time I'm economically solvent, or financially solvent. I sometimes worry about those kind of things. I won't be able to pay my bills or my car will blow up and insurance won't cover it. (laughs to self) It's not quite that extreme. I, I, I worry about finances. I would like—I'm not driven by money, but I'm partly driven by how much income I can bring in, I guess. I've changed jobs over the last three years. It was all for financial gain as well as increasing my responsibility and authority with the company I was moving to, and I . . . I guess men in their thirties have those career uh, I'd like to think I have a career, and I believe I do. I'm a little concerned about becoming a father. Sherry and I have talked about having kids. I would like to be a father. And I don't think it's an easy task. My friends are fathers and don't find it easy. A challenge, but something I know I can do.

TH: How do you know?

PT: Well, the lady I was engaged to before Sherry had two sons. They were with us a lot, and I was a pretty good father to them. They weren't my sole responsibility; they still had their father but, uh . . .

TH: Were you together a lot?

PT: Yeah, we lived together for two years.

TH: Why didn't you marry her?
(The therapist has just had a countertransferential reaction. For her own reasons she has indicated to Dick that she thinks there is something wrong with not marrying the woman he lived with and had, in fact, planned to marry. It is important to watch the way in which the therapist's reaction works on Dick, who tries over the next ten minutes to understand and then conform to how the therapist sees this issue. Our sense is that Dick is quite willing to be told what he felt and what was wrong with him.)

PT: Um, we, uh, I basically just didn't want to marry her. I think I was, uh, I was sexually attracted to her. We had, uh, career goals in common, but, uh, I decided I didn't love her enough to marry her. So we broke off the engagement, or I broke off the engagement.

TH: How much before the wedding did you break off the engagement?

PT: We were perpetually engaged—engaged to be engaged. We had set a date. She and I both worked for Southwestern Bell. We set a date. She changed jobs, and went to work for a company in Sharpsville, and we postponed getting married, which was probably a wise decision. We never did set another date after that, and that went on for another year and a half. And then I just decided it wasn't, it wasn't a good thing for us to be married. I loved her, but I loved her like you would a friend. I didn't feel like I loved her the way you should to marry her. And I decided I didn't want to be the father of her kids.

TH: Was there a problem with kids?

PT: No, I loved her kids. Smart, they were smart, pretty much outgoing. Well, one was outgoing; the other had a perfectionistic, uh, personality. He wasn't as easy to be with. They both liked me and liked being around me.

TH: You seemed really sad talking about her.
(Actually, he has not sounded sad at all. His tone has been conversational with an occasional dramatic pause. However, immediately after this comment, he drops his head, speaks more slowly, and sounds a little choked up. It is an open question whether the therapist intuited a mood that was just below the surface or offered a role for the patient to play.)

PT: Well . . . I guess we met in '85 and dated for a couple, a couple of years. And I guess we had, we had our rocky times. We'd date and break up and date and break up, and then we got engaged and lived together for two years. We spent a lot of time together. And it's, it's, it's sad. It was a big part of my life.

TH: (inaudible).

PT: Yeah, well, (inaudible).

TH: Were there triggers to that?

PT: Were there what?

TH: To you deciding you didn't love her enough to . . .

PT: I think I was going into a deep depression. I withdrew really bad. I think it really started before I quit Southwestern Bell. And she and I, we worked together, we were both assigned to the same site. We were both assigned to the area and worked together for that one-year period and stayed together and my contract ended and I went up and for a couple of months and then we both came up to here. I felt I needed to do something; I didn't want to marry her.

TH: You decided that while you were separated from her?

PT: Yeah. I decided before we got separated, physically.

TH: Do you remember how you came to that? I'm sensing this pattern here (laughing).
(If there is a pattern here it is not obvious to us and seems more the result of a beginning therapist's wanting to find one, joined with her overly personal reaction to this theme. The patient, however, is willing to cooperate. In what follows, he does not seem to know what the therapist wants, but he appears to be trying hard to produce it. He agrees with the therapist but obviously has no idea how to develop the point. He pauses, apparently hoping for some clues and then experiments with the theme of being controlled by someone else.)

PT: (laughs) Yeah, I do have a dating pattern or had a dating pattern.

TH: Your marriage was like that, I mean, um . . .

PT: Yeah, um . . . (long pause) As to how I came to that decision . . . We had a hectic life. The kids stayed with their dad during the week while we, uh, came up here on weekends, and we'd have the kids on the weekends and work during the week. I didn't like the life-style we had if that was going to continue. There was nothing [in the town where the kids stayed with their father] that I was happy with or wanted to do. I like being on the road and I knew that she liked being on the road and so I knew that our lives were not going to be settled. And then I get back to the thought of someone else controlling . . . my life was being controlled by someone else, by her and our jobs and living arrangements.

TH: And that was while you were still at Southwestern Bell?

PT: That started at Southwestern Bell and went on into the next job.

TH: But when you started thinking about not being with her, there were still all these forces?

PT: Yeah. I did, I did get very withdrawn. I didn't, I didn't enjoy much of anything. We'd still go on vacation. We'd still do a lot of things. We went to Dallas on vacation. We'd go snow skiing with our friends. We'd do a lot of things I enjoyed doing but . . .

TH: When you say you started withdrawing, what do you mean by that?

PT: Uh . . . Uh, I didn't interact with people like I usually did. I, uh . . .

TH: Stayed home more?

PT: I stayed home more. I wouldn't participate in conversations. Basically, I'd sit and listen. Daydream. Figure out a way to break the engagement. (laughs a little) And that was really a recurring conversation I had with myself, was how to break the engagement. And I would dwell on that so much it was about to drive me crazy.

TH: So you withdrew in response to reaching the decision to break off the engagement, in response to all these forces that were sort of impinging on you. Right?

PT: Uh huh, right. And, uh . . . I still functioned, I still went to work, still did my job, went out to eat with the people we worked with. (He describes whom he ate with at some length both at work and outside work.)

TH: So when did you break up with her?

PT: Broke up in May of '91.

TH: You already knew Sherry then?

PT: Yeah.

TH: Did that have any effect on, uh . . .

PT: I didn't break up with her because of Sherry.
(The exchange is suddenly interrupted when the therapist notices the time, and a discussion about schedules ensues. The patient reassures the therapist that he can stay longer, saying that he has dinner reservations at a Mexican restaurant and briefly exchanging information about places to eat. He warms to the subject and talks at some length about it. He ends by saying that his eating habits have changed.)

TH: Tell me why your eating habits have changed.

PT: Well, work and exercise.

TH: What do you do for exercise?

PT: Well, I used to run a lot, but Sherry and I do a gym in town two or three times a week. Bicycle, track, lift a few weights.
(The exchange moves far afield again as therapist and

patient chat about places to work out, traffic patterns, and other irrelevancies. This goes on for about ten minutes.)

TH: Do you respond to stress physically?

PT: I get tense. I get headaches. Depends on where the stress is coming from. If it's work stress, I tend to get kind of quiet, try to figure out what I'm going to do to solve it. Personal stress—I haven't had any personal stress for a while. I guess getting married. Even if you love somebody else it's a little stressful getting married. We had a small wedding, so we didn't have the hassle of tuxes and the church and all that.
(It is a little surprising to hear the patient say that he has had no personal stress recently. Presumably it is conflict with his wife that has led him to seek treatment. One might begin to suspect that the patient has no idea why he has come. At this point, he is chatting amiably with the therapist as though the two were at a party getting acquainted. The therapist, being new to interviewing, does not know how to change this, and the patient seems not to care that she cannot. In short, he does not seem bothered or troubled by anything, and it is very far from clear why he is here.)

TH: So the stress you had was mental? And how do you experience that?
(The therapist asks a question that makes no sense. Nonetheless, the patient tries to answer it. He seems throughout the interview to avoid anything that would produce even mild tension with the therapist.)

PT: Well, um . . . (long pause) I really don't know that I felt stressful getting married. I was nervous. I had been single for ten years. I say I was single—I hadn't married in ten years.

TH: It was a big step.

PT: I enjoyed being a bachelor. Part of the time I enjoyed being engaged. But, uh, all in all, I enjoyed being single, so it was a big step. (laughs) And there was another thing I wanted to talk to you about, finding ways to, uh, put my past behind me. You know, you say you detect some sadness . . .

TH: Some sadness . . .

PT: And I want to get over that, I need to get over that. And I don't really think it affects me a whole lot, but I guess it probably does because I know I reflect some on people I've dated and probably hurt by, by not, not, uh, con-continuing the relationship.

TH: (nodding vigorously) Uh huh.

PT: And for a long time most of the girls I stopped dating immediately got married. (laughs) Not immediately but I assume that was part of the reason we were dating. In my search for companionship and fun they were in search of a lifetime relationship.

TH: (nodding again) Uh huh.

PT: And, uh . . . I forgot where I was going. Sherry has a little difficulty. Because she, she knew, she knows my ex-fiance. We all worked together. She knows that relationship and probably one or two other people I've dated. She has a little difficulty that I'm, I'm more experienced or had more opportunities for relationships. And I'm trying to put that, that, it's my life, and I don't want to discard it, but I'm trying to put it aside and move on, to, uh, my life with Sherry. And I want her to put her past behind her as well as mine. I don't know how to do that.

TH: Does that come up between the two of you?

PT: It comes up, not to the point of arguing, but it comes up.

TH: Can you think of an example?

PT: Yeah. Actually, Sherry told me I needed to come see you guys. Had to go out of town to take care of some business in, in January, and I was adding her to my checking accounts and bank accounts, and I found out that Donna, my first wife, was still on one of my checking accounts. For some odd reason it had got taken off all the other accounts at that bank but this one. So I had to try to call her to get her to sign a release form. I tried two or three times but I didn't reach her, so I left two or three messages. So I called Sherry to tell her I was leaving town. My voice was on the recorder, and I had just hung up the phone from trying to [call Donna], and when Sherry picked up the phone I said, "Donna, this is Dick"—it was subconscious. I wasn't thinking about what I said; I thought I had said, "Sherry, this is Dick." But I said, "Donna, this is Dick." I had just left her two or three messages in the last five minutes. So I got home and I walked in the door, and she said, "Are you feeling okay? I'm kind of worried about you." And I said, "Why?" and she said, "Go listen to the message you left me." And it said pretty clearly, "Donna." And I'm embarrassed because we both talked about our past to a degree. And she kind of shrugged that one off. If it hurt her feelings or felt really bad about it, I think she was more concerned about my mental state as to whether that was just a slip or if I was regressing. You know, if, if, uh, I don't know why I said it. I was upset she was still on one of my accounts, and it was important to me to get her off, and, and for that reason she was on my mind. And having said her name two or three times in the last five minutes it just kind of came out.

TH: And Sherry wasn't angry about it?

PT: No, she wasn't. She took it kind of well. I expected to get beat on the head or something. (laughs)

TH: Yeah, that was bad!

PT: And that was one instance. But, uh, I have some female friends that I didn't date, but they're also female friends who introduced me to their female friends who I did date, and they want to stay in con . . . they want to stay in touch. Most of them I've been friends with for eight, nine, or ten years. I tried to explain to Sherry that it was nothing sexual; I don't want anything sexual. It's a friend-ship, and most, most of them are married, and I know their husbands. Sherry hasn't had a chance to meet 'em because they live in different cities. She has a problem with that. She'd like me not to have any contact with ex-female friends or females I dated or females I'm just friends with. That's I guess another example of where she's having difficulty with my having, with my being . . . And I guess that gets back to, that's another problem that I have. I've had ten more years of life and so I'm bound to have had a few more additional experiences.

(Dick has come for therapy because his wife is apparently insecure. What is striking is that he is buying into his wife's insecurity instead of challenging it. He is trying to find something wrong with himself that would justify therapy. The question again arises whether Dick is a naive and perhaps hysteroid man or whether he is willing to play whatever role he is assigned.)

TH: Did you talk about these things before you got married?

PT: Yeah, yeah, we did. I think she's just having a little more trouble with it than she, she expected to. Well, I haven't given any of my old friends our new phone number or our new address. But they've called my old work place in Atlanta, and they gave them my new work phone, so if, you know, one of them, you know, I haven't actually talked to any of them. They've called and left messages, and I told Sherry when I got home that Joanna called, and that upsets her. And, uh, other than trying to be reasonable and explain to her the situation, I don't know how to help her deal with that.

TH: So is that why you're here?
(The therapist notices that she does not know why Dick has come for treatment. Her question seems to imply to Dick that there should be something wrong with him, not something wrong with his wife. He spends the rest of the session trying on one kind of pathology and then another, as if he were hoping that the therapist would confirm one of them and give him an identity as a patient.)

PT: That's one of the reasons. My Bill Clinton impression: Does he start with his thumb or like this? I'd like to put the negative parts of my past aside. Like I said, I don't want to remove them or get rid of them but put them aside and not think of them as negative parts of my personality or past behavior.

TH: This is by yourself? This is not Sherry?

PT: That's right; this is just me.

TH: You have some negative feelings about some things that you've done?

PT: Um, yeah, well, may . . . This may be presumptuous, but I think I may have hurt a few people's feelings.

TH: And so would you call that guilt?

PT: Yeah, you could call that guilt.

TH: See, I need to know why you're doing this.
(The therapist again tells Dick that she needs some explanation for his being here. We would not have concluded that Dick felt guilty, either from his manner or from the content of his productions. It is largely the therapist's suggestion; Dick, however, tries hard to play the part, just

as he earlier tried to find a pattern to his dating relation-
ships when the therapist suggested there was one.)

PT: Okay, yeah, I would like to, uh, remove my guilt feelings for past relationships. I would like to get some insights or . . . way . . . I need, uh, guidance I guess in how to help Sherry deal with it. From my side. She's going to have to deal with it from her side. When that confrontation arises I guess I feel guilty, at that point. Maybe that's the same thing. I feel guilty I've got friends, and I don't want to feel that.

TH: Does it make you mad?

PT: It frustrates me, uh . . .

TH: You talked earlier about this issue of having things control you, of having forces control you.

PT: Yes, uh huh, yes.

TH: Would you say that you feel that way about this situation?

PT: It could be, it could be. It'd be fair. It'd be a stretch, but, uh, I could, uh, categorize it as that, that Sherry's trying to control who I'm friends with, and I experienced that with, with my previous fiance more strongly, because then I didn't care. I didn't care that I had these female relationships whether, whether, you know, they were somebody I had dated or somebody I was friends with. I didn't care if she got mad or not, and I care about Sherry's feelings. So, you know, I, that's one difference in the two, that I guess is her attempt to control me. I don't think she recognizes that. That may be a concession I have to make, to, uh, tell my friends we'll be friends but we won't have any contact! (laughs) We'll be friends in spirit.
(Dick is again trying hard to match up with what the
therapist suggests is wrong with him, even though, as he

*says, "it'd be a stretch." The therapist is correct to focus
on the marriage, but Dick is going out of his way to find
some role for himself as a patient, as though he wants to
let his wife off the hook.)*

TH: Have you ever done that before?

PT: No. I don't think so. One girl I broke up with last
year I said I really don't think we should date because I
don't see our relationship going anywhere. She said, "If we
can't date, I don't want to be friends." And I said that we
had friends in common and we're going to see each other
sometimes, and there may be times you don't have anything to do, and as bad as I am I may be your best
alternative. If you want to be by yourself rather than be
with me, that's fine, but so . . . she decided she didn't want
to see me at all, but she called me up a few days later and
said she'd, she'd thought about it some and thought that
friendship was a better way to go than just canceling the
thought of ever having known me. I guess that friendship
after dating can happen, but friendship in spirit I don't
know. (laughs)

TH: Okay, so you'd like help dealing with the guilt of
some of your past, and you'd like help . . .

PT: I would like, I would like, help, in, I guess in feeling
like one hundred percent or at least ninety-five percent of
my mental capabilities. I just, I just don't concentrate well.
Either I've got a short attention span, or it's not something
I noticed until I started working. You know, again, when
you're going to school you've got a lot of different influences. You've got a lot of different activities coming at
you, and your day's pretty much broken up. You're not
sitting in one place eight or nine hours doing, doing work.
*(Dick is looking for symptoms. The problem is that he does
not seem to have any. The therapist's next comment seems
accurate.)*

TH: Maybe, maybe you're bored.

PT: Maybe. Could be I'm bored. But I'd like to figure out what I am feeling. Am I depressed at work? Bored at work? And just don't know it? (laughs)
(Dick is correct that he is out of touch with his private wishes, intentions, and feelings. He does not know what he thinks or feels whenever these would lead him into conflict with others—hence his difficulty in breaking off his earlier engagement. He has so far postulated [or agreed with the therapist's suggestion] that he suffers from worry, sadness, fear of being controlled by others, pathological interpersonal patterns, guilt, poor concentration, and now depression. We see no real evidence that he suffers from any of these and think instead that he is trying hard to be who his wife and also the therapist need him to be.)

TH: If you were depressed you would know it. You would know if you were depressed.

PT: Yeah, but I don't know what depression feels like.
(There are probably few adults who could make such a statement. When a patient makes such a remark and it is believable [and in this case we find it believable], the therapist should wonder about as-if pathology as well as narcissistic pathology.)

TH: People who are depressed—if you were depressed your bearing would have been very lethargic, you would have had no intonation to your voice. Depressed people are very monotone. They just sit there and don't move at all. Insomnia, problems eating, sleeping, sexual difficulties, overwhelming sadness, crying, suicidal thoughts.

PT: I've been glassy eyed. (laughs very loud) Yeah, well . . .

TH: Let me ask you—I have to ask about this: Any drugs or alcohol?

PT: I don't have any with me, but I could get some. (laughs ingratiatingly) We have a code of conduct at work and fitness for duty, and I don't use drugs. [He goes on to relate learning to drink in college and rambles as he talks about the subject. He covers boating and working out in the course of this discussion.] I wouldn't want to say that I have a drinking problem, but someone else might. I never went into rehab or withdrawals or anything. I never had the DTs; I don't think I ever hallucinated when I quit thinking.
(The statement "I wouldn't say I have a drinking problem, but someone else might" is instructive. Dick is signaling a willingness to be defined. In addition to guilt, depression, poor concentration, et al., Dick is apparently willing to consider alcoholism as one of his problems.)

TH: Well, speaking of hallucinations, is there any history of mental illness in your family?

PT: No. I had a grandmother who had Alzheimer's. I came from a relatively sane family, I think.

TH: You sound like a relatively sane man actually. I'm wondering . . . it seems like what might be most beneficial for you might be marital therapy.

PT: Could be.

TH: Cause I don't hear you saying that you're experiencing any problems with living.

PT: Well, I think my biggest problem is I get up in the mornings, and I feel like my head's foggy, and I go to work, and I feel like my head's foggy. And in the afternoon I feel like my head's foggy.
(The therapist has made a sensible suggestion, and after initially agreeing with it, Dick tries again to find some-

*thing wrong with himself. He wants to stay out of conflict
with his wife and would rather sacrifice himself, as it were.
This is what would be expected of an as-if individual, since
Dick is willing to play out whatever role his wife [or the
therapist] needs but is unwilling to press what he wants.)*

TH: It's foggy all the time?

PT: Yes.

TH: When they did those medical tests, nothing showed
up?

PT: No.

TH: Did you have the same complaints then?

PT: Yeah. My doctor suggested I have a psychological
evaluation. Kind of as a last resort. Not a last resort, but he
told me there was nothing else really he could look for, and
he said they had a therapist, a psychiatrist, on staff and just
let him know whenever I wanted to have an evaluation,
but I never got to that stage.
*(The session ends at this point, although not without
Dick's raising another possible pathology for himself. As
another session is scheduled, he raises the possibility that
he suffers Attention Deficit Disorder, returning to his
earlier complaint of poor concentration. Throughout the
session, he has been unfailingly pleasant, conversational,
and even chatty. He has neither shown nor convincingly
referred to strong feelings of any sort and seems, in the
therapist's words, "relatively sane." In short, he appears
untroubled, has little idea why he has come to treatment,
wants to avoid any tension with others, and shows that he
is very eager to play out the role of patient if only someone
will give him clues on how to do so. All of this is enough to
raise the possibility of an as-if diagnosis, even though it is
far too early to settle the question.)*

6

Precocious Ego
Development

THE MINIATURE ADULT

Quiet borderline patients generally have very distinctive histories: As children they were, in effect, miniature adults. Their immaturities seem to have fallen away rather early and to have been replaced by traits more representative of hyperconforming adults. They are remembered by parents, teachers, and those who worked with them in religious groups, scouts, or other youth activities as "good" children, and they are sometimes referred to as "perfect." What is meant by this is that they gave no one any trouble—in sharp contrast to most youth. They seem to have taken on mannerisms, attitudes, and behaviors that were adultomorphic quite early, certainly by grade school, which gave them the appearance of precocious maturity. These individuals did not seem to need others in the way most children do. They were not dependent or needy, and they almost never allowed themselves the luxury of falling apart and needing to be comforted, even under stress. They do not seem to have leaned on peers much more than on parents or teachers. It is not accurate to say that they were socially isolated, but they seemed fairly uninvested in who they were with; it is as though they had no strong preferences. All in all, they did not show the usual cycles of storminess and placidity that attend growing up.

Of course, precocious development of ego functions can occur with healthy children as well as in those who will become quiet borderline individuals. Many children can show an early frustration tolerance, patience, verbal fluidity, synthetic capacity, and ability to observe the self. These are most frequently seen in children who possess superior intellectual abilities. Such children seem unusually self contained; they are able to turn away from the social world in favor of entertaining and occupying themselves without help from others. Their self-sufficiency and obviously bright minds make them seem suddenly mature.

There are clear differences between children whose early maturity follows a precocious intellect versus those who show pathological precocity. To begin with, children who are developing in an as-if direction do not usually show gifted intelligence. Further, children whose precocious ego functions follow a precocious intellect usually seem self-contained to an observer. Not only are they less dependent on the social world, but they do not seem to realize how advanced they look. Children who are pathologically mature, by contrast, are seldom out of touch with how they seem to others and what impact they are having. They seem to try to create situations and interactions that the other person would want to respond to. It is true that they remain uninvested in the people they are with, but they certainly do not ignore them, and they seem to want to be with someone, even if they are not attached to anyone in particular.

Finally, children who show healthy precocity do not mind being in the world of the child; they are not trying to avoid the dependency that usually goes with growing up. They behave precociously simply because they can, not because it is the solution to a problem. It is, however, the solution to a problem life has presented the future as-if individual. These children behave with premature self-sufficiency because both dependency and aloneness are dangerous for them. They are prematurely self-sufficient as a way of dodging the perils of needing others while yet carving out a place with other people. These are the children we describe in this chapter, and they must not be confused with those whose gifted intelligence has led to precocious coping skills.

In many respects, early childhood is a matter of indulging the child's natural grandiosity or at least not disabusing the child too quickly of feeling that he or she is the center of the universe. There is a megalomania that is healthy for the young child, although it is dealt progressively harder blows by such events as discovering that the mother is a separate person, that one's body must be controlled, and that there are qualitative differences between adults and children. This last discovery ends the oedipal phase (Chasseguet-Smirgel 1984, Grunberger 1989) and sends the child off to school with a kind of sad disillusionment that is nonetheless a good preparation for the tasks of growing up and fitting in. It is hard to want to do all that is required between first grade and college if one is still as much the center of the universe as when the mother beamed and smiled for no other reason than that the baby was there.

When we say that future as-if patients showed precocious ego development, we mean that these children were forced out of infantile megalomania far too quickly. They were disillusioned much earlier than normal and much earlier than healthy, as though the world simply did not do enough to support this natural illusion. Normally, children are helped to deal with this disillusionment by forming identifications with their parents—they lose their status as centers of the universe, but they gain the hope that they may, with work, become like their admired and idealized parent(s). These identifications become building blocks of the personality, as it were, foundations for identity. When disillusionment comes too early, the identifications that replace infantile megalomania are not available. The child is too young to form them. The child is no longer (or perhaps never really got established as) the center of the universe, but neither is he or she connected to the parents and to the future through a set of identifications. The problem is obvious: How can the child grow up?

The as-if patient's solution is: all at once. Instead of oedipal identifications that can become a foundation for the personality, primitive identifications are all that is available. The hallmark of such identifications is that they are imitative and transitory (cf. Jacobson 1964). Anyone who has watched a preoedipal child for any length of time has seen those sorts of identifications as the child watched and then imitated the movements or words of an older child or caretaker. These imitations are fleeting, however, and do not seem to have a lasting impact. It is as though the child were trying the behavior on for size, so to speak. The child who is about to start the road to a quiet borderline development begins a series of such primitive identifications, acting like the parents, no doubt reinforced by their delight at his or her attempts at adultomorphic self-sufficiency. The child learns that the semblance of maturity offers some sense of being in the family. The problem for the child is that it is not really he or she who is given a role but the child-acting-like-an-adult who has a place.

Such a child lacks a real place and is thrown back on him- or herself too early. There is an absence of friendly intimacy between these children and their families. To be sure, there are exchanges that look intimate in a sense, but it is not the usual intimacy between adults and children. What is missing is the child's dependency on the adults, or firm generational boundaries. The child is accorded parity in these seemingly intimate exchanges. What this usually looks like is a reversal of the typical family—the future as-if individual does for the parents those things parents generally do for their children, offering praise, support, encouragement, and help with tasks. The child manages to carve out a role, certainly, but it is a twisted role.

Or is it? Perhaps we should at least raise the question of whether all this is as pathological as it seems. If these children are acting like adults, perhaps it is not such a problem after all. One might argue that these children are getting a head start on their peers, learning adaptability, responsiveness, and social skills earlier than most. What makes this a problem? Our best answer is one that would be hard to defend to, say, a strict behaviorist and quite possibly to an insurance reviewer, namely: It's not real. What makes human beings real to one another is some element of affective attunement on the one hand and revelations of variability (a capacity to retain identity but to be different across different times and situations) on the other hand. The future as-if individual is engaged in a sham in this regard. These individuals can make other persons feel known, as though there were a genuine tie, possibly even as if there were empathy and affective resonance. However, these children (and, later, these adults) cannot follow through on what it means to establish a connection with another person, which involves the ability to declare that person as special. Seeing others in this way entails experiencing them as unique and irreplaceable. With time, however, it becomes clear that the as-if child treats everyone in such a fashion; anyone could have come into the child's life and received the same type of response. The apparently precocious ability to adapt to the social world is a sham because there is no basis for enduring attachments; there is only a series of interchangeable objects.

Therapists can learn of this pattern in their patient's childhood by asking closely about peer relations. Most adult patients will remember the cliques or groups they were part of in childhood and a succession of "best friends," and those who lacked these cliques and friends will report having been lonely. It is a different matter with quiet borderline patients. They do not appear to have had any close playmates, nor do they seem to have missed this. The therapist may get the sense that everyone was the same to them, that they were not especially invested in anyone in particular.

Yet it is also the case that the future as-if individual did not want to be alone. In this respect, quiet borderline patients are different from schizoid patients; the latter do not appear to have found aloneness uncomfortable as children, or at least not any more uncomfortable than being with people. By contrast, as-if patients generally remember wanting to be around people when they were children and not liking aloneness. Other people were not a problem or a source of anxiety, as is usually the case for the future schizoid patient. The child who is on the way to a schizoid development harbors a deep fear that his or her love is dangerous (cf. Laing 1960), and hence it is not easy to be comfortable with other persons. Others can awaken hungers that the child fears will harm a loved one or lead the child to be harmed in turn, and in this situation, aloneness can come as a relief. The child who is taking an as-if road, however, does not seem afraid of doing damage to others or, in fact, of being damaged by others. There seems to be some other agenda altogether that does not turn on aggression, anxiety, hope, or fear.

Here again we may use a contrast with the schizoid patient to bring the as-if individual into focus. Schizoid patients give the very clear impression of having tried to contact others and having found it so painful an experience that they abandoned the effort and, with it, the object hunger that led to the attempt. They seem, in other words, to have suffered, and their suffering led to their pathology. As-if patients do not give this impression, however. They do not seem to have encountered great pain, disappointment, or privation.

As-if patients were not trying to get away from pain but, rather, from confusion. What the as-if individual needed during early childhood from the adult world was as basic as the vicissitudes of love and hate but nonetheless different: *The future as-if individual needed help in organizing experience.* As we argued in Chapter 3, the inner world is inchoate, fluid, and chaotic for the very young child. The chaos is gradually organized and mastered through the help of interactions with caretakers; through their responses, they define and articulate the child's emotions, urges, and intentions. If major elements of that chaos remain unseen by caretakers, or if the child is not able to make use of what the caretaker sees, the inner world is correspondingly undeveloped and remains in chaos. For the child to remain in touch with his or her own hitherto unseen and therefore undefined feelings and intentions is, in effect, for the child to remain confused and overwhelmed by a jumble of fantasies and feelings.

In normal development, the parents' mirroring responses gradually bring definition to the internal world; children feel real for the first time while looking at the mother's face and seeing there a representation of themselves. This process contributes significantly to the young child's dependency on the parents and, through the eventual achievement of object constancy, to the child's ability to move toward independence. Even before the child begins to suspect (and, shortly thereafter, to fear) that the mother is separate, seeds of lasting attachment are being sown. The child needs the mother and other caretakers to feel real, defined, and alive; he or she grows attached to the mother as the jumbled and surging mass of rising and falling tension becomes clarified, growing gradually manageable.

In as-if development, the inner confusion largely remained. Either the child's caretakers were not able to mirror what the child felt, or the child was not able to make use of what was mirrored. In either event, early parent–child interaction was not successful in beginning to clarify the child's inner world. Private experience, such as experience of feelings, wishes, and impulses, remained equivalent to confusion. As we discussed in Chapter 3, under these circumstances the child may flee confusion through an important reversal in the mirroring process. In normal development, the mother mirrors the child's moods and other subjective states, thereby bringing some order to the chaos, but in as-if development *the child mirrors the parents' moods and wishes*. While this also brings order to the chaos, it does so by splitting off the confusion rather than through the preferred process, mastery. Nonetheless, it is the best the child can manage. The desire to escape confusion is legitimate; given that the child either cannot receive needed help from caretakers or cannot make use of the help that is available, flight from confusion is the best option available.

In this situation, the child no longer asks (as it were), "Am I real?" but "Is this role being played right?" The child who is on the as-if road is focused on getting the transitory (imitative) identification right, on imitating the other person well enough that there will be some recognition and acknowledgment. Such a response from the other is quite important, since it offers definition and, thereby, prospects for organizing the experience. Indeed, the as-if child's growing ability to intuit what others might want or respond to positively is built on the desire to organize experience. There is nothing magical about the child's ability to "read" the other person; rather, there is simply the sense that, "If I'm not confused, I must be on the right track." The child is learning to behave in ways that elicit organizing responses from others. While the child appears to be more and more mature, in fact he or she is learning to get away from confusion through sensing what other people will respond to.

Much of what the as-if individual did as a child was an attempt to keep anything confusing from ever happening. To state the matter a little too simply, the child learned to stay away from the inner world and instead to pay constant attention to the social world. Unlike normal (or even most abnormal) children, the as-if child was relatively unburdened by selfish interests. A child who enters into an interaction without some selfish purpose or desire will look remarkably mature to an adult, who will doubtless be pleased at what seems to be a willingness to share, cooperate, and help out in general. Of course, from our viewpoint the child is showing none of these traits. The child is simply avoiding the confusion that goes with his or her private feelings and wishes and, instead, pursuing the sense of order that comes with the other person's acknowledgment of the child's compliance.

THE APPEARANCE OF INDEPENDENCE

The child who seems to be an adult in miniature will doubtless strike observers as remarkably self-sufficient. It hardly needs to be said that the reverse is the case, since the child needs frequent feedback from others in order to function. Those near the child may not notice this need for feedback, since the child is not necessarily seeking praise or recognition. Any reaction indicating that a role has been played out well is adequate for the as-if child to feel that he or she knows what is expected and how to meet expectations. Thus, certain seemingly mature and independent behaviors are built up precisely because the child is utterly dependent on a response from the other that will organize experience and offer some definition.

It is not correct, then, to say that these patients were independent as children. They were quite dependent on the reactions of others. All this, however, was in the interest of avoiding *dependency,* which is dangerous for several reasons. First, the as-if child finds it difficult to discriminate between persons who might be able to offer what is needed and those who cannot. Both are met with a pseudo-openness in which the child appears to be receptive but is actually operating at a certain distance. Second, dependency entails dropping one's guard, which in turn allows the other person to excite hungers, hopes, and fears. These children have not been able to master such private experiences, and so dropping their guard would entail the possibility of again becoming confused. As-if children are trying to avoid anything that might stir up feelings. They cannot venture into the world of affect because they do not trust the adult world to contain or interpret affect.

Third, these children may vaguely fear that others would take advantage if they were more open with their dependency. Adult patients often carry memories of having reached out as children only to have their neediness thrown back in their faces, as it were, or at least of having felt that this was the case. Curiously, they do not relate these stories with anger, and there does not seem to have been a paranoid reaction. It is as though the individual did not take it personally. Generally, instances in which neediness led to being taken advantage of are remembered and told in a matter-of-fact way. The patient appears simply to have made a (thoroughly adaptive) mental note that dependency was not especially safe and should be avoided.

One patient said that his mother would laugh at him if he wanted help of any kind. He remembered her ridiculing him with, "You say you're a boy, but you can't do anything." The patient reported this in a flat, indifferent way as one fact among many others, but not as a complaint.

Among other things, dependency involves the willingness to become emotionally receptive to another person and allow that person to be responsible for what happens. There must be some measure of trust that the other person will know what to do with us and will neither try to hurt us nor be so clumsy that we are harmed by accident. Different degrees of openness and wariness are appropriate to different periods of life, but at any age there can be no dependency without a willingness to let the other make an impact.

The as-if adaptation, by contrast, is a step away from the shared world of other persons. For all its seeming responsiveness to others, the as-if style is emotionally insulated, an attempt to get away from the impact others might make. To let others make an impact is to grant them some sort of personal significance, and this is something the as-if style does not allow. There is a paradox in the as-if style: The child is dependent on the outside world in order to organize experience, but the child is dependent in a thoroughly impersonal way. There is no strong attachment to or need for a particular person, just for *some* person.

Dependency starts with the feeling of being seen (known) by the other and comes to include relying on how the other sees us. (In any adult-level relationship, dependency will also involve being willing to say how we see the other person as well.) If we do not feel seen by the other, we cannot rely on that person for any lasting definition of ourselves, which is to say that we cannot depend on the person. If we are not seen by important others, then the only self-definition that is possible is: I am not allowed to be seen (known)—I can appear and perform, but I cannot be known.

There is a kind of delicate balance the as-if child must attain and maintain over time. The child must stay enough in contact with other persons to have roles to perform but not so much in contact that others could make an impact at a deeper level. *The appearance of self-sufficiency is therefore a replacement for dependency.* It is, as already mentioned, a sham self-sufficiency, since others are constantly needed and without them the child has little idea how to proceed. We might say that the child needs to be seen but not to be known. When with others, therefore, the child does not allow anyone to make a personal, intimate impact. When alone, however, the child is in danger of becoming confused or disorganized and yearns for someone who can give clues on how to structure time, someone, that is, to say what is expected and acceptable. The balance that is sought is between being dependent on others for definition without allowing dependency needs to become aroused.

The as-if individual's appearance of independence, therefore, is more accurately understood as an attempt to avoid dependency. It will be far from obvious that this is the individual's underlying intention, however. By the time quiet borderline adults present themselves for treatment, they have had years of praise for their seeming independence and possibly even for their ability to take care of others. One of the first tasks of treatment, then, is for the therapist to see through the appearance of independence. In contrast to classic, or noisy, borderline patients, who must be weaned from an aggressive, hungry dependency that is evident from the start, the as-if patient must be taught genuine dependency. The therapist must note first how dependent the patient is on others for roles to play and must note then that the patient perpetually avoids any actual reliance on others emotionally.

THE QUESTION OF DEPENDING ON THE THERAPIST

The quiet borderline patient has earned a place in the world through not needing anything from others and from seeming instead to be remarkably self-reliant. Discovering how to do this was, after all, the key to finding a role in the family during the growing-up years, and the as-if individual honed this skill in school, church, social settings, and on the job. By the time such individuals come for treatment, they expect the therapist also to encourage independence and the ability to take care of themselves. These expectations doubtless contribute to the ability to present themselves to the therapist as virtually normal or at least without obvious problems.

Therapy is an odd setting in which to practice not needing anything, but this is what should be expected from quiet borderline patients. As children they showed precocious maturation, and as adults they rigidly hold to the pseudo-independence that won praise and acceptance during childhood. As-if patients do not try to need or depend on the therapist. These are not patients who call between appointments for help or reassurance, who have crises, or who ask for extra appointments. It is an ironic matter to be in therapy trying to maintain a stance of not needing anything. Therapists should be aware of the paradox involved and also of the fact that the patient sees no paradox. For as-if patients, therapy is just one more role to play, one in which they accept the one-down position of patient and yet nonetheless manage not to need anything from the therapist: They play the part of someone in a dependent posture but they do not seek really to depend on the therapist. As-if patients experience the relationship in largely impersonal terms, which keeps the subject of dependency far away.

> One patient, a mental health worker, canceled an appointment in her second year of treatment. At their next session, the therapist asked about the cancellation, and the patient replied that she had just met a new lover and wanted to take a break from therapy while she and her lover got to know each other. The therapist replied that this was not acceptable to him and that he would not work with the patient further if she canceled another appointment for such a reason. The patient was surprised and asked if the therapist would throw her out of

treatment "just for that?" The therapist said it was not a matter of throwing her out; it was a matter of whether she wanted therapy and the commitment it implied. After reiterating that the cancellation was in his opinion for a superfluous reason, he added, "My patients don't do that sort of thing." The patient was surprised by the therapist's stance, in particular by the phrase "my patients." She asked with genuine puzzlement what he meant and seemed touched by the implication that the therapist was willing to define her in a personal, almost parental, way. She said that she couldn't think of herself as "your patient." She said the most she could do was to "think of myself as part of your caseload."

It is hard for quiet borderline patients to believe that others will tolerate their needing anything from them. They have, rather, the sense that they hold value for others to the extent that they make no demands. Their experience as children was that their role in the family rested on being independent, and they seem as adults to have the idea that this remains the only possible role. For one thing, as-if patients are not that sure about other persons; they are not sure it is a good thing to let others make that much of an impact. For another thing, as-if patients are not any more sure about themselves; they do not believe that they could have enough meaning for another person to want to meet (or at least endure) their needs.

In addition, quiet borderline patients take a secret pride in not needing anything from others. We mentioned earlier that as-if children are disabused too early of normal infantile grandiosity. Normal children use the pain of gradually relinquishing infantile megalomania to fuel idealizations of, and, later, identifications with, the parents. By contrast, as-if children come to feel a secret pride in their precocious independence. Having been praised by family members, teachers, and others for not needing anything, they can easily overestimate their abilities. This is another motivation for not leaning on the therapist, since, as mentioned earlier, they have no reason to believe that the therapist will respond differently to their seeming independence. When they learn that the therapist is neither pleased nor finds them especially competent, they will feel the loss of this source of pride and will be as slow to surrender it as most patients are to give up their narcissistic resources.

In consequence of these different factors, therapists will have trouble bringing as-if patients to depend on them. These patients do not want to entrust their well-being to the therapist, and they feel easier in a more conventional conversation. One way quiet borderline patients may seek to avoid dependency is through excessive interest in the therapist. Therapists can be seduced into talking about themselves for a variety of reasons. They may mistakenly believe that it is good to model self-disclosure for patients who have trouble with intimacy, or perhaps they receive narcissistic gratification from the patient's attentiveness when they talk about themselves. Whatever the motivation, therapists are simply mistaken to talk about themselves with quiet borderline patients. Therapists who do this are encouraging the patient's illusion that there is no difference between this and the other relationships in his or her life. Dependency is not furthered; it is made less likely.

> One therapist noticed that several as-if patients seemed to know quite a bit of personal information about previous therapists. It turned out that they had spent much of their time in sessions talking about the therapist. By the patients' descriptions, sessions seemed to have had a conversational tone to them, as though two people were simply passing some time together. One of the patients clearly intended to continue this pattern. She had learned a surprising amount of information about her new therapist before seeing him and started the first session by pleasantly chatting about what she had learned. She was unaware that there would be any difference between therapy and a conversation between two acquaintances.

Therapists may also find their as-if patients talking excessively about other people. This has the effect of diluting the therapist's impact on the patient, since the therapist's attention will be on someone else. Whatever intimacy is needed for dependency to form is thereby avoided. While most patients spend part of at least some sessions discussing various persons in their lives, as-if patients tend to do this too much. Moreover, they talk about others in a particularly countertherapeutic way. Their discussions seem bland and empty, even when they are discussing important people in their lives. The therapist may form the impression that they are simply talking to fill up the time, not because the subject matter is important to them (curiously, the therapist may feel the subject matter is indeed important, as though the patient has left it to the therapist to experience its importance). What patients say and how they say it would be more appropriate to a gathering of friends or family where people are simply chatting or trying to bring one another up to date. The therapist may (and should) eventually ask, "What does this have to do with you?" The answer, no matter how it is actually phrased, will be "nothing."

A more subtle way for quiet borderline patients to avoid dependency is through using the therapist more as a consultant or advice giver than as a therapist. Patients who are themselves mental health workers may want to discuss cases with the therapist, and other patients may seek advice on child rearing or how to handle a problem at work. At first, these requests for help may look promising, since the patient is leaning on the therapist for something. Whatever dependency is involved, however, is at arm's length, since it is always someone else who is being discussed. The patient has not really dropped his or her guard but is still standing off to the side emotionally, as it were. In addition, any feedback or suggestions to the as-if patient can easily be used as further cues for role playing. The patient gains information on how to look as if he or she were a therapist, parent, or committed employee. Certainly the therapist is not being depended on in a personal way; at best, the patient uses the therapist as a kind of acting teacher.

It will be up to the therapist to bypass the patient's attempt at establishing a conventional relationship and thereby avoiding dependency. The therapist should keep in mind that as-if patients are not familiar with any other type of relationship, however. They are not showing resistance in the classic sense of the term; if they are resisting dependency on the therapist (and they are), it is because they do not know how to do otherwise. Dependency strivings have been split off, and the patient does not really have access to these. If the therapist makes an intervention about avoiding dependency, the patient is not likely to feel the tension or anxiety that, with most therapy patients, usually attends an on-target confrontation. Rather, as-if patients will take the confrontation to indicate that the therapist's expectations are not being met, that a role is not being played adequately. Beyond this, these patients will be genuinely puzzled about what is being asked of them.

To the extent these patients are able to experience some yearning to lean on someone and be cared for, they are also likely to feel confused and disorganized. Earlier, we observed that quiet borderline individuals do not use their as-if orientation to escape pain but, rather, *to escape confusion*. We suggested that the inner world—affect clusters, fantasy systems, and rudimentary series of wish and impulse—is undefined, primitive, and unintegrated with the rest of the personality. The as-if style is an adaptation to avoid the inner world and the cognitive disorganization that accompanies even brief contact with it. Thus, what the therapist wants of the patient is something that will necessarily lead to deterioration in the patient's adaptive functioning.

This point has been seen with particular clarity by Khan (1960), who, as we noted in Chapter 2, made a number of observations about schizoid patients that we believe actually apply to quiet borderline individuals. Khan suggested that when these patients regress it is to fundamental stages of dependency, stages at which affectivity is undifferentiated and therefore unintegrated with the rest of experience. From very early in life such individuals have tried to keep internal chaos under magical control, effectively splitting off and denying that aspect of psychic life. Khan argues, and we agree, that the real task of treatment is to help the patient experience in the therapy setting the "total fragmented reality" the patient tries to keep under magical control. The experience of needing the therapist will necessarily be disorganizing and primitive, then, and the patient will (in Khan's opinion) resist it, or (in our opinion) simply not see it.

Dependency is disorganizing to as-if patients because it propels them into an experience of the world in which there is no firm difference between self and other. We are not, after all, talking about the dependency shown by oedipal-level patients, who already know that they are real and substantial and can therefore form attachments to other persons without risking the complete loss of identity. By contrast, the quiet borderline patient's dependency does not rest on a firm distinction between self and other. The therapist invites the patient to a dependency in which the patient need not recognize that the therapist is separate and distinct. Indeed, for a time, the patient may not be sure that there is a difference or at least not be sure where the boundaries are. Just as infants initially find themselves in the external world, out there in the mother's mirroring face, so a quiet borderline patient who is dependent on the therapist will not be fully certain whether "I" is in here or part of being with the therapist.

> One as-if patient began to depend on her therapist in the second year of treatment, gradually allowing herself to become aware that she was unhappy with her marriage. She was reluctant to make a decision to end the marriage, however, and kept asking the therapist whether he could help her through the turmoil she felt would follow the decision. When she finally decided that she was indeed ready to end the relationship, she felt intensely guilty. She began to suffer dissociative episodes, at least two of which were psychotic in nature. After each episode, she called the therapist, clearly afraid of what had happened. It seemed to be enough for her to talk with him briefly, and she was then able each time to return to the day's activities. Eventually, these episodes disappeared. They were part of the disorganization that came from this patient's allowing herself to form feelings about her marriage (she had previously said that she felt little about it) and to consider reaching out to the therapist for help.

When the as-if patient feels some dependency on the therapist, therefore, confusion is inevitable. Therapists should be pleased to see evidence of disorganization if this occurs in the context of growing dependency. The therapist must not panic at what looks to be evidence that the patient is getting much worse; in fact, it is a sign that the treatment is on the right track. Confusion signifies progress, because confusion is the most real thing the patient can feel. The task for the therapist is to tolerate the resulting tension without feeling a need to take away the chaos the patient is experiencing.

In trying to think through what response—if any—to make to the patient's disorganization, the therapist should remember the specific dynamics of quiet borderline pathology. This is a situation in which it is important to be aware of the differences between as-if and schizoid patients. With the latter, the therapist must avoid impinging on the patient's private reality, since a central question for schizoid patients is whether others can be encountered without complete loss of the sense of private self. For the as-if patient, however, the problem is not preserving a sense of private selfhood but gaining one. Therefore, the therapist is not a threat to take away the patient's privacy but is instead the avenue to gaining it.

BUILDING DEPENDENCY ON THE THERAPIST

When the as-if patient begins to show confusion, it means that the stresses of "holding it together" have become too great and also that the patient is no longer hyperconcerned with preserving an image or role. In turn, this means that the patient is willing to be taken seriously by the therapist, no longer clinging to a purely external definition that protects the patient from the inner world and its accompanying disorganization. The most genuine or authentic thing about the patient is confusion, after all, and its gradual appearance is the emergence of a real self, if we might put it in those terms. The question, of course, is what the therapist might be able to do to help the patient relinquish the safety of playing out roles given by others and move toward dependency and its inevitable confusion (for the patient).

In earlier works on borderline patients (Cohen and Sherwood 1989, 1991) we have argued that there are no specific techniques or problem-solving strategies that can be used in a how-to-do-it manner to repair the borderline patient's basic deficits. We have instead argued that therapists must adopt a certain posture or overall approach to borderline patients. Such postures or overall approaches may begin a therapeutic process that eventually leads to growth and healing. It would be a mistake to believe that there are exercises, tactics, or specific interventions that will in and of themselves build, for example, object constancy or, in the present case, make the patient depend on the therapist. It is not the case that the therapist can intervene in any specific way and thereby produce a willingness to risk dependency.

The therapist's overall approach to as-if patients is to take them seriously, more seriously indeed than the patient wishes to be taken. When therapists refuse to talk about themselves or others in sessions and when they refuse to become consultants and advice givers principally, for instance, they are taking the patient seriously. They are saying, in effect, that the patient is worth consideration and that they believe there is meaning in the patient alone. We might say that whatever the therapist does to insist that the therapy hour not be business as usual for the patient is a way of taking the patient seriously. If, therefore, we are to discuss how the therapist leads the as-if patient into dependency, we must focus on what the therapist plans to do to interfere with the patient's attempt to find a role and play it in the therapy hour.

As-if patients tend to speak in an overly abstracted, propositional language (cf. Cohen and Sherwood 1991, pp. 244–251); evocative language tends to be avoided, since such language carries an affective charge. The overall impression from this sort of language is that the patient is better integrated and more autonomous than is actually the case. The therapist must see through this appearance of integration and find ways to move the interaction toward more emotionally charged, evocative speech. The therapist may, for instance, use language that is more crude or laden with vulgarities than would normally be used. The therapist may also do such things as clap the hands together to make a noise as emphasis for a point; this brings more liveliness to the exchange. Finally, the therapist may (and should) refer to the patient's posture, bodily tension, and body language. As we noted in Chapter 4, the body is a fundamental support to the sense of one's own reality. It interrupts the patient's overly propositional, affectively arid language to call attention to the patient's body, referring to what the body says as a counterpoint to the patient's words.

In these sorts of interventions, the therapist is simply trying to interfere with the patient's attempt to produce an interaction that carries the appearance of normalcy and conventionality. In and of themselves such interventions will not lead to any particular movement in the case; they must be part of an overall determination to challenge the patient's presentation, asking in as many ways as possible whether the patient wants (or can imagine) being taken seriously.

> An as-if patient sipped a soft drink during her session. At one point it was clear that she was uncomfortable and was trying hard not to burp. The therapist mentioned this and asked, "Why don't you burp?" The patient resisted even answering the question, trying to pretend that the matter had not come up. The therapist pressed the question, seeing that the patient and her body were much at odds and preferring the body's spontaneity to the woman's characteristic superficiality. The woman finally replied that she could not burp. To the inevitable question, "Why not?" the woman said, "Women in my family don't do that." This unusual exchange gave the therapist a way to raise the problem of genuineness and to present the therapy hour as a time when spontaneity could be experimented with. The patient, however, was too far away from depending on the therapist to take such a risk.

As the therapist challenges the patient's attempt to appear integrated and essentially normal, there will very likely be indications that the patient is at sea once he or she is forced away from a pseudo-independent posture. The therapist may notice that the patient's communications make less sense. The therapist's own mental state can be a source of information; the therapist who feels confused while listening to an as-if patient may find his or her own disorganization to be a template of the patient's thinking. The patient may still talk as though he or she is saying something cogent and meaningful, but the therapist may sense that the patient is not far from losing coherence. A comment such as, "Do you know what you're talking about right now?" may be helpful. The facial expression and tone of voice are crucial, as the therapist cannot afford to appear critical or as though the patient has just been caught at something. The tone must be somewhat playful and affiliative, conveying the possibility that the patient can share in the therapist's discovery, thereby making it a joint discovery.

The patient's reaction to such a comment will show something of how close he or she is to a willingness to lean on the therapist. If the patient makes an honest response, there is a greater willingness to embark on the road to dependency. As-if patients will show affect or confusion only if they trust the therapist to help them manage it. Management, however, must not include trying to take the confusion away. The therapist does well to sit with the confusion, neither trying to interpret it nor make the patient less confused. Indeed, we believe it is advisable for the therapist not even to use the word confusion. It will not hurt to let the patient know the therapist is aware the patient is feeling differently from the way he or she used to feel, but the patient should be allowed to put his or her own words to the experience. The therapist needs only to confirm that the patient's experience is seen or known and, moreover, that the experience may be a scary one.

The therapist must not jump in to make sense of what the patient feels. That imposes the therapist's organization on the patient and, in the process, runs the risk of taking away the only real thing the patient has produced. Any attempt to clarify the patient's feelings will not feel real if it comes too fast. The therapist must communicate that he or she is aware of what the patient feels and respects the patient's courage, or the willingness to tolerate what is felt.

What is at issue here is the type of dependency the therapist is trying to establish. The therapist wants the patient to feel ownership of his or her own growth; while the therapist sees and knows what is happening, the growth is the patient's own accomplishment. This is the kind of growth parents try to bring about with their children, where growth is something the children do themselves and is much more than simply carrying out the parents' wishes. If growth is a matter of carrying out someone else's wishes, there is only the semblance of maturation; compliance lies underneath, and dependency is replaced with embeddedness.

The therapist, by not rushing to define or organize the confusion, allows a dependency that is not built on compliance. Needless to say, this is different from how the patient grew up, where private experience was quickly replaced with compliance. The therapist must let patients take risks, in this case the risk of facing inward looseness and disorganization. We believe that patients can do this if they have some assurance that someone sees and confirms the courage they are showing. This sense of being seen but not controlled makes it possible to move away from the embeddedness of compliance (and its attendant role playing). By contrast, if patients feel they are simply doing what the therapist wants, or defining experience as the therapist dictates, there is no launching away from embeddedness. The patients then remain in a pseudo-independent posture, quite embedded in how the therapist defines their experience.

Quiet borderline patients typically have childhood histories of precocious ego development and of adultomorphic traits. What appears, however, to be early maturity is actually an attempt to avoid the confusion and disorganization that is experienced whenever the child (and later the adult) tries to depend on someone. As-if individuals are not actually mature or independent; they remain quite dependent on others for roles to play and thereby for definition. However, they are not really dependent either; theirs is a surface level relatedness that avoids spontaneity, affect, and leaning on the other person. They bring this style to treatment, where work must be done to help the patient depend on the therapist, which in turn usually entails exposing the patient to some measure of confusion and disorganization. Until genuine dependency becomes possible, however, the patient will alternate between needing to be seen (or defined) on the one hand and making sure that what is seen remains at surface level, on the other hand.

TRANSCRIPT: THE NEED TO BE SEEN AND THE FEAR OF BEING KNOWN

The following transcript illustrates the way as-if patients alternate between the need to be seen by someone and the equally great need to avoid being dependent. This particular patient was unable to be alone and felt keenly the desire to be someone else's object whenever she was by herself. This need to be seen or known disappeared when in the presence of others, however; she then began trying to determine what was expected of her so that she could get on with the business of meeting expectations. She could not really be herself in either case, then, and was defined by the presence or absence of someone to see her.

This patient came for therapy at age 35. At first it was hard to know why, since she seemed calm and relatively untroubled in the way she interacted with the therapist. She initially made several vague and hard-to-define complaints and seemed, alternately, hysteroid, depressed, and mildly obsessive. By the end of the first session, the therapist felt he knew very little more than when the patient had begun. The overall impression was of someone who was attempting to communicate distress without saying aloud that she was unhappy. It seemed important to the patient to appear normal, as though she were trying to dodge the accusation of being a complainer. Indeed, throughout treatment, the therapist was repeatedly surprised to find that what the patient appeared to be feeling bore little resemblance to what she actually experienced; she always felt far worse than she showed.

Little by little, information came out that led the therapist to see the woman as having as-if traits, although she was not fully an as-if patient. First, she had assumed an almost caricatured, adultomorphic stance in her preschool years and never relinquished it through adolescence. She was remarkably self-contained and "mature" as a child and teenager, never showing defiance, anger, or distress. As a child she grew up on a small farm and had many responsibilities which she apparently handled remarkably well. She also had to spend much time alone. Privately she hated this and wished desperately for company, but she never said anything about it to anyone. The patient seems not only to have been a perfect child but a perfect adolescent too—the parents of her friends would let their children attend any party or function she attended, since "They knew I would never do anything wrong."

Second, this woman had little ability to define herself and in fact often referred to herself as "nobody." (She had dreams in which she was introduced to people as someone else or by the wrong name.) She felt guilty whenever she tried to say aloud what her own wants and interests were, insisting that it would be better to pay attention to what others wanted of her. She did not seem to mean this in a masochistic way (she was not usually taken advantage of by others) but seemed instead to be saying that she needed others to tell her who to be. For instance, in one session she said: "It's easier just doing what others expect me to do. It's got to the point I don't even know what I want to do . . . I'm supposed to do whatever the other person wants me to do, and if you don't tell me, I don't know what it is." Not surprisingly, during sessions she frequently insisted that the therapist should tell her what he wanted her to talk about.

Third, the patient was exceptionally passive. Although she was not docile, she was unable to make even the most rudimentary expressions of assertiveness. She tended to allow others to make important decisions for her without venturing her own opinion. Often she found that she had no opinion on important and personal matters, and at other times she discovered that she had opinions only after the decision had already been made for her. She felt truly comfortable only when playing out roles assigned by others.

Finally, the patient found both aloneness and intimacy to be highly problematic. The therapist once asked what it was like to be alone with no role to play, and the patient said, "It's like I'm not." This is the patient described briefly in Chapter 1 who suffered dissociated states of mind for hours when alone at home. However, interactions with others were not necessarily better. She resisted any truly intimate involvement with others and usually wanted only not to be alone physically. She was insulated interpersonally and had a repetitive dream in which "it's like I'm behind glass, away from everybody else, although no one notices it."

Treatment was exceptionally slow and difficult. The patient had a hard time talking and would often sit staring at the therapist, occasionally asking for guidance on what she should say. She was genuinely distressed when he would not tell her, since she was virtually unable to produce any content spontaneously or on her own initiative. Often the patient mumbled when she talked, as though she wished both to say something and keep it to herself at the same time.

This session took place in the tenth month of once weekly therapy after a working relationship and some measure of dependency were beginning to form. The previous session had been very hard for the patient due to the therapist's silence. Partly as a consequence, the therapist is more talkative in this session than usual (and more talkative than is wise).

PT: (mumbles unintelligibly)

TH: What did you say?

PT: I said, "Are you just going to sit?"

TH: (after a 30-second pause) We often do.

PT: (mumbles again)

TH: What did you say? Did you say, "I know"?

PT: I know. I hate it. (pause) This week has been a fast week. You know how last week I talked about how you just have to go, I've been that way all week. Zooming along at 90 miles an hour. I've been doing a lot of work for this seminar. She gives us a lot of homework and stuff to do. So. It's work stuff (mumbles). I'm enjoying it.
(This patient hates having time on her hands, finding it hard to structure empty time. The problem for her is making decisions about what to do next. Without someone to tell her what should be done, she obsesses and falls inert. She has a hard time making any independent decision, afraid that she will somehow make a mistake. By contrast, she does quite well when a schedule of activities is laid out for her. In this case, the work-related seminar is filling her free time and dictating what she does.)

TH: Yeah. I'll bet you are enjoying it.

PT: I'm going to do it and get it all done. I wanna have it all (mumbles). Right then, if I can't do that.

TH: I'm not with you. What do you mean?

PT: Anything that we can do. It's a child-care seminar that I'm talking about, instituting some new things at work. We make a lot of the things that we use, and I want to make it and have it all right there. When I walk back in the door [at work] I want every bit of it done. I mean it takes years to get all of this stuff together, to do this, unless you want to fork out a fortune and buy the kit, you know. Which I won't do. But I want to start it and I want to get it all done. And then I want to jump ahead and do everything else that there is to do. And I can't do it, and I get aggravated because I can't do it. (mumbles something) (30-second pause) Oh please, I don't want to sit and stare. (sigh) (mumbles to herself) (sigh) I didn't make it to (a restaurant she had planned to visit) this week because of the seminar.

TH: (laughing) Do you think I'll talk more if you go there?

PT: I don't know, you might. I cannot stand quiet. I cannot stand it! If I am in a quiet room by myself I make my own noise. I mean I talk to myself or else I'll sing a song. But I can not stand quiet . . .

TH: What's it like?

PT: Oh, it just drives me, drives me nuts. It's like you're in a little box . . .

TH: Makes you tense?

PT: Oh yeah, I can't stand it! I don't like it . . .

TH: You feel hemmed in?
(The therapist is trying to make the patient aware of her inner life by calling attention to how she feels. The patient is usually oriented to the external world and cut off from her inner world. She tends to feel affect only in vague, undefined ways.)

PT: Uh huh. I mean it's like you're under a magnifying glass.

TH: Who's looking?

PT: Everybody.
(This is an unexpected answer. The patient has trouble feeling real when she is alone. Thus, the patient might have been expected to say something to the effect that she

feels anxious over having no one to define her when by herself. However, she says that she is anxious because she imagines many people looking at and scrutinizing her. This turns out to be a very important theme, although the therapist does not realize it here and lets the issue get lost. Fortunately, the subject comes up again late in the session.)

TH: You surprise me. I would have thought it would be nobody.

PT: Everybody's looking.

TH: If you're home alone and it's quiet, everybody's looking?

PT: Oh yes, everybody knows what you're doing, everybody sees, I mean, it's awful. It's like you're under a magnifying glass, and everybody's just sitting back waiting for you to do something. (pause) Or . . . or like you just kind of fade away. (sighs) Like everything stops. Nothing else is going on. Everybody's waiting to see what you're going to do . . .

TH: You're home alone, and it's quiet. It's not just that you feel boxed in but it's as though you're being watched by a bunch of people who have suddenly come to a stop and are waiting to see what you are about to do? Either that or did you say that everything fades?
(The therapist is confused by what the patient just said and is trying to define it more clearly. As the session continues, the therapist notices that the patient is frequently confusing; she contradicts herself frequently, making a comment and then retracting it. At first glance, there is an obsessive quality to these confusing segments. Closer inspection, however, suggests that the patient is showing the confusion typical of an as-if patient who is starting to feel dependent on the therapist.)

PT: Not, not everything else, well, yeah. *I mean it's not like, well it's not like you don't exist . . . but it kind of is. (pause)* But it's never quiet—I never give myself the opportunity to be any place that's quiet. I can't stand it. I mean I will sing, I will do anything to keep it from being quiet . . . I'll talk to myself, I'll do anything. (pause) Was that funny?

TH: You don't sing in here.

PT: Well, no, because you're in here.

TH: If there really is somebody watching, is that different? Does it matter whether I'm real, or would it be the same thing if I were in your imagination?

PT: (long pause) No, no, you couldn't do the same thing. Because you can actually hear me if I, say, sang. That's why I mumble like I do.

TH: Hmmm.

PT: These people think you're nuts if you're talking to yourself all the time. So I talk to myself silently a lot.

TH: In here or at home?

PT: Oh! At home! Oh, sometimes I've done it here when . . . (laughs nervously) I don't want to (mumbles) when it's quiet! I mean sometimes it's like impending doom, like something's gonna happen, and I don't know what it is . . .

TH: That is the way you look. You look agitated, like something bad's about to happen.

PT: Sometimes it feels that way. I mean there's this sense of not knowing, and either everything is going to hinge on what I'm going to do or else . . . it wouldn't matter a hill of beans what I do—nobody would care anyway. I mean, you know it's like being caught between a rock and a hard place? Like a Catch-22? If you do something, either that's going to cause everybody to notice you and look at you, but if you don't do anything, everybody's still standing there and looking at you, waiting for you to do something. So you're just kind of stuck. Don't know which way to go . . .

(The patient has essentially said that she feels she does not exist unless she is in the midst of noise, activity, and other people. She finds aloneness so painful that she imagines other people looking at her when she is by herself. She says that these imaginary others seem to be waiting for her to do something, and the therapist hears the idea that these imaginary others expect something of the patient. In what follows he tries to personalize this theme by focusing on whether the patient imagines that he too expects something from her. The therapist is missing the key theme, however, that the patient cannot feel real without someone to see and define her.)

TH: You seem to believe I have some expectation of you.

PT: Well, I think everybody does. Everybody always has, so I think everybody does.

TH: Do you think I have some secret expectation that I'm not letting you in on?

PT: I'm sure you do. I think everybody does. (pause)

TH: You don't trust me when I say that you can talk about whatever's on your mind?

PT: No, no, I think I can.

TH: You think there's more?

PT: What do you mean, more?

TH: That I have some other agenda that I'm not telling you about.

PT: Well, no, because that's too broad a topic. I mean you're supposed to tell me what stuff to talk about. I mean that's too broad. And I don't, I don't like focusing on myself! (mumbles) I would rather focus on somebody else, or something else. It would be easier for me to sit here and talk about you than to sit here and talk about me . . .

TH: You could do that if you wished.

PT: I tried that and you didn't talk back . . .

TH: You wanted me to sit here and talk about me.

PT: Yeah, I wanted you to jump in every once in a while.

TH: I see.

PT: But you won't do it. But you do, you do expect . . . Well, no, you don't . . . I feel like you do, you expect me to talk and whatever, and (very quietly) I just don't feel comfortable with it. I mean I don't think I'd do anything, I don't think anything I have done or anything I will do or whatever is that interesting, is that important. What does it matter? Who cares? So (mumbles) . . . (sighs)
(This is a good example of the confusion mentioned earlier. It is no accident that it takes place as the therapist has tried to personalize the interaction.)

TH: You don't think that you as a person matter.
(This is probably true, but it is not the point here. The patient correctly believes that the therapist has expectations of her; although it is hard for her to say it aloud, she voices the opinion that he expects her to talk. If the therapist didn't have some expectations about this, he wouldn't have made several comments early in the session about how hard silence was for the patient—he would

have demonstrated his own comfort with silence by being silent. The patient, who is a skilled observer and who has a lifetime of experience drawing conclusions about what others might expect of her, noticed this. She now concludes that she is expected to talk. The therapist should probably confirm that she is correctly picking up an expectation he was not aware of. He should also notice that the patient is not exactly saying that she does not matter as a person; she is more likely saying that she doubts she could claim another person's interest and attention, that she is boring or uninteresting.)

PT: (about one minute silence) I don't . . . I don't think that it's I don't matter, it's just I'm not important . . .

TH: Perhaps there would be a problem with being important or with wanting to be important.
(The therapist is off the subject, which is this patient's need to be seen (and to a lesser extent her fear of being seen). The patient tries to get back to this theme and eventually does. For a while, though, the therapist keeps returning to questions of valuation, that is, questions of whether the patient fears criticism and rejection. These themes are essentially narcissistic in nature, but the patient is dealing with issues that are more related to doubts about her own reality, not doubts about her value.)

PT: Well, if you were important, then people would notice you. And I don't want people looking at me. I mean if I know . . . well, no, that's not true either. I mean even at work if I'm being observed or whatever, I don't like it, because I feel like people are judging me; they're not judging what I'm doing . . .

TH: It could be hard to separate the two. I can see why you'd be nervous.

PT: I don't like it. It drives me crazy (mumbles).

TH: What did you say?

PT: I said I can't stand it; it drives me crazy. I don't like it. I mean I'm a basket case for days when the regional manager comes in. I've been doing this for ten years. You'd think . . . but I don't. I feel like he's judging me more than what I'm doing . . .

TH: I think what you're saying is that you have a hard time distinguishing you as a person from whatever role you're playing.

PT: Yeah. Well, if . . . It's like I've always had a role to fill. Like there never was a time when I could just be myself.

TH: Is there a "yourself" to be?

PT: There used to be.
(The patient consistently maintains that she used to be very different from what she now is. She returns to this theme later.)

TH: Where did you go?

PT: I don't know. I mean I think that's why so much now I feel like I'm fighting with myself so much of the time. I mean you know it's like I had an evil twin. I'm at myself all the time. And I don't know . . . I don't know if I expect too much of myself? Or if I expect too much out of other people. But it's like I can't, it's like I'm on the bottom looking up instead of being on the top looking down . . .

TH: And what's the difference?

PT: I have to do, I have to do things or be things to come up to someone else's level rather than already being on that level. (pause) Then I would rather just sit back and not say or do anything and let everybody else do it because I can't or I don't feel like . . . it's not that I can't compete but like I can't be an equal. Either, either you get people who know everything that I went through growing up—either they feel really sorry for you . . . and it's like, oh how wonderful you've turned out with the life you've had or else the people who don't know what I went through will look at me now and then say, well, forget it, you shouldn't even be in a public profession, let alone being on the same keel that I'm on. It's like there's nothing that I can do to be equal with everybody else. Does that make any sense?

TH: I think I understand what you're saying. But the last thing you said, about people who say you shouldn't be in a public profession, that's a reference to the supervisor? *(The patient once had a supervisor who criticized her style with the public.)*

PT: Well, yeah.

TH: Is it also a reference to people you know now or is it a reference to what you imagine?

PT: Probably, probably, more a reference to what I imagine than to what people say . . . *(This is close to the earlier theme, that this patient creates a network of expectations, judgments, and interactions in fantasy when she lacks a definite role to play, and then lives out of these imaginary interactions. The therapist goes on to pick up on one aspect of the subject, that the patient's time sense is too narrow. He addresses the way the patient seeks premature closure when she is uncertain rather than wait to see what happens next. This is a key issue with most borderline patients, but the therapist is probably unwise to pursue it here. The patient, after all, is imagining what others think because she needs roles to play, not because she is uneasy with ambiguity.)*

TH: When you're faced with uncertainty, such as not knowing what's on other people's minds, when faced with uncertainty, you fill in the blanks, and you usually fill in the blanks with believing that other people are critical of you and rejecting. That's your way of resolving ambiguity or uncertainty.

PT: Uh huh. I automatically assume the worst with almost everyone.

TH: How come you can't just hold the uncertainty and content yourself with not knowing what other people are thinking, just like the rest of us don't know what others are thinking?

PT: I don't know.

TH: Did you know that was possible?

PT: I don't guess I ever thought about it.

TH: Well, I just want to make sure you know it's a possibility, that all of us go through lots of situations without knowing what other people are thinking about, even whether they're thinking about us. We simply accept that's an uncertainty—they might be critical, they're probably indifferent, but in any event we don't know and don't have to know. I mention it because you seem to think you have to fill in any uncertainty in a self-critical way.

PT: I never thought of it that way. I mean when I was growing up I had teachers who did it in school and classmates who did it in school and I guess I just automatically assumed that everybody does it. It's just always been that way.

TH: It might have been that way when you were a child, but it has not always been that way since. You have just thought it was that way.

PT: (after a long silence) Well, I just don't feel comfortable not knowing what anybody wants (mumbles). I mean if I can't do what anybody wants, then I feel guilty like it's my fault that I can't do it. I don't ever stop to think whether it's in my power to do. I just think it's my fault I can't do it. I did something to cause . . . whatever. (after another silence, this one lasting several minutes) Well, I know there's stuff I don't have any control over. I have no control over whether the sun comes up every day or whether it rains or . . . (mumbling) but everything's my fault. It's my fault if everybody's not happy. Because that's my job, to make everybody happy.

TH: You do a lousy job!

PT: (laughing) Oh, I know, but I didn't used to.

TH: I have some other patients who keep asking me why they're so unhappy; now I can tell them.

PT: Thank you.

TH: When you were sitting there quietly a few minutes ago, you looked more comfortable than usual. Did you feel any different than usual when we're silent?

PT: Uh uh.

TH: No? I misread you.

PT: I felt (mumbles inaudibly). Somebody said something about that to me yesterday, that I appeared so low key and easygoing that I must never get upset about anything, which is true—everybody thinks that, but on the inside I'm like this (makes a shaking motion with her hand). I'm going ninety miles an hour . . .

TH: Yes I can see that. To feel comfortable sitting quietly with me you would have to trust me, and that would be difficult for you.

(The therapist is inviting the patient to a more personalized interaction. She briefly responds more intimately, saying then that there must be something the therapist wants of her that she can match up with. She then veers back into more general, less personalized content. The therapist makes one more effort to personalize the exchange with a paradoxical intervention about trust; see the following.)

PT: (30-second pause) Yeah. I mean there's gotta be something, there's gotta be something . . .

TH: You lost me there.

PT: Oh gosh. (sighs) There has to be something that either I'm not doing or, I mean it can't just be . . . (mumbles) *There has to be something that you want! There's something everybody wants!* And I can't always figure out what that is to make sure I do whatever it is that everybody wants me to do!

TH: Okay. I want you to trust me.
(The therapist is using humor to try to reach the patient. He knows that what he suggests is impossible for the patient, who also sees the therapist's humorous intent.)

PT: (laughs) Well you'll have to define it.

TH: Oh, okay. By trust I mean that we can sit quietly together and you will feel confident that I still hold a good opinion of you and find you a valuable person.

PT: I can't feel that way. (sighs and mumbles inaudibly)

TH: Yeah, but don't you feel better, because now you know you're not matching up with my expectations?

PT: Now I feel guilty because I don't! (laughs) There's no happy medium. And there used to be. There used to be a medium in there. Well I don't know if you'd call it a medium, but, I mean like when I was a kid if anybody in the room would speak their opinion about anything it was me. You could always count on me speaking up and saying something. If you needed anything done, or whatever, I was always the first one up there. I mean I was always in the middle of everything, and I liked being in the middle . . . of everything. And then gradually or all of a sudden that started changing . . .

(We noted earlier that this patient consistently maintained that she used to be different, that there was a time when she knew who she was and felt confident of her place in the world. The therapist never found any evidence to suggest that this was so. It may be that the patient confused having had more definite roles to play as a child with having a more solid identity. Her precocious independence as a child certainly brought her much praise, and she probably felt more sure of herself due to the frequent feedback. She goes on to talk about showing animals in livestock shows as a child.)

TH: When?

PT: I don't know. I . . . I don't know if I could say when that started changing. But, I mean, when I had my livestock to show, I could be in the center and be noticed, and it didn't bother me. Of course, I wasn't the only thing people were looking at. Looking at the animals too. And I knew I was good. And I could do, I could do it. There was always something else to try, always something more challenging to do, but I could do it. And it's the same way with [managing the child-care center]. I can get in there, and I can do it. And it's like that's what I am, and that's the way that I am. But when I get out into the other world I can't be that way. People are always passing judgment.

(In fact, there is no evidence that anyone is taking enough notice of the patient to be passing judgment. This seems to be entirely her fantasy and reflects a desire to be seen by others. The patient does not feel real when she is not

*playing a role given her by someone else. She wants to be
seen, to be defined by others, and she is willing to imagine
such a circumstance even when she is not being seen or
noticed. As she has already said, she imagines being seen
even when she is perfectly alone. Curiously, at this point
in the session the patient starts to think a little more
clearly and seems to be fighting off the therapist less. She
is able to do good work for much of the remainder of the
session.)*

TH: Certainly in your mind they're always passing judgment. It's almost as though—I know you'll disagree with
this—it's almost as though you'd rather they pass judgment
than not notice you at all.

PT: I'd rather they pass judgment?

TH: Than not notice you at all.

PT: (pause of about one minute) So by, by feeling this
way, or doing the things that I do, I'm calling the attention
to myself that I don't want?

TH: What's your thought there? Can you spell that idea
out?

PT: Like attention-getting behavior?

TH: No. Because you don't actually draw attention to
yourself. You imagine it. It's like you're trying to create a
fantasy of the other person thinking about you. You want
them to be thinking about you. Even when you're alone,
you manufacture a host of people thinking about you. That
suggests to me that you're someone who doesn't want to
be forgotten.

PT: I will admit I don't want to be forgotten. I have a fear
that when I die no one will show up at my funeral. I
discovered that about myself when I worked at a nursing

home. I would never leave anybody, if I had to stay, if I had to go off the clock and stay, if someone was going to be by themselves and we knew they were dying, I'd stay all night if I had to. So now I have this fear (mumbles) coming to my funeral. My friend Linda promised me she'd come to my funeral and then steal all the stuff out of my office! (laughs)

TH: You are grinning and you make light when you say this, but I gather it's a serious subject if you would stay all night with people at the nursing home rather than have them be alone. That was a compassionate thing to do. I gather the compassion was born out of your ability to identify with them. You feel that you too are in danger of being forgotten and left.

PT: Well, that might have been, that might be, but to me it was like it was the other way around. Because of the staying and realizing that people die alone or are alone, then that made me think about it, to say that I don't want that to happen to me. But I was left alone a lot as a child.

TH: Yes, you were!

PT: Well that may have been why—I never thought about why I stayed.

TH: You may have seen some of your own predicament in theirs?

PT: I never thought of it that way. (pause) I think that may be. I can't say it's not. But I turn around now, and I lock myself in my house, I close off the house so I can wall myself off in one room. I mean I ostracize myself.

TH: Yes, you do. But when you do that you either imagine a world of people staring at you or you dissociate for the entire day.

PT: Uh huh.

TH: It appears to me that the only way you can stay present by yourself is to imagine that there are people looking at you. Otherwise, you truly are not there.

PT: Well, either that or I have to be doing something. (pause) If I can get totally absorbed into something, which used to be the animals and used to be [her son], and then during the school year it was school stuff, and if I could constantly be doing something, then I don't feel like everybody's waiting for my next move or that the world is standing still or whatever. But it's not like I'm doing anything for myself; I'm doing it for somebody else. I'm not supposed to be doing it for myself. I mean I would never—well, I won't say I would never—I probably would never say, "Well, I want to go see this movie" and then go see the movie for myself. Because I'm supposed to be doing something else. I'm not supposed to be doing that. I should be home doing, whatever, anything. And then I go home and there's the laundry, and even that gets overwhelming, just sorting the stupid laundry. You know, then I have to talk to myself about which load I'm going to do first. Who cares? It doesn't make any difference, but then I do it and I say to myself I should have done it differently. It's not like the world is going to end tomorrow because of the way I did it. I go in the kitchen and I close it all up, and nobody knows I'm home (mumbling, getting quiet).

TH: Did you say nobody knows you're home?

PT: Nobody knows I'm home. Even if my car's there nobody knows I'm home.

TH: In some odd way you seem to want a private self, but if there's even the possibility that somebody's around you feel you have no private self. You're immediately taken over and consumed by their eyes.

PT: Because I've always had to do whatever anybody else wanted me to do! I've never had any—well, yes I did,

no, I didn't—(pause) I never had any time when there was just me. The times that kids normally have when they're growing up when it's just them and their time to be kids, I didn't have that. Or it didn't feel like I did.
The patient's confusion has returned during the last few exchanges.

TH: I believe that's true, but it's not true now.

PT: But I don't know what to do with that time or that self now that I have it. I don't know what to do with . . . (tape runs out—session ends a few moments later).
(The theme by session's end is that the patient cannot feel real when she is alone and yet is not easy when other people are actually present. When alone, she feels unreal and imagines others who can see and define her. When others are actually there, however, she feels captured by their expectations and unable to define herself as separate from them. She both needs and fears being seen by the other.)

7

The Absence of Identity

IDENTITY

There is a lifelong dialogue between personal identity and our relationships with others, between our private sense of self and who others take us (and make us) to be. At times, this dialogue may seem like a battle, while at other times the conversation between the private and social self may be enchanting and free of struggle. It is hard to imagine a person whose identity is not influenced by the way significant others see him or her. Our sense of self is initially given by others, and it is thereafter a lifelong decision whether the people in our lives add to or diminish what they originally gave.

Very early in life we discover ourselves in the other. We first catch a glimpse of who we are (or might be) in the reactions of those around us, at first in the mother's mirroring responses (cf. Chapter 3). While the infant's own feelings and intentions may be jumbled, unintelligible, and overwhelming, these gain definition and clarity as they are reflected in the mother's face, voice, and general manner toward her baby. Feelings and urges that flood the infant with terrible and compelling tension become (over time) defined, organized, and manageable when they appear outside, on the mother's face and in her intonations. Babies thereby find themselves in their mothers' faces.

Of course no mother is an accurate, passive mirror, saying and reflecting solely what is "in" the child. Mothers and other caretakers are selective in what they see and respond to, and certainly they respond as much to their own fantasies about the baby as to the baby's moods and feelings. For that matter, mirroring is a reciprocal affair; the baby is also selective in responding to the mother, and this, in turn, influences the mother's view of herself and her experience of the baby. This is both the beauty and the difficulty with the mirroring process: In part the parents merely give back to the child what is already there, but in part what they put "in" the child is alien, coming from their own hopes, fears, and moods. The process that begins our sense of who we are is, then, partly a matter of discovering what is already there, but is also partly a matter of filling us with someone else's fantasies about us.

It happens, therefore, that significant others can (and do) give us our selves through defining what we feel and seeing what we are like. Persons who are important emotionally can also take us away from our selves by seeing us differently from the way we are or by seeing aspects of us we do not want to acknowledge. For relatively healthy persons, the other's ability to give or take us away from our selves becomes muted with maturation. This muting does not occur to the same extent with unhealthy persons; we might say, in fact, that the degree of pathology present in any individual is proportionate to the degree to which another person has the power to alter the experience of self. Traditionally, identity has been thought of as intrapsychic and belonging solely to the individual. Identity is also interpersonal, not something that resides only within us.

The as-if individual is an extreme example of the interpersonal elements in identity. For most persons, the other's ability to affect identity is buffered by abiding fantasies and perceptions of self. For the as-if individual, however, there is no buffering; anyone who is at least temporarily important to the as-if patient can influence his or her identity. This is so for the simple reason that as-if individuals are by and large without abiding fantasies or perceptions of themselves (although they certainly have fantasies about the other people in their lives). In saying this, we reiterate a position to which we have referred throughout this book, that quiet borderline individuals have no sense of self or identity. Their experience of themselves is discontinuous in the sense that there is no ownership of whatever self experience is available at any given time. The individual is not committed to who he or she is at any given moment and can, with a minimum of distress, become different.

Consequently, there is no private identity available for dialogue with the other: There is only the way the other sees the as-if individual and, through seeing, offers definition. We are not sure whether to say that this type of identity differs from normal identity in that it is not truly interpersonal (since there is only one individual who is being personal) or whether we should say that it differs because it is radically interpersonal (since the as-if individual is all too willing to be who and what the other asks). However one might choose to say it, the dialogue of identity is different for the as-if individual. While others may give such an individual his or her identity, they are not a threat to it. Other persons may not take as-if individuals away from themselves. What identity as-if patients have is ever on loan and seldom something to which they are committed.

For normal persons, the danger that comes from other people is that they may disrupt our sense of self, imposing their own fantasies of who we are. This may be initially exciting, as when we are idealized, or painful, as when we are denigrated, but it is a disruption nonetheless to feel the impact of the other's image of us. This disruption does not exist for quiet borderline individuals, however, since the other's image of them is not at odds with their own. Psychologically speaking, they themselves do not exist; they *are* the other's fantasy of them.

When we speak of the absence of all but transitory identities in the as-if patient, we are referring to the absence of those personal commitments that serve as the foundation of identity.

By commitments, we do not necessarily refer to conscious and deliberate choices but, rather, to an individual's ongoing intentions, to patterns of behavior and attitude that are clung to across time and changing circumstances. While we may not be conscious of having made such a commitment, we become aware of the commitment itself when placed in circumstances that conflict with it. A youth, for instance, may not be aware of a commitment to the well-being of a younger sibling until he or she sees the sibling being picked on at school and feels a protective impulse. Most persons carry such commitments with them, even if there was no particular instant when the commitment was entered into.

Two such commitments support identity. The first is a commitment to sexual differences, which is, in turn, a commitment to a particular way of experiencing our bodies and our relationships to others. This is a matter of acknowledging that there are differences between males and females and that the two are not interchangeable. Experiencing ourselves as either male or female (and feeling that we are not the other) offers immediate access to a set of social roles; although these roles come from others, they belong to us as well. The roles are rooted in our bodies—once gained from others, they are part of us because they have a basis in our bodies.

The second commitment underlying identity is a commitment to growing up, which in time becomes a commitment to an occupation or vocation. This commitment rests in the dual sense that there is a difference between adults and children and that the task of children is to become adults. It goes without saying that a commitment to growing up is built on identifications with the adults in our lives. As with the commitment to sexual differences, these identifications come first from outside us but are gradually made our own. Finally, we are not growing up to become like our mothers and fathers but to become ourselves.

With maturation, the commitment to grow up becomes a vocational or occupational commitment. If asked to tell about themselves, most adults begin with a statement of their occupation or the lack of one. This serves as a statement of where they fit in the scheme of things, of how others should see them. Even an occupation that one plans to change later can lend a sense of belonging or definition. Identifying with one's job gradually replaces the identifications of childhood as the bedrock of identity. While a vocational identification is less personal than identifying with one's parents, it serves much the same function in underwriting identity.

The quiet borderline individual lacks these two commitments. We have referred in previous chapters to Deutsch's (1942) observation that as-if patients appear inclined to a casual sexual morality; most of the patients she discussed showed "sexual perversions." Our clinical impressions support Deutsch's observations. It is our experience that a disproportionate number of as-if patients have not only been promiscuous but have had bisexual experiences. It may, in fact, be an aid to diagnosis to learn that an apparently conventional and seemingly marginally disturbed patient has a history of bisexual relationships or flirtations. Such information should immediately raise the question of whether the patient lacks one of the two chief commitments that underlies a sense of self, the commitment to sexual differences. Whereas sexual identity entails feeling that our bodies irreversibly commit us to certain patterns of behavior (and that we cannot escape these because they adhere to our physical selves), the as-if individual's behavior indicates a sense that nothing about oneself is irreversible, that everything depends on what the situation requires rather than on who one is.

Similarly, we find a lack of vocational commitment in quiet borderline patients. This is not the case with more classic, or noisy, borderline individuals, whose vocational choice and functioning are often islands of stability in an ocean of chaos. By contrast, quiet borderline patients seem to have fairly little investment in their jobs after an initial burst of enthusiasm dies down. Even jobs that have been held for some time are surrendered with little distress. We believe that, as a rule, these patients change jobs more often than most, although not because they are in pursuit of a vocational goal. Rather, they change because "something else came up" or "I guess I was bored." Most of their job changes are lateral moves.

Behind the quiet borderline patient's lack of commitment to a vocational identity lies an absence of generational boundaries. At some point in the preschool and early grade-school years, children must submit to their roles as children. Healthy children are thoroughly egocentric in the first years of life, not questioning that they are the center of the universe until unwelcome realities (e.g., the birth of a sibling, starting school) begin to crowd them out of self-centeredness and into the larger world and its multiple perspectives. The oedipal struggle seems to be the central event in this process of benign disillusionment (cf. Chasseguet-Smirgel 1984). During the oedipal period, children learn—to their dismay—that "no matter what they have thought, and no matter what people tell them . . . they are not little men or little women but little children" (Cameron 1963, p. 74). Such a discovery, so important in establishing the parental identifications that underwrite the desire to grow up, establishes generational boundaries or the sense that, first, there are essential differences between adults and children, and, second, children must grow up in order to become adults.

We have already argued that the later sense of vocational identity is rooted in the commitment to grow up, or in generational boundaries. It is easy to see the way generational boundaries contribute to identity in other ways as well. Children who know that they are children and that they are in the hands of adults know what, in fact, is their situation. They have a place in the scheme of things that defines their role now and also gives them a future. There is also the security of knowing that adult potentials are not expected too early and that there will be time to grow into who and what the child is to become.

The child who becomes a quiet borderline individual does not grow up this way, however. One of the hallmarks of such children is precocious maturity, which is to say that these children suffered the illusion that they were already grown up or that there were no essential generational differences. Such an illusion is not unique to as-if pathology; we believe that pathological narcissism also rests on the denial of generational differences (cf. Sherwood 1990, pp. 381–382), and Chasseguet-Smirgel (1984) proposes that this denial plays a central role in the perversions. What is unique in as-if pathology is that the denial of generational differences does not support the child's natural grandiosity (in pathological narcissism and perversion the denial of generational differences leads the child to become his or her own ideal) but, rather, leads the child to become a mere extension of the parents. The roles and status of different family members are confused, and the child takes on adult mannerisms and traits far too early.

The absence of generational boundaries contributes to a weakening of personal boundaries. When we talk of boundaries, we refer to the dichotomy self-world or, possibly, private–public. The task is to effect a firm difference between self and the world without making that boundary too rigid on the one hand or too permeable on the other. The as-if individual errs in the latter direction. The wishes of the parents automatically become the child's preferences; in the process of making the self to be an extension of the parents, the child loses all that goes with being a self: autonomy, initiative, and integrity. There is, in effect, no private world. There are simply the wishes or expectations of others, and these fill up what would have been the self.

Given these circumstances, it is not easy to imagine how the quiet borderline individual could achieve the commitments to sexual differences and maturation/occupational identity that are part of the sense of self. Earlier, we spoke of the dialogue with others that leads to identity and said that the as-if personality reflects that process gone awry. As-if pathology results when only one side of the dialogue is heard, when the individual is filled with the fantasies and expectations of the other, and what is already there in the individual is simply not seen or recognized.

PROBLEMS WITH ALONENESS AND RELATEDNESS

The identity difficulties suffered by quiet borderline patients lead to two problems, discomfort in being alone on the one hand and inability to be genuine in relationships on the other hand. Perhaps it sounds incongruous that as-if individuals should have trouble being alone. After all, they do not allow themselves to be dependent on others, and so it may seem that they would not miss having others in their lives. Yet, in our experience it is rare to find a quiet borderline patient who is comfortable between relationships. These are not persons who do well outside relationships, and we have found that they tend to exchange one person for another fairly quickly when a relationship ends.

Even though as-if individuals do not become dependent on other persons, they might be said to be dependent on having someone available for feedback and definition. Their dependency, then, is a matter of plasticity, a matter of needing someone to conform to as opposed to becoming attached to a particular person. At this level of relatedness, people are virtually interchangeable. There is fairly little to recommend one person over another, since anyone who offers a role to play will suffice. Thus, the patient's problems with aloneness become problems with relatedness. Since almost any relationship will satisfy the desire to be defined, there is no genuineness to relationships. It is not the other *person* who is encountered but simply a role the other person holds out. Relationships tend to be impersonal at the same time that they are urgently sought.

Perhaps it will clarify the quiet borderline patient's style of relating to others if we compare it with another pathological form of relatedness in which persons are interchangeable, the narcissistic style. The narcissist relates to others only to the extent that they become the focus of his or her immediate intentions; the other is wanted for an audience or to meet the narcissist's needs. There is, therefore, always some manipulation involved; others are (subtly or none too subtly) asked to give up their own wishes and enter the narcissist's world. By contrast, as-if individuals do not seem to be manipulating others; all they seem to want from other people is some role to play. The narcissist has a much better sense of *wanting*. The narcissist wants, demands, and expects and visits these upon the people nearby. As-if individuals are not like this. They can patiently wait as long as they are in someone's emotional sphere. They generally become agitated or impulsive only when they are alone and want to get away from the lack of definition that comes with aloneness.

One might be tempted to say that what the quiet borderline patient needs is a touch of narcissism. Those who are involved with such a person might well say this—it can be a disappointing experience to get into a relationship with an as-if individual. There seems at first to be nothing amiss really. The as-if individual is exceptionally sensitive and responsive to what the other person wants, and this can be gratifying. If anything, as-if individuals may be especially pleasing and exciting at first, as they willingly comply with the other person. The relationship does not progress or deepen, however, since the as-if individual can do little more than follow the other's lead. Curiously, what is missing is the possibility of conflict. For adults, intimacy involves—and perhaps comes from—conflict. Conflict may not be pleasant while occurring, but it reassures each party that the other person is real, that there actually is someone else there. The possibility of conflict shows that the other person must be taken seriously, and, in turn, this produces respect and concern for the other's wishes.

Conflict also reveals that the other person is capable of commitment and of fighting to hold to the commitment. The quiet borderline patient, however, has no personal commitment to anything. Quiet borderline individuals are utterly dependent on the social environment; consequently, they do not risk tension with that environment, a fact of which their plasticity is evidence. The problem with tension, of course, is that it produces a sense of separateness from the other person. Tension highlights the individual in his or her aloneness, shining a spotlight, as it were, on the fact that there are differences between self and other. The as-if individual is certainly not trying to highlight these things and is in fact trying not to see them at all. Commitment is given up in favor of plasticity, then, since failure to do this eventually threatens the as-if patient with aloneness.

Since it is not possible to have an intimate relationship without risking tension and conflict, relationships cannot progress beyond a certain enthusiastic beginning. Deutsch (1942) gave an illustration of this process. She described how one of her patients, "a clever and experienced man" (p. 75), met one of her as-if female cases at a party. The man spent his next session with Deutsch praising the young woman for her attractive qualities but ended with the sad comment that something seemed vaguely wrong with her nonetheless. Deutsch submitted paintings of the same as-if patient to an art authority for evaluation, and the patient eventually entered training in the authority's school. The art authority and the patient's teacher were originally enthusiastic about her abilities but after some time grew rather less enthusiastic, feeling that the original promise was not fulfilled. This is the pattern for as-if individuals. Initially, they can engender excitement in the other person, but this cools fairly quickly if the other is looking for something that can grow and be sustained.

The quiet borderline patient is not seeking intimacy. Closeness is problematic, first because it entails being asked to provide something personal to the other, and the as-if individual does not really have anything personal to offer. Second, intimacy brings the risk of being made into an extension of the other person in a way that involves surrender rather than plasticity. That is, intimacy necessarily means abandoning separateness for periods of time and becoming, as it were, an extension of the other person. Abandoning separateness is not a problem for as-if individuals as long as plasticity is the vehicle for doing this. However, intimacy involves surrender, not mere pliancy, and as-if personalities have not learned how to surrender. They have learned how to use others to define themselves, interacting in a pliant way, but not in a way that gives up anything personal. Finally, intimacy entails spontaneity, a level of freedom that as-if individuals are not likely to risk. By definition, spontaneity is genuine, while, at best, these patients are as-if-they-were-genuine.

When quiet borderline individuals enter into an emotional relationship, it is not likely to last very long. As already noted, most persons will grow disenchanted with the as-if patient over time, as the relationship fails to progress and deepen. It is the absence of mutuality that is the problem. In the early stages of a relationship, we subtly suggest to the other person how he or she might see us; through our behavior and style of interaction, we disclose some of our fantasies of ourselves (the more pathological an individual, the more disparity between self-fantasy and behavior). These fantasies, in turn, pull certain responses from the other person, and through these responses we feel known and accepted or unknown and rejected. Particularly in the early days of a relationship, there can be a euphoria that comes with feeling accepted. This occurs when the other person responds to our fantasies by confirming those that are essentially positive and disallowing those that are negative.

If the relationship progresses, the other person gradually stops accepting our fantasies about ourselves at face value; the other begins to make changes, as it were, keeping some elements of the fantasy but changing others. We then have to decide whether we feel known and held in the corrections made by the other person, versus whether we feel that the other person's image of us is "not-me" (Sullivan 1947). We are, of course, doing the same thing with the other person all the while, and the result is a most fluid process.

This process is essentially a type of projective identification. To use a spatial language, we put images of ourselves into the other person, and they respond at first as though we were the person we suggest we are. However, genuine relationships cannot continue indefinitely on such a fantastic basis. In a healthy relationship, the other person does not accept indefinitely our fantasies and perceptions of ourselves. Rather, the other's fantasies and perceptions of us start to come into play.

In turn, their fantasies and perceptions modify our original self-presentation. If the relationship is to thrive, their image of us cannot be totally incompatible with the fantasies of ourselves we have conveyed to them. Yet the other cannot simply accept our fantasies of ourselves carte blanche. They must make changes, and we must, in effect, let them put their fantasies and perceptions of us into us. When this occurs, we feel known, held, and defined. This process deepens the relationship and is what we mean by mutuality.

In the case of the as-if individual, this process is arrested. The exchange is less fluid, stopping with the initial projective identifications. In effect, the as-if patient simply accepts without modification the other's self-presentation. As a consequence, the relationship really never changes and has something of a static quality in contrast to the living, growing nature of healthy relationships.

A further problem is the way as-if individuals present themselves to the other. Since they lack abiding fantasies and perceptions of themselves, they do not suggest an image of themselves to the other. Rather, they wait for hints of how the other might be willing to see them and then react in a complementary fashion. They are, in effect, becoming the other's fantasy of them. Initially, this may lead the other person to feel especially close, as though boundaries had been dropped and separateness dissolved. Eventually, however, the other begins to sense that it is not a matter of two separate persons who are intimately involved but, rather, two people acting out a fantasy proposed by only one of them.

> A patient told her therapist she had broken up with her boyfriend. He had complained, "You are telling me that you need to do this for yourself and your own life, and I need to leave you alone so you can lead your own life. But you don't have a life. You just lead part of everyone else's." The patient was perplexed by this comment but remembered that her therapist had several times spoken of the way she seemed to lose her identity in others. She brought the subject up in her next session.

Inevitably, relationships cool between healthy persons and as-if patients. The former find themselves either disillusioned or simply bored; in either event, they tend to drop out of the relationship. As-if individuals may themselves end a relationship if they feel that too much is being demanded of them, that is, if they feel that anything personal is being demanded of them. Being plastic precludes being intimate and also makes leaving less traumatic; if (pseudo)attachments are easy for plastic individuals, there is also an easiness to letting go.

When relationships dissolve, the as-if patient may feel bad about it at first but with surprising speed moves on to the next pseudo-attachment. There is no deepening of the personality from the pain of separation and loss when a relationship ends. Whatever pain is felt does not go very deep and is at best quite transitory. Certainly it does not obscure the ability to find a replacement for the lost object. There is an "out-of-sight, out-of-mind" quality to the as-if individual's relationships. These individuals do not seem to retain cherished memories of lost relationships; rather, the relationship simply ends.

Of course, quiet borderline individuals can and do have sustained relationships. Certain types of people may not find the as-if patient's incapacity for mutuality and intimacy to be problematic. As we mentioned in an earlier chapter, narcissistic individuals may not notice the absence of mutuality and may, in fact, prefer other persons to remain simply a mirror of themselves. In addition, persons who themselves have problems with intimacy (for example, those with schizoid tendencies) may welcome the fact that no demand will be made on them for genuine closeness. Thus, many as-if persons have histories of sustained or enduring relationships.

The therapist has a unique problem with the as-if patient. The therapist must not tolerate an as-if relationship and so is not content to avoid demands for genuine involvement. While others might walk out of the relationship because it is unsatisfying, the therapist cannot, of course, since the therapist is not in the relationship to be satisfied. Neither can the therapist simply insist on a genuineness that the patient cannot—at least at the start of treatment—produce. The therapist is therefore in the position of having to recognize the patient's attempts at avoiding a genuine relationship and working gradually to effect one.

In the course of this work, the therapist is also addressing the patient's core issue, the absence of identity, or the absence of any sustained sense of self. It is due to the absence of a continuous, integrated experience of self that the patient cannot enter into a genuine relationship and must instead avoid aloneness on the one hand and intimacy on the other. Our earlier proposition was that there is an ongoing dialogue between who we are and who others take us to be. Quiet borderline individuals, we argued, enter into only one side of the dialogue, that which involves who others take them to be, since the other part, namely identity, is essentially missing. In the course of pursuing a genuine relationship, the therapist is trying to make the patient capable of genuine relatedness. This means gaining the ability to articulate wishes, preferences, and intentions and to be committed to some of these. Such an ability is the core of selfhood or identity. It is not possible to try to establish a relationship with the quiet borderline patient without at the same time directly or indirectly playing midwife to the patient's sense of self.

PSEUDO-RELATEDNESS IN THE SESSION

As we have discussed, in the early stages of a relationship each individual reveals some of his or her fantasies about the self and, by implication, the other, inviting the other's experience to match up with these. In sessions, of course, it is a different matter; therapists take pains not to reveal their private fantasies about themselves to patients. As much as possible, therapists try to be hidden personally—it may be that this (probably unintentionally) changes with time in a long treatment, but at first, all but poorly trained therapists try to keep a large measure of anonymity. There is probably no complete anonymity; the office itself will say much about the therapist, or will at least suggest much to any patient looking for information. The quiet borderline individual has years of experience reading just these sorts of cues and will be attentive to whatever might be suggested about the therapist. In spite of these unavoidable sources of information, therapists will try not to reveal their fantasies about themselves to a new patient. They will want the patient to provide as much of the material for the therapeutic relationship as possible.

This therapeutic reserve leaves most non-as-if patients revealing their fantasies about themselves to the therapist and also producing fantasies about who the therapist is. *There is therefore a lack of mutuality to the therapeutic relationship that parallels the lack of mutuality in the as-if patient's style of dealing with others.* The difference between the therapist and the as-if patient is that the therapist could produce fantasies about self and other, while the as-if patient cannot. Despite this difference in potential, therapy starts with a sticky similarity—two people, each waiting for the other to reveal a fantasy to react to. In effect, the therapist has preempted the as-if patient's characteristic role in relationships: Instead of the patient, it is the therapist who insists that the other (in this case, the patient) reveal fantasies about the self and also about the other (in this case, the therapist). As-if patients are used to being in the position the therapist has taken. They are accustomed to prompting others to reveal fantasies about the self and about how the other sees the as-if individual without mutual self-revelation.

Of course, there the parallel between the therapist and the as-if patient ends. The therapist, unlike the as-if patient, is not trying to avoid genuineness in relationships and is, in fact, trying to produce such genuineness. As-if individuals avoid mutuality in order to evoke definition from the other person and thereby avoid having to define themselves. There is no question of being genuine or of being genuinely involved with the other for the quiet borderline patient. However, under normal circumstances it will not be evident that as-if individuals are avoiding genuineness—the other person will fill in the gaps in the relationship for a long while, as it were, assuming that the as-if individual could make demands, show mutuality, or risk tension if he or she chose to do so. In the therapy session, by contrast, it should be clear within the first few sessions that the patient is not being genuine. The therapist has usurped the as-if individual's role by deliberately avoiding mutuality and therefore not filling in the gaps in the relationship. There is no screen or cover for the patient in the therapy session; since the therapist is not filling in the gaps, it gradually becomes clear that the as-if patient does not know how to enter into a relationship.

The quiet borderline patient, however, is not aware of what we are calling problems with relatedness. It is not as though the patient were choosing pseudo-relatedness deliberately and had more authentic forms of involvement at his or her disposal. The as-if patient is simply doing with the therapist what he or she does with everyone else. It is not exactly correct, then, to say that the patient is at pains to mask any problems he or she has with relatedness; what the as-if patient wants is simply to fit in and to give the appearance of normalcy. Consequently, one of the first signs of pseudo-relatedness is that the patient is trying to look normal. The therapist may notice a chit-chatty style on the patient's part, even while talking about subjects that might ordinarily be thought of as laden with emotion.

> One as-if patient told her therapist of a truly traumatic event that had occurred during childhood. The event was so distressing that the therapist inadvertently blurted out, "Oh, how horrible, you poor dear" even though this sort of remark was not at all her characteristic style. The patient was genuinely puzzled at the therapist's sympathy and wondered, "Why is she making such a big deal about it?"

The patient will not know how to move beyond the casual sorts of chatter typical of social encounters, and even the therapist's interventions will not serve to deepen the material or make the encounter seem more intimate. In this case, the patient is behaving with the therapist much as he or she behaves with anyone else. In the absence of cues from the therapist on what is expected, the as-if patient is adopting whatever role is played out in casual social situations.

The therapist's response to the patient depends on how the therapist understands the situation. A patient who, in the first sessions, sounds more as if he or she is at a dinner party than in therapy will probably appear to be in a resistance phase of treatment. We have already argued in earlier chapters that we do not believe this to be the case with the as-if patient, but the therapist at first does not know that the patient suffers as-if pathology. Thus, the therapist will probably intervene with the patient as though resistance were the problem. The patient is not likely to be changed much by these interventions and will probably continue to talk in a somewhat casual manner, or at least in a manner that does not reveal the self so much as it avoids the possibility of tension.

The absence of resistance rests on the lack of firm identity. Resistance presupposes greater separateness and autonomy than the as-if patient brings to the session. Even though as-if patients are not psychotic—and therefore can distinguish self from world—they do not bring their own projects or intentions with them to therapy. The patient comes for treatment with the silent assumption that the therapist is substantial and real and that the patient can, as it were, borrow this reality for the duration of the session. The idea is not to resist but to comply, to live in the shadow of the therapist's reality. The patient does not fear engulfment by the therapist, nor does he or she want to become or merge with the therapist, as a psychotic individual might; the patient wants to share the world the therapist will create or provide. Since the patient does not initially understand what is required in the therapy hour, he or she will begin as if the session were any other social setting. As the patient gains a sense of what the therapist wants, this will change, and the patient will attempt to sound like a therapy patient. The initial appearance of normalcy or chit-chat should not be taken as resistance, nor should the later change to sounding-like-a-therapy-patient be taken for a treatment alliance. In both cases, the patient tries to intuit and comply with whatever the rules appear to be.

As quiet borderline individuals begin to sense what is expected of a therapy patient, the therapist will begin to hear a combination of the earlier chit-chat style along with what popular culture imagines goes on in therapy. As-if patients may begin to report and discuss problems that sound as though they might have come from television talk shows. For example, they may talk vaguely about "problems with relationships," "fear of intimacy," "maybe I was sexually abused," or "I think I've been depressed." The therapist may notice, however, that none of this is accompanied by much conviction, and the patient seems to be trying different subjects on for size, as it were.

There are several cues that none of this is genuine. First, no matter how seemingly potent the issues discussed in a session, as-if patients frequently have trouble remembering those issues in later sessions. Upon noticing this, therapists might think that the patient is defending against anxiety-arousing material. However, when the patient is reminded of the material, there is no evidence of distress or anxiety on the patient's part. Rather, it seems that the patient does not identify with the material, as though it had happened to someone else.

> One patient reported to her therapist that "I think I may have been sexually molested by my uncle, but I can't remember the details, and I hope you can bring them back." In a later session the therapist made a reference to the impact of having been sexually molested by an uncle and, to his surprise, the patient responded, "Oh, that sounds terrible!" The therapist, taken aback to say the least, reminded the patient that she had said that she might have been molested by her uncle. The patient replied, "Oh, did I? I guess I must have blocked it out." It turned out that this patient had not repressed a traumatic event. Rather, the patient had recently seen a television talk show on the subject of

women who had been sexually molested but could not re-member it. She had adopted the topic as something a therapy patient might talk about, even though it eventually became clear that it had nothing to do with her.

A further cue that the patient is not being genuine lies in the therapist's reaction to the material. Even after a number of sessions, the therapist will find that nothing has come up that arouses strong, painful, or conflicted feelings in him or her. The material seems too easy to listen to; there is nothing personal being stirred up in the therapist by the material, as should be the case if the material is personal for the patient. Nothing is being demanded of the therapist, and the therapy hour may even seem to be an exceptionally easy one for the most part. The therapist may alternate between looking for-ward to the (easy) session and wondering, "What are we doing here?" Certainly, these patients do not present the strong emotional responses that, for instance, noisy borderline pa-tients arouse.

Therapists will also notice a lack of spontaneity to as-if patients, and it is of a sort that precludes the possibility that something genuine will occur. Certainly, other seriously dis-turbed patients may avoid spontaneity, for example, if they are being withholding with the therapist or if they are virtually daring the therapist to try to approach them. These ways of avoiding spontaneity, however, actually serve to create a rela-tionship. They reach out to the therapist and bring him or her into a struggle with the patient. As-if individuals, by contrast, seem almost like contestants on a quiz show. Even though the therapist's questions and comments may go to highly personal issues, as-if patients handle these like people who are simply playing the game. As Deutsch and others have noted, there is a staged quality to the entire interaction.

The therapist's final cue that nothing genuine is happening is that there is no sense of connectedness with the patient. The therapist does not have a relationship with the as-if patient, only an appointment. This might, of course, be said of patients suffering other types of pathology, for example, narcissistic patients and also schizophrenics. There is an impersonality to the therapeutic relationship with these patients, as with quiet borderline patients. However, it is a different type of impersonality. Narcissistic and schizophrenic patients assert their own subjectivities and in the process dismiss or negate the therapist's (the narcissist is trying to one-up the therapist, and the schizophrenic hopes to avoid annihilation through annihilating the therapist first). With as-if patients, however, there is no question of asserting their subjectivity and so no question of negating the therapist's.

The therapist must understand that the as-if patient's inability to enter into a genuine relationship reflects the absence of a sense of self. It is not as though the patient could behave differently with the therapist: What the therapist sees is all that is there. The therapeutic task is to help a sense of selfhood come to life. The only tool for this is the relationship with the patient, which begins as a pseudo-relationship and which the therapist hopes to change into something more genuine and substantial.

THERAPY OF PSEUDO-RELATEDNESS

Treating the patient's pseudo-relatedness is the same thing as treating the patient's lack of identity. For us all, identity is born and refined in an interpersonal matrix. It is the same for the quiet borderline patient: If there is to be a growing sense of self, it will occur through the therapeutic interaction. In Chapter 4, we proposed that the general tenor of therapy should be a focus on genuineness, on whether the patient wants to be taken seriously. Needless to say, the idea is not to present this as an intellectual problem, something to be talked about or reflected upon. Rather, the therapist must interact with the patient in ways that present problems for the patient's pseudo-relatedness.

Interventions should try to create a certain tension between the as-if patient's pseudo-relatedness and the therapist. One way to accomplish this is by raising the question of how the patient decides if someone is genuine. The therapist ought not try to answer this question (or any other early in treatment) but, rather, use it to establish the foundation on which the patient decides who is real versus who is not. The therapist will usually find that the patient has no foundation at all but simply assumes that everyone else is genuine. It does not seem to occur to the quiet borderline patient to search for a discrepancy between appearance and reality but, by contrast, to take appearance for reality. The virtue of raising this question is that it subtly challenges this equation.

The therapist should not, however, raise the question of whether he or she seems genuine to the patient or of how the patient could tell if the therapist were genuine. This question aims at too much intimacy (far) too soon and also has a gamey quality to it. It is better to keep the question more general or to aim it at relationships outside of therapy. The quiet borderline patient is not comfortable with intimacy, and the question of the therapist's genuineness makes the therapeutic relationship too personal long before the patient can tolerate a personal relationship and, even more importantly, long before it is a personal relationship. The as-if patient should eventually be able to sense or feel that there is a genuineness to the therapeutic relationship and not have to be told that there is or be asked to decide that there is. At best, the patient will not know what the therapist is talking about. At worst, the patient will give an as-if answer, thereby making it harder to see that there is a difference to the therapeutic relationship.

Rather than personalize the topic of genuineness, therapists can build on it by asking patients about the motivations of other persons in their lives. As just noted, quiet borderline patients do not typically distinguish between reality and appearance but take what comes at face value (hence their assumption that other persons are genuine). It is useful, then, for therapists to suggest that there is something in addition to appearance that needs to be considered. The very question invites patients to flesh out their images of other persons, adding a new dimension, that of critical thinking, or the ability to question what is presented by the other.

Unfortunately, it will be a long time before the question really goes anywhere. Quiet borderline individuals usually cannot fathom the other person's intentions in a relationship. While they can often be adept in the work place at divining the motivations of colleagues or those with whom they do business, personal relationships are another matter. Looking beyond appearance requires the ability to step back, as it were, and look from a broader perspective; another way to say this is that it requires a certain healthy paranoia. Yet paranoia presupposes the ability both to see other persons as a threat and also to oppose them, and these are things as-if individuals cannot generally do. They do not usually let themselves be aware of tension with others, blending in passively instead and often not even letting themselves be aware that opposition was an option. Until quiet borderline patients become more capable of paranoid thinking, they will have little success trying to know the motivations of others.

Therapists can help patients in this process by trying to reconstruct sequences of events in order to discover the intentions of others. As-if patients seldom seem to know why things come about; they know *what* happened but have no idea *how*. They constantly find themselves in situations with no clear idea of what they or the other person did to bring it about. A side effect of this is a relative incapacity to feel guilt. Since there is little awareness of the self as a causal agent, there is no experience of making a choice. After all, the as-if individual is imitating others, and so it is hard to experience oneself as the author of a decision. There is, therefore, little sense of responsibility.

If quiet borderline patients have little sense of their own responsibility, the same is true for their sense of what others are responsible for. They do not seem to track the other person's overall intent but stay aware only of the last thing that happened. Since they do not have active plans or intentions of their own, quiet borderline patients do not appear to watch closely those of others. Consequently, therapists will find it very hard to trace a sequence of events backwards to try to determine how an event unfolded.

> An example is the woman mentioned in Chapter 4 who reported on her weekend by saying, "I had this blind date and then suddenly we were in bed." It took a number of questions for the therapist to learn that six hours had passed between meeting and going to bed. The patient really had no sense of the sequence of events between meeting the date and having sex with him. She was unaware what her date had done to suggest sex or of how she had agreed. It was not that she was amnesic or otherwise dissociative for the evening. She could relate what had occurred but did not understand how events were related causally. It was not that she was confused; she simply did not think in linear terms. The events of the evening were not organized in her memory in any causal sequence.

The therapist's problem is how to explore someone's life when there are virtually no details or causal sequences. Asking questions and receiving vacant answers is frustrating, and the therapist may eventually be tempted to create fictions. Of course, the therapist does not think of it as creating fictions; rather, it will seem as if missing details are simply being filled in. The therapist postulates plausible sequences and motivations to cover the gaps in the patient's rendition of what took place, not quite realizing the extent to which he or she is manufacturing those details. The patient does not mind very much and usually agrees that, yes, that could be just how it happened.

There are therefore significant problems that confront the therapist who tries to help the patient identify the motivations of others through reconstructing events. The less the patient seems to know, the more the therapist may feel tempted to solve this problem, pushing to gain far more certainty and detailed knowledge than is likely with as-if patients. This is a situation in which it is best to remember our earlier point not to try to do anything deep or substantial in the first months—perhaps the first year—of treatment with quiet borderline patients. The therapist should accept the fact that there will be many gaps in what the patient can recover. It is better to highlight the gaps than to try to fill them; leaving the gap open may create a small tension for the patient and build some motivation for seeing more of the picture next time.

In pursuing questions about motivations and sequences of events, therapists are partly trying to correct distortions in the patient's time sense. We mentioned earlier that quiet borderline patients do not live their personal lives in linear time. Events seem to occur in a vacuum, without the usual context of what came before and what might come after. There is a dissociated quality to experience even though the patient is not dissociative, as though whatever occurs comes from nowhere and goes to the same place. These individuals lack a firm sense of causality in their personal lives.

Psychologically, causality rests on one's sense of linear, or historical, time, on the sense that our time flows in one direction and is not reversible. The discovery of historical time rests, in turn, on the discovery of personal agency. If we do not feel able to make an impact on events, to take initiative, or to create or alter what happens to us, we neither need to experience the linear flow of time nor are we able to do so. The feeling of personal agency allows us to project ourselves into the future and establishes the connection between the present and what comes next. In the absence of personal agency, however, one lives in an enlarged moment that may last a few minutes, an evening, or years, but which eventually simply fades and is replaced by another, unconnected moment. Establishing a *sequence* of events replaces disconnected moments with linear time. In turn, seeing that events are linear makes it possible to see order in them and to ponder the question of agency and the attendant questions of responsibility, motivation, and genuineness.

Initially, the question of responsibility will confuse as-if patients, who truly do not feel that they are the authors of their actions. They know what they did, and so in this sense they are not psychotic or dissociative; but they do not fully realize that they had choices, that actions can be deliberate and the result of intention. Thus, they have a mental grasp of what happened, but not as their own personal choice. The events of their lives are things that seem just to have happened, not actions or responses they authored.

One patient's husband grew tired of her pets and without asking her gave them away. The patient did not know this was going to happen and stood surprised when a friend of her husband's showed up one morning, loaded her pets, and drove away. For years afterwards she held a resentment against her husband for this insensitive act and brought it up repeatedly in therapy as a painful event. Curiously, she was only aware of her husband's actions. She was baffled when the therapist asked why she decided to stand by and let her pets be taken away. She had not experienced herself as having more than the role of bystander. The same patient was not happy in her marriage and wondered whether her husband might be led to pursue a divorce. With her marriage as with her pets, she could not experience herself as a center of initiative.

FURTHER CONSIDERATIONS ON THERAPY OF PSEUDO-RELATEDNESS

To this point we have been describing types of questions therapists might pose to highlight the as-if patient's problems experiencing others in ways that would allow for a genuine relationship. The intent of these interventions is to call the patient's way of experiencing self and others into question. As far as these verbal interventions go, they are useful and help, we believe, to set the stage for making the therapeutic relationship into a different sort of relationship for as-if patients. Verbal interventions will not, however, be enough. Eventually, therapists will have to use the impact of their presence to introduce new ways of dealing with people. The style of dealing with the patient will have to carry more weight than the actual words the therapist might use. Therapists must make an impact as persons if as-if patients are to see them as persons.

As-if patients see their therapists (and the others in their lives) in homogenized, generic ways. Relationships are built, that is, on stereotypes, which are used to make sense of other persons and to understand their intentions. There is a cognitive basis for the way these patients rely on stereotypes in order to understand people—the cognitive focus is impaired with these individuals. In our experience, as-if patients cannot easily determine what is the most important thing to look at in a situation. Most persons have an intuitive grasp of what are the most important features in the interpersonal perceptual field and use these to organize how they see what is happening. By contrast, as-if patients really are not able to pick out the most salient features. They tend to fall back on stereotypes in order to make sense of the other person.

> One as-if patient was having a lively discussion with her date on some intellectual subject. As her date made a point, the patient suddenly blurted out, "You're just a male chauvinist oppressor!" Her date was surprised, since the topic they were discussing had nothing at all to do with women's issues and nothing else had happened in the course of the evening to call forth such a remark. The comment seemed to come out of nowhere and was met with a bewildered silence. The date asked the patient why she made such a remark, and the patient seemed to have little or no idea. Indeed, although the patient tried to develop the theme, her remarks seemed, as the date remembered it, to have been part of an entirely different conversation with someone else. Eventually, the date assumed the patient must be joking and said, "You've got to be kidding." At this the patient obligingly changed the subject completely. It appeared that the patient did not know how to handle the discussion and had resorted to an irrelevant stereotype to get her bearings.

> A therapist was in the early phases of treatment with a patient who he later came to understand was an as-if individual. The

therapist was aware that nothing of significance was coming up in the patient's productions and sought a way to deepen the material. He suggested that the patient lie down on the couch, seeking to introduce a regressive influence. The patient brightened and said, "Oh! I know what you're going to do!" She cheerfully explained that she had seen a movie about Freud and assumed that the therapist was about to hypnotize her. In this case, the patient had drawn on a readily available stereotype to explain what the therapist wanted from her.

This reliance on stereotypes illustrates an aspect of pseudo-relatedness. In the early stages of a relationship, as-if individuals invite other persons to express something of their individuality (usually through being receptive and interested when others talk and through not imposing much about themselves). This is pleasing and flattering to other persons, of course, who feel as though the as-if individual truly wants to know them. However, much of what others tell as-if individuals about themselves will be recast in stereotyped terms. As-if individuals cannot understand people in individualized terms; the cognitive deficit we described earlier—that as-if patients cannot focus on the most salient feature of a situation—keeps these patients from understanding the way others are unique. By contrast, others will be seen in terms of preformed expectations that are largely culturally determined. In some situations, for instance, in the classroom or work place, this may be quite adequate, but it is likely to be disappointing to anyone who seeks a genuine relationship with the as-if individual.

We have, then, a paradox. As-if individuals coax others to reveal their subjectivity, or their individuality. This individuality, however, will be understood in a way that negates the other's uniqueness. By virtue of relying on stereotyped perceptions, as-if individuals *level,* as it were, idiosyncratic and personalized features to a more homogeneous picture of the other person. Others are not experienced with any sensitivity to their specialness but are instead seen in generic and ultimately impersonal ways. There is the appearance of relatedness but not the substance. The relationship can go only so far before it becomes plain that there is no genuine regard for the other person as a unique individual.

This pattern will be evident in therapy, of course. As-if patients will understand treatment in stereotyped terms, since there is no greater ability to enter into a genuine relationship with the therapist than with anyone else. The therapist must, in turn, intrude into what is essentially an insulated reality that cannot open up enough to learn what others are actually like. The problem for the therapist is how to do this, how to create a situation in which the therapist's words can have a genuine impact. As long as the patient translates the therapist's comments into a stereotyped format, the therapist is not getting through. The problem, then, is how to interact with the patient in a way that will communicate the possibility that something authentic can happen in the session.

Interventions made in the usual way will not accomplish this goal. Most interventions rely on verbal content which, it is assumed, will have a shared meaning between therapist and patient. Therapists believe in their words, if we may put it that way, and the assumption is that therapeutic language will relate to the patient's life. However, the as-if patient's whole way of being is designed to glean a certain amount of information from words without letting anything personal take place. Thus, the therapist who aims to say something personalized and intimate to the as-if patient will not get through. The patient will translate the intervention into an affectless and impersonal communication; the personal element will be lost. What we are saying, in effect, is that just as the content of the patient's communications is hollow, the content of therapeutic interventions will also be rendered hollow by the patient.

If the problem is stereotyping, therapists must behave in ways that bypass whatever generic image of them the as-if patient has. We do not mean that the therapist is to behave in bizarre, off-the-wall, or unethical ways. Therapists will have to fall back on their theoretical understanding, training, and their own therapy to create effective interventions; these are, as always, the wellsprings of fruitful interventions, and there is no place for wild, undisciplined behavior on the part of therapists. Therapists will, however, have to break out of their usual verbally governed frameworks. Such a change requires that therapists be comfortable with their own spontaneity and be able to exercise spontaneity without losing therapeutic discipline.

We believe that manipulating the tone of the session is a key. Therapists must learn to use gentle humor on the one hand and master the ability to challenge patients in sobering ways on the other. Which the therapist does depends on the patient. When patients are too caught up in themselves and unable to catch sight of alternatives, humor can be quite helpful. By contrast, when patients go out of their way to say, in effect, "Don't take me seriously," therapists must take pains to take them very seriously, emphasizing a different attitude altogether.

To begin with humor, as-if patients strike us as especially lacking in this quality. While they may be able to laugh at jokes, they do not seem to be able to laugh at their own foibles or regard themselves with ironic detachment. And yet, humor is precisely the way most persons start to triumph over the immediate concrete facticity of their lives. Through being able to laugh at ourselves, we take an alternate perspective, leaving what is and adopting another way of experiencing the same predicament that changes the feeling tone. To the extent that stereotypes are built on avoiding alternative ways of looking at an event or person, humor has its place. It can be a form of intrusion that breaks through by being so unexpected and at the same time preserving the possibility of a friendly alliance (in analytic terms this is sometimes termed bypassing the defenses).

When the patient cannot laugh, the therapist must see the humor in the patient's situation. Needless to say, therapists cannot do this in the first months of treatment; there must be some solidity to the therapeutic relationship, even if there is little genuineness, before humor is attempted. Otherwise, therapists are likely to be expressing sadism (possibly stemming from their frustrations with the case) rather than behaving with any therapeutic intent. To be sure, sadism is probably embedded in all humor, but it must be sublimated for the humor to have any utility in treatment. If the sadism remains figural, then humor has the effect of placing the patient one-down and inviting a power struggle far too early. At best, sadistic humor highlights the way the patient and therapist are separate from each other. The risk is that the patient is left feeling that the therapist is potentially dangerous or dangerously unpredictable. By contrast, we want to use humor to create a certain useful tension through which genuine contact can be made. The patient must be invited to join with the therapist in taking a bemused attitude toward the patient's verbalizations. At the least, the humor must break down the as-if patient's stereotyped, generic modes of experience by suddenly revealing a different way of looking at things.

> One as-if patient was apparently irritated with her therapist, although she denied this. However, she began to tell the therapist of a party she planned to give, adding pointedly that he was not invited. She proceeded to discuss the menu in some detail and then reviewed the guest list in even greater detail. The therapist listened to all this with an attitude of mild amusement combined with some impatience at the ever-lengthening report. He responded by saying nothing but smiling pleasantly as the patient went on. The patient noticed the smile and seemed irritated that she might not be having the intended effect. She asked why the therapist was smiling. He said affably, "I think you're very funny." The patient became briefly indignant and said, "I don't see anything funny," an out-of-character response. She then caught herself and returned to her as-if style, saying in a friendly way, "But if you do, that's all right. I guess all you therapists are a little weird." Before she said this, tension had started to build, and her last comment served to dispel it. In this case, a genuine interaction had occurred for an instant, but the patient returned to an ingenuine style of relating and to stereotyping the therapist in order to avoid the tension she had started to feel.

Another patient complained that her therapist was too silent. She grew genuinely distressed by his refusal to tell her what to talk about and felt truly wretched after sessions. She complained that she did not know whether she met his expectations and had no way to know how she was doing without more feedback. In the midst of one such complaint, the therapist nodded and smiled but said nothing. The patient burst out with, "There you go again, not saying anything." The therapist responded playfully with, "And there you go again, telling me there I go again." The patient was stopped by this and laughed for a moment. She eventually resumed her complaints, but she seemed more at ease in spite of herself.

In these examples, humor was used to interrupt pathological behavior and induce at least briefly a more honest interaction. The overarching intent of therapy with quiet borderline patients is to raise the subject of whether they can come to want to be taken seriously. The use of humor is a gentle way of saying that they cannot be taken seriously when they interact on the basis of stereotypes.

There is an additional benefit. As-if individuals grew up trying to be "good" and without imperfection. The use of humor introduces the possibility of being seen as less than perfect and yet finding that the therapist is not going to humiliate or be judgmental on account of what has been exposed. It is also a chance for the patient to see that the "judge's" needs have not been thwarted because of the patient's imperfection. This is different when compared to what patients feared while growing up. At that time, they feared that their failures would reflect badly on the parents or would be taken by the parents as a narcissistic wound. In such a case, patients felt that they would be responsible for someone else's disappointment.

The exposure of imperfection creates the possibility of genuineness. This is in contrast to exposing imperfection in other types of patients. Obsessive patients, for instance, may well become guarded and paranoid when an imperfection is exposed. As-if patients, however, are allowed to be separate from the therapist and yet connected in a genuine way when humor is used to highlight their weaknesses. As long as these patients feel that their imperfections directly reflect on or influence someone else, they cannot feel separate; their behavior is virtually fused with the other person's self esteem. Using humor, therapists reassure patients that, first, they are not fused and so the patient is separate, but, second, that the therapist has not taken offense, and so patient and therapist are still connected. In this case, the imperfection creates the possibility of genuineness; humor allows the patient to catch a glimpse of this truth.

Humor, of course, will not be useful when the patient is being too light, chatty, or otherwise behaving as though the therapy session were a social gathering. In such a case, humor would simply add to the already too-casual tone. In Chapter 4, we stated that the overall focus of therapy with as-if patients should be to raise the question of whether patients wish to be taken seriously. We reiterate this point here. When as-if patients present themselves in a casual way, they do so with the hope that they will not be held responsible for what they say. In such a circumstance, therapists must maintain a detached but interested stance. If therapists are too intense or serious, patients will stereotype them as being humorless. On the other hand, therapists cannot allow themselves to be sucked into a chatty interchange. If therapists are seduced into a casual interaction, it undermines their subsequent ability to produce a more honest relationship.

> One as-if patient talked early in treatment of having faked an orgasm and fooled her husband the night before. She presented this in a humorous way, much as though she were chatting with women friends on sexual matters. The woman went on, saying that she had been doing this for years, not having found sex with her husband to be very satisfying. She added that she was not particularly bothered by any of this. The therapist said nothing, feeling that anything he might say would contribute to a too-casual ambience. The patient appeared to be looking for some

reaction from the therapist, but there seemed nothing to say that would be therapeutic. The therapist set his sights on resisting the patient's attempts to establish a lighthearted tone, accomplishing this by silence.

One problem is that nothing as-if patients say is ego dystonic. They are not bothered when they avoid genuineness. Thus there is no inward push toward something more honest, and the therapist must create whatever momentum toward genuineness will arise in sessions. It is the therapist's job to convey that "I am someone who helps people who are concerned about their problems." Eventually, therapists must communicate that it does no good—the patient will be in no position to be helped—if he or she is not concerned about the issues that come up in sessions. Therapists may even have to suggest that the patient has come for treatment too early, that therapy is not what the patient needs or wants at this point. Paradoxically, the most effective way a therapist can convey the importance of the patient's being concerned about his or her problems is sometimes to refuse to offer treatment. While this may be difficult if therapists find too many openings in their schedules or feel that they need cases, it can nonetheless be the most effective intervention available.

This is not, of course, the same issue as the appearance of normalcy. Throughout this work we have advised therapists not to be put off by as-if patients who seem untroubled and normal. Our concern here is with patients who do raise issues, or at least who present subjects that would be problems for most individuals, but who lack any measure of concern for these matters. Therapists certainly cannot try to argue as-if patients into being concerned. At best, a power struggle results in which the therapist is likely to sound somewhat caricatured or perhaps like a clerk trying to make a sale. Rather, therapists must manipulate the tone of sessions to get across the point that the therapist takes him- or herself seriously and does not undertake treatment with the expectation of wasting time (although, of course, some time is unproductive in any treatment). That is, therapists must convey a kind of self-importance that implies selectivity about how time is spent. The fact that the therapist can be selective does something useful for the patient, who may be shocked to find that the therapist is willing to turn away "business." The patient's stereotypes about therapists may thereby be undermined. This is therefore one way that therapists can communicate that people can take themselves seriously, that the therapist does so, and that the patient is expected to move in that direction.

As-if patients are an extreme example of the interpersonal elements of identity. People who are even temporarily important can influence their sense of who they are and how they are to experience themselves. There seems to be no core of private selfhood that continues beyond encounters with others. The chief consequence of this lack of identity is interpersonal. As-if patients cannot be alone, since they need someone through whom they can define themselves. However, they cannot be genuine in relationships. They are incapable of intimacy, commitment, or willingness to risk conflict. Plasticity and pseudo-relatedness replace these usual hallmarks of genuine relationships.

Pseudo-relatedness is the way identity problems will show themselves in therapy. There are several signs that the patient is dealing with the therapist on a pseudo-relationship basis: a chit-chat style, the absence of meaningful resistance, trouble remembering discussions of seemingly traumatic events, and an absence of spontaneity. Therapists may find other cues within themselves; they may find that they are not grabbed or aroused by the patient's productions and that they do not feel connected with the patient, even after some time has passed.

The therapist works with the patient's lack of identity by addressing the lack of genuineness in relationships. In general, therapists must try to create tension between themselves and the patient's pseudo-relatedness. There are verbal interventions to begin this process, but the therapist must also manipulate the tone of sessions. If as-if patients are not aware that their productions are empty, therapists can use humor to highlight this. Therapists must also be ready to make the session more tense and serious if patients continue with a chatty style. At times, the best intervention may even be a refusal to continue treatment.

TRANSCRIPT: IDENTITY ISSUES

Sharon is a divorcee in her early twenties, having divorced her husband because, "I was bored." She is a college graduate and at the time of this session was working in a department store as a sales clerk. She came for treatment at the urging of a friend, who noticed that Sharon tended to get into and out of relationships quickly and tended also to become sexually involved before she had the chance to know whether a relationship could develop. When a relationship ended, Sharon usually started a new one quickly, seldom using good judgment, with the result that the new romance, too, was generally short-lived. She seemed perpetually to be breaking up with someone and starting to date someone else. At the time of this session, Sharon had been seen for six months at a training clinic.

Sharon's manner of speaking is unusual and hard to describe. She tends to talk in a dreamy, breathless way, making it very hard to take seriously anything she says. Sharon draws out her words, and there is something absent-minded about her, even when she is trying to communicate important themes. Although her intellect is slightly above average, she manages to sound unintelligent. Her composure bears comment as well. Throughout the session that follows—and indeed in all her sessions—Sharon keeps an ingratiating smile on her face. The effect of the smile is to say, "I'm harmless—don't take offense." She seems intent on trying to please, and it would be easy to mistake her for a hysteroid patient.

This is the first session in three weeks for the patient and therapist. At the end of the last session Sharon mentioned that she was trying to change jobs and hoped to be hired at a popular restaurant in town.

PT: Did you enjoy your time away?

TH: I did. How have you been? It's been a long time.

PT: Yeah. It has been a long . . . Nothin's really happened, you know.

TH: How've you been feeling?

PT: All right. I've had my ups and downs. (pause) I still don't know if I got the job at the restaurant.

TH: You've been waiting on that, gosh, a month?

PT: I talked to both the head manager and the assistant manager. And I'm gonna call them back today. And my friend works there, and she works for them, and they like her a lot, and my interviews with them went really well and they liked me. Danny's been out of town, the manager, but he's supposed to be back tonight, and I'll call him and see.

TH: Are you ready to get out of your other job?

PT: I am. I realize I won't make as much money waitressing, but I'm ready for a new environment and setting. And I want to be around different people.

TH: What do you imagine that will be like?

PT: A lot of different people work at (the restaurant) and there's a lot of different people you can interact with. They like gettin' out and havin' a good time and they've got a young frame of mind. They are young. And that's all I want to be around right now. (pause of about one minute) I've gotten so pale; I haven't been in sunlight in ages. (another pause) Things are kind of confusing with Connor, of course. I decided I wanted to break up with him over the weekend.

TH: Did you?

PT: Yeah, and now he wants to be friends and wants to come over and that confuses me. I like hanging around with him and talkin' to him and jokin' with him but it kind of makes things start all over again, which I don't really want. (pause)

TH: Do you know what you both want from that relationship?

PT: I guess I like talkin' to him and would like to be friends with him. I don't want to continue to have a sexual relationship with him. He was askin' me about that. He stopped over at my apartment before I came over here. And on the way over here he asked me, "Do you just want me to back off? Do you want me to back off sex like?" And I said, "Yeah." And I could tell it was like a flash of anger in him; he was mad about it. He was supposed to take me to lunch afterwards but (mumbles inaudibly) . . . It's a really good movie.
(Sharon has brought up an angry exchange with the man she is trying to break up with and then blandly moved to the subject of a movie. As-if patients often seem not to know what bears being upset about versus what is an ordinary, nonemotional subject and blend the two together. Unfortunately, the therapist lets Sharon do this. It would have been a good time to focus on the relationship with Connor and on the question of what Sharon thinks a genuine relationship would be like.)

TH: I've heard about it. It's supposed to be good.

PT: I read the book for one of my college English classes and really enjoyed reading the book. The movie's good too.

TH: What did you like about it?

PT: I liked seeing the different ways people view things and the sisters are real strong and havin' their own opinions and definite personalities.

TH: You've talked in here about wanting that for yourself.

PT: Yeah . . . When people say, you know, I'm just, I should just be myself and people say "just be yourself." I wish I knew what that was. God, I wish I could just do that naturally. Somethin' I want.
(The patient introduces an important theme. She feels that she can't be herself. She seems to mean that nothing is spontaneous for her, that she is too aware of what the other person expects of her and too concerned with trying to meet their expectations. She is probably trying to say that she feels inauthentic.)

TH: If you were just going to be yourself, what would you be like?

PT: There would be a degree of comfortableness, of not having to think about what you're going to be doing in the next few moments or what you're gonna be sayin'. So there would be feelin' comfortable.

TH: Sounds like security.
(It is a temptation for many beginning therapists to see patients in terms of anxiety. Seeing the patient as frightened offers the therapist a measure of security against the uncertainties of the therapy process. The temptation is to see the patient as needy or more particularly as in need of the therapist's strong protection. The patient seems weak, and by comparison the therapist must be strong. In this case, however, security is not the issue. Sharon shows no hint of anxiety, fear, or inner conflict in the entire session. Sharon gradually tries to get the therapist back to what bothers her, that she feels completely defined by whomever she is with, not by herself.)

PT: I guess so. Knowin' that you have a personality and not have to be afraid there's something wrong with it, just be able to show it. (pause) I think I'm gradually . . . beginnin' to . . . to do that.

TH: Um hmm. How does that feel?

PT: (pause) I'm not as afraid, that there's somethin' wrong with me? (pause) And not as afraid to be around people and meet new people.

TH: Um hmm.
(We see the as-if process at work. Sharon wants to please her therapist and is using words consistent with the anxiety theme introduced by the therapist. She makes a clever transition back to the real issue, however, in the next line, using the word "afraid" but moving back to the problem of being real. The therapist remains committed to the theme of fear, however, and to seeing Sharon as weak and helpless. Much of what Sharon goes on to say about superficiality probably refers to her perception of how she is interacting with the therapist at this point.)

PT: I'm still afraid that there's a degree of falseness about me. And it is hard to really open up.

TH: I think that is difficult for you. I know it's been hard.

PT: I think that I connect with people at almost a superficial level. It's hard for me to get beyond that.

TH: Um hmm. Is there a fear about getting beyond that?
(The therapist is still stuck on the subject of anxiety, and Sharon finally says openly that this is not the subject.)

PT: It doesn't seem so much a fear as a complete experience of not knowing what to do. And it's not natural because it's never occurred and not knowing how to get it started. (pause) And also I'm afraid, or I feel an inhibition, about gettin' close to people.

TH: And what's your fantasy about what would happen if you get closer to people?

PT: It would be very nice and comfortable, and satisfying.

TH: What's your fantasy about the fear?
(The therapist is back on anxiety, but Sharon returns to authenticity or feeling fake.)

PT: Just knowin' it's unnatural and them knowin' it's unnatural.

TH: So even being closer to other people you feel it would be unnatural.

PT: Um hmm. (pause) (mumbles inaudibly).

TH: Um hmm. Takes practice.

PT: (pause of about 1 minute) Now I feel like I'm kind of growin' apart some from Lisa. Worried about it. I mean she's great and I really like her a lot but as far as what we like and what we like to do we're not very similar.

TH: That's what you've said in the past. She has a wild streak that's hard for you to keep up with.

PT: (laughs) Yeah, and the things I like to do, like they like to hang out at the Single Pony all the time, and I just don't care for the place at all. I've started hanging around the (muffled) more, and one thing I like about Ramona is she's a bit on the intellectual side—she's very intelligent. And like the movie I saw last night, Ramona might have enjoyed it, and I doubt Lisa would have liked it. They would have hated it!

TH: So your interests are different.

PT: One thing I like about Connor is that his interest as far as reading good books and trying to improve on the intellectual is somethin' he has always been interested in, and I am too. And he, uh, he uh enjoyed going to the movie with me. And he's the only person I know who would have wanted to go to the movie with me.

TH: Oh, really? The only one?

PT: Just about. Ramona might have wanted to go with me, but the people at work, oh golly. You know, most people I know they want comedy! (pause—she twists and turns in her chair) We ran into his friends Jim and Dally there, the people that he lives with. We had seen them just before we left, and none of us had talked to each other about the movie and then we were standing there gettin' popcorn and Cokes and then they walked in. They couldn't believe it either, it was such a coincidence. They said there'll probably just be ten people in this movie. Jim was an English major. He got I think his masters in English . . . I like Dally a lot.

TH: That's what you've said before, that you're intrigued.

PT: I would like to be friends with her, but I don't feel I should pursue it because it would be an intrusion because (mumbles) because it's his roommates and his friends.

TH: And so that's invalid?

PT: Um hmm, I'd be movin' into his space. It wouldn't be really fair.

TH: He has this sort of ownership of these people. Is that how you see it?

PT: I don't feel like I ought to be steppin' over boundaries (mumbles inaudibly). I hope I get the job at (the restaurant). I like Angie a lot! Angie lived with Jim for . . . several years. And she's, uh, she's real free spirited and liberal and very intelligent. She's recently got her degree. I think she was in the scholars program and spent a lot of her time doing research work in South America and, and she's just really sweet, I mean, just open and affectionate type person. And I would really love to get to know her and even be friends with her.

TH: Um hmm. Sounds like that might be enjoyable.

PT: And I, since meetin' Ramona I have a little more confidence meetin' friends because I thought the same of her like she's really cool and I might not fit in with her at all. But I made the move towards her and now we get along really well.

TH: Um hmm. That's worked out. That's different for you. You've been friends with Ramona, that's still real recent . . .

PT: It's still not completely natural but I'm hopin' it will become more that way as time . . .

TH: What feels unnatural?

PT: Ramona can just chat on and on and on about everything. She'll tell me the little details about goin' shopping, about sewing on buttons and all these little details of her life she can go on and on about. And she'll say, "What's goin' on with you?" And I'll have nothin' to say. I don't have that kind of gift of just gabbin'. You know, small talk and bein' able to talk about my life like it's interesting.

TH: I guess I'm struck by that, Sharon, because you're able to do that in here and I wonder what the difference is.

PT: (breaks into a slightly embarrassed smile and laughs) I don't know.

TH: If you stick to the part about telling the details of the day to day of her life, because it sounds like she's talking about sound buttons, sort of the same conversation (sic).

PT: Sometimes I just draw a blank, I just draw a blank. I say I just went to work but I can't think of any . . .

TH: (interrupting) It's hard to elaborate or tell a story?

PT: (nodding) I've never really been a storyteller, you know. Occasionally I can. I can really go into details about Connor—afraid everyone's gettin' sick of that.

TH: So if you're really involved in something, it's easier to talk about.
(It seems to us that the therapist is off track here. She seems to be focusing on Sharon's lack of confidence in herself as a good conversationalist. However, Sharon lacks confidence that she could hold another person's interest as a person, not as a conversationalist. The reason Sharon does not want to talk to others about herself is that she is afraid they will see her as empty and worthless if they learn more about her. She hopes to hide from them what she perceives as her emptiness.)

PT: (long pause) In my work there's absolutely no fascination (sighs). Can't wait to leave, can't wait to give notice!

TH: Yeah, you've been wanting out of that job for a long time, since last January.

PT: A big part of it is the hours. If the hours was different it would be a different story. I'd like to have another side to my life, to be able to do things . . . I just want another side of life rather than just 9 to 5.

TH: What do you imagine doing with this different life?

PT: Well ideally, ideally, it probably won't be this way, but ideally just doing common, everyday things. Keepin' my apartment straight, cooking, I'd like to bake, and and havin' friends over and building a comfortable life.

TH: So your job represents a lot of changes.

PT: I hope so. I hope my whole life will change just because I'm waitin' tables rather than sellin' electronics.

TH: Do you think that's possible?

PT: I think just like that it's not.

TH: Um hmm.

PT: (pause) But I'm hopin' maybe havin' the extra time . . .

TH: (interrupts) Do you think that will make a difference?

PT: I'm hopin' so that I won't just waste it and hate myself for wastin' it. Because there's been times in the past when I've been grateful to (the electronics store) because it's kept me from havin' the free time I'm uncomfortable with.

TH: Right, and when you say you waste time, what does it mean to waste time?

PT: To be sitting in that apartment that's in total disarray that you're totally ashamed for anyone to drop by and yet you're doin' nothing except maybe reading.

TH: And that's bad?

PT: Yeah, I mean just reading would be fine if I could get the apartment in order first. But the fear of acting, of straightening it, of just sittin' there miserable because it's dirty but not doin' anything about it, I hate that feeling. I hate it.

TH: What do you hate about that feeling? What's so difficult about it?

PT: I know I would feel so much better if I would clean it but yet for some reason not doin' it, just not doin' it.

TH: Sounds like a little battle or struggle.

PT: (absently) Um hmm.

TH: Or like the struggle you've had with your mother when she would say you can't go out until you clean your room?
(The therapist senses that this is an important subject but does not know how to get to it. She looks for genetic material. However, it is far too early in this treatment to begin trying to make genetic interpretations. In addition, there is no good basis in the patient's verbalizations for believing that this has something to do with Sharon's mother.)

PT: (gives a little laugh) Sounds like what I deserve, to be just sittin' there.

TH: Deprived?

PT: Um hmm. (long pause) I want to change that. I want to change that.

TH: Do you think the rules are different as an adult?

PT: They shouldn't be.

TH: Or if your room's a mess you can still have friends.

PT: See, that's the thing. I can go over to Ramona's, and it's a mess, and I don't think anything about it. That's fine, I don't care. And I can think that there's some order to it, but my mess is totally different from anyone else's mess. My mess denotes a totally screwed-up personality.

TH: So, your mess in the apartment represents the inside of you. It's like what's inside of you is on display.
(The therapist is on target. This is what Sharon has been trying to say. It is an unusual experience for Sharon to feel heard or to feel that what is inside of her can be seen and accepted by others. Thus, in what follows it is not surprising that Sharon is somewhat loose at first. As we have commented, any time a quiet borderline patient allows some dependency, confusion will be near at hand.)

PT: (losing her ingratiating friendliness—more somber) Yeah, I'm scared for people to see it.

TH: What will they see?

PT: See that there's something wrong with me, that I'm not worth bein' around. That there's no order, that I have absolutely no order to my life, no reason, no purpose . . . A disintegrated personality! (laughs in a slightly mean fashion).

TH: Is there a part of you that wants people to see that side of you?

PT: (almost frightened) No, I don't think so. I don't, I don't want anyone to see. I want to hide, I want to hide; I'm not very good at hiding it. 'Cause I can't get the damned place cleaned up!

TH: Um hmm. No matter what you do it's still messy.

PT: (dreamily) I can do a little surface cleaning, but there's still that moldy spot in my bathroom floor from water from the shower. My tub is dirty. (laughs) Sounds crazy.

(An analytically oriented therapist would hear fantasies related to urethral and anal sadism in Sharon's last statements along with a hint that Sharon fears she would lose her sanity if she explored this. However, we believe it is too early in this treatment to respond to these issues or to fantasy systems. The only issue here worth pursuing, in our judgment, is whether Sharon can have the experience of telling another person about her "bad" feelings and have these be heard and accepted. If the therapist were to interpret the sadistic content here, Sharon might well feel that the therapist could not withstand the tension produced by these themes and wanted to resolve the tension by making these themes go away. This would simply duplicate her experience growing up, when her "bad" feelings were not acknowledged in the family. Her response then was to disown and ignore such feelings, and she will do so again if the therapist seems too uncomfortable or in a hurry to be done with the disorganization Sharon feels inside herself.)

TH: Sounds important to me.

PT: I would love for it to lose its importance, for it to no longer be such an issue for me.

TH: Um hmm, but it represents something inside of you.

PT: I used to have the same sort of hang-up about my weight. I used to be heavy, heavier. And I saw that as a reflection of my personality and my lack of strength, lack of will, not being able to change my . . . and I'm afraid I'm gaining it back. I'm on a pasta binge; I've been eatin' at Pasta Plus four days out of seven. (laughs) I thought about it constantly. It was on my mind. It never left. It was an obsession.

TH: Before?

PT: Yeah, it was so uncomfortable. When I finally lost the weight and never had to think about it, it was such a free feeling.

TH: Like you had gotten it off your (inaudible)?

PT: Yeah, something you no longer have to worry about. It's such a free feeling. And I want it to be the same way with this obsession about the places I live. I want to get rid of that burden so I'll be more free.

TH: You think it's related to the hiding? To the sense wanting to hide (sic)? Losing the weight, so you're not so visible?

PT: The part these other people can't see? See, when I'm out, people can't see it. When they come in, they will.

TH: Before, when you say you were happier, when you were out, everybody could see you. But the truth is, you were home.

PT: (pause) I always want to go to someone else's house. I don't want anybody in mine. (pauses, looks around, sighs) So that's the problem—how do I fix it? (This is said in a slightly petulant, childish way.)

TH: Figure out what it means.
(The preceding has been loose and confused. The therapist, too, has been slightly disorganized, as can be seen from her small breakdowns in syntax and grammar. The patient has put pressure on the therapist with her question, "How do I fix it?" The therapist's answer is probably an attempt to regain control. The therapist's apparent desire to restore order and control is further seen in the suddenly escalated frequency of her responses. The session is turning into an interview, as if the therapist does not

want the patient to get very far into a subject. It is not clear what is disorganizing the therapist.)

PT: (looks abruptly away) Means I'm still scared there's somethin' wrong with me.

TH: Can you say what you're afraid, uh, in terms of what might still be wrong with you?

PT: It's a very vague thing. I can't even point it out. That's one thing I'm afraid of, an overall vagueness of mind. There's nothing that I really stand for or believe in. There's just this vagueness. I jump from one thing to another. There's no cohesiveness.

TH: And the fear is . . . that that means what?

PT: There is no real personality. It's all just surface that I try to make up as I go.

TH: I think there's someone there that's very frightened.

PT: (pauses about one minute and looks away) I guess I'm afraid I'm not really becomin' a more real person. I'm just getting better and better at acting.

TH: There's too many dangers of acting all the time. (Long pause) I think there's a reason for it.

PT: (another long pause) Huh. I guess I'm afraid if I just totally reveal whatever my real self is, it might be so completely boring that everybody will leave.

TH: Then you won't have anyone to hold you.
(This intervention strikes us as a serious mistake even though it is built on material from earlier sessions. The therapist seems to be trying to see the patient as a weak and lonely child in need of mothering. This was also probably the intent of the preceding statement, "I think

there's someone there that's very frightened." In spite of these mistakes, the patient seems to intuit the therapist's interest and concern and is producing important material. However, a quiet borderline patient will eventually give in to what he or she perceives the therapist wants. If the therapist continues inviting the patient to appear helpless and childlike, the patient will conform and play the part, as her next two statements show.)

PT: There won't be anyone, no comfort (mumbles inaudibly).

TH: That's a scary fear.

PT: I have to keep my friends, and my family is of no comfort to me at all.

TH: They disappoint you. (long pause) What's your thought or feeling about letting that real self come out in here?
(The therapist recovers and makes a better intervention. In contrast to the previous invitations to play the part of a small and frightened child, the therapist brings matters back to here-and-now reality and in the process invites the patient to resume exploring the fear that she is boring and unable to hold another person's interest.)

PT: (pause of about thirty seconds) Maybe if it comes out it's completely boring. I won't be able to put it back and be active.

TH: So you're afraid that somehow once it's out, this thing's just out.

PT: (absently) Um hmm.

TH: So it doesn't sound too boring to me. It sounds pretty powerful.

PT: (pause of about one minute) I don't see why I have to see it as something that's totally unknown to me, like it's a stranger.

TH: Um hmm. You keep your distance from it.

PT: (covers her face with her hands and then starts sweeping her hair away from her face) Sounding silly now. Like the movie, book *It,* Stephen King. I'm just bein' melodramatic.

TH: I don't think you are at all. That's what our work is about here.

PT: Like I'm being self-indulgent.

TH: What feels like being self-indulgent?

PT: Like I'm talking about this just to entertain myself.

TH: I sense that it's really hard for you to talk about this.

PT: It's like I'm hopin' there's something there and so I talk about it.

TH: I think there is something there, and it's important to talk about it. But if you talk about it, it feels indulgent. Where do you think that comes from?

PT: (long pause) I'm supposed to be sensible. Not think so much about . . . myself.

TH: Who told you that?

PT: My parents.
(Unhappily, the therapist has now let the focus get completely away from the patient's fear of boring the therapist. The patient has just made several statements to the effect that she is not worth the therapist's attention. She is

probably worried that she will start to talk about herself only to have the therapist confirm the fear of being seen as boring and worthless. The therapist hints that the patient ought to blame something on her parents, and the patient tries to comply.)

TH: Um hmm.

PT: It's not who you are but how you act.

TH: Um hmm, it's (inaudible). When your parents tell you that, what does that feel like?

PT: Feels like it's selfish to consider yourself too much and just need to follow the rules and try to treat people . . . fairly.

TH: I think it feels like a lot of things as you tell me that. You seem to be getting more distant and more withdrawn. That message renders you more (inaudible) in some way?

PT: Any time I would see someone when I was growing up, or even when I was married, acting in a way that expressed themselves, it was either too dramatic or rude or I'd think, "Man, what's wrong with them? Why can't they just get over the dramatics and just act right?"

TH: Um hmm. And get under control.

PT: Yeah, what makes them think they can just . . . do that?

TH: Their parents didn't explain the rules to 'em, huh?

PT: (laughs) I guess not. My parents did kind of teach that self-expression was just indulgence, and conformity was the thing. Learn the rules and follow them.

TH: Seems to have a pretty high price.

PT: Hm hmm. They must have believed it too, for them to have taught me that. I know my dad believes in conformity.

TH: As someone who's conformed, how do you understand what it's like? When you see what the person who's conformed perfectly is like, what do you see?

PT: Not much richness and experience. Just a day in and out of the same thing. We have friends. He doesn't have a single friend. Not even one. And he looks forward to retirement, but all he looks forward to is running, and watching TV, and reading the newspaper. He never cares about goin' anywhere or trying any hobbies or bein' with any people. That's how he lives his entire life.

TH: How do you feel when you think about that and see that?

PT: Scary (mumbles). I'm afraid that's what I am. It's not what I want to be.

TH: Right. It's sad and lonely.

PT: Yeah, it's isolated. (pause of about one minute) I'd like to convince myself that it's okay to be unreasonable.

TH: There's a side to all of us that's unreasonable.

PT: I'd like to have . . . (mumbles) whatever it might be and still be a caring and loving person as far as open to people but not just by following whatever rules I think are supposed to be followed but just from naturalness. That's what I would like.
(This is the theme the patient raised at the start of this session, the question of whether she can spontaneously be herself without being defined by the expectations ["rules"] of others.)

TH: Natural must mean, natural must mean spontaneous?

PT: Um hmm. Yeah, spontaneous just from inner feeling of liking people and being nonjudgmental. Accepting people for being uniqueness, I love the uniqueness of people! I feel like I don't have any myself. (sighs) (long pause) I'm always attracted to people who are, I think, in some way unique or natural and nonconforming. People like my dad or people who see things in black and white and, you know, I'm this way and people who are this other way, I don't want anything to do with people like that. I don't want to be anywhere near.

TH: Um hmm, people for whom it's all clear.

PT: Yeah, I hate that. Hmm. (sighs and fidgets in chair) I feel lightheaded! (long pause)

TH: Does that have anything to do with what you've been talking about?

PT: I think so. But how to wake up?

TH: This has been sort of dreamlike to talk about this?

PT: Um hmm. I guess one reason Connor's hard to give up is the, the way I see it in other people he sees it in me.

TH: Um hmm.

PT: He's got sort of admiration for me.

TH: That gives you hope that you're not gonna be like your dad.
(At this point the session winds down as the therapist raises the question of a future appointment time.)

Part III

BROADER
CONCERNS

INTRODUCTION

The final section of this book consists of only one chapter. It is born of our growing fear that as-if traits may increasingly become the norm in Western society. A culture built on rapid change and the need to adapt quickly may find the inner life to be an unwelcome distraction. We believe that there are decided cultural trends and also changes in child rearing that favor the development of as-if traits.

We also confess to fears about the future of psychotherapy, a craft we have hitherto felt lucky to practice and proud to identify with. We see, however, influences on training and practice that lead us to believe that the world of the future may know a more truncated, degraded, and simplistic version of psychotherapy than what we have studied and known.

This chapter is a record of our fears.

8

As-If Trends in Culture and Therapy

INTRODUCTION

When we began work on this book, we were faced with a troublesome question: Is the as-if personality an instance of pathology, or is it rather a supremely adaptive personality style? In earlier chapters we have several times noted that as-if individuals are well suited for change and may adapt much better than other persons to some of the demands placed on them by an era of rapid change. There are, after all, times and circumstances in which it may be an advantage to an individual to have no lasting or non-negotiable commitments. Individuals who are regularly moved to new towns by their businesses, for example, will be less troubled by those changes if they are the sort of people who do not get deeply attached to other persons. Similarly, it may be best for individuals not to identify very strongly with a particular trade or profession when technological changes and periodic corporate downsizings make it likely that they will have a succession of jobs, trades, and companies across the years. There can be advantages to being able to put on and take off relationships and jobs like clothing—to be worn for a time and then exchanged for something newer.

The individual's identity is affected by the absence of lasting commitments, however. The simplest definition of identity is the capacity to commit and, consequently, those things to which an individual is, in fact, committed. Commitments may range from the mundane to the sublime, from something as ordinary as the intention to go to work every day in order to support one's family, on the one hand, to less typical commitments, on the other, such as a passionate devotion to the needs of handicapped children. Whether mundane or exotic, we are defined by our commitments. We *are* students, spouses, employees, believers in causes, and practitioners of religion. To the extent that nothing matters very much to us, we are like Camus's (1955) stranger, indifferent and more spectator than author to our lives.

There is an inevitable collision between rapid change and identity. More than thirty years ago, Wheelis (1958) studied this collision, concerned with the question of whether it is possible to maintain a solid sense of self and at the same time adapt to frequent change. Of course, our era is not the first to experience cultural change; there has always been change in human society. Yet Wheelis makes a good point when he notes that change has never been so rapid as in post-World War II Western society. He observes that for the first time we can be aware of change while it is occurring. Through electronic media we can watch nightly (and indeed hourly) summaries of cultural and political changes as though we were mere observers when in fact our lives will be influenced by much of what we watch—and also by the fact of having watched.

Rapid change poses two problems for identity, according to Wheelis's (1958) analysis. First, it is hard to believe in set values when everything keeps changing. Identity, however, depends on stable values, on the sense that what gives life meaning is constant. Hence, in the midst of rapid change, it can be difficult to answer the question, "Who am I?" because those things that once guaranteed the answer have suddenly come to seem relative and transient.

Second, the more solid the sense of identity, the less flexible the individual. To the extent that an individual is committed, he or she has lost flexibility, since commitment means that some things are not negotiable and therefore cannot be forgotten or bargained away. When circumstances change, the individual whose commitments remain constant may not be able to change with them. Commitments and identity are built on allegiances that are both transcendent and at the same time highly personal—for example, that communism is evil, that one must be faithful to one's spouse, or that those who have been treated unfairly should be given some advantage. These commitments, which may have been maintained over a lifetime, however, may make it difficult for the individual who holds them to adjust to the end of the cold war, the sexual revolution, or to a shift in the political climate away from affirmative action. Indeed, the more firmly any set of values is held, the more likely the individual is to run afoul of changing times.

Ought we then speculate that the pressures of rapid change undermine identity and, as a byproduct, encourage as-if tendencies? This is precisely our hypothesis. In the mid-sixties, Ross (1967) was apparently thinking along similar lines. He suggested that excessive valuation of conformity, emphasis on material values, and a growing disregard for the inner world created a cultural atmosphere that encouraged as-if adaptation. He speculated, in fact, that in such a culture, "the 'as if' personality may be a far more common type than we have encountered in analytic practice" (p. 81). This is our opinion as well. Rapid change necessarily pressures individuals away from intransigent commitments and toward a desire to adapt, that is to say, to conform. The private space that is generally called the self is overrun by the desire to belong to the public sphere. This leads, in turn, to a loss of depth in the individual's experience of the world. Depth of feeling and a firm sense of self are replaced by superficial, highly plastic categories of experience.

We think this is what Marcuse (1964) called "one-dimensional man," what Kierkegaard (1962) referred to as a leveling of human life and loss of the capacity to be an individual, and what Deutsch (1942) labeled the as-if personality.

Of course, the preceding argument is not, strictly speaking, a psychological one. We have been talking, perhaps, more at the level of social criticism or social philosophy. In Chapter 2 we proposed an etiology based partly on mother–child interactions and also on patterns of family interaction. We are not now trying to say that social forces, rather than personal and interpersonal factors, are the real key. Rather, we want to argue that certain social trends shape the parent–child relationship and that these same trends will reward and punish individuals as they later make or avoid lasting commitments. In addition, we intend to argue that the enterprise of therapy is influenced by these same cultural winds.

CHANGING EXPECTATIONS OF PARENTS

In the 1950s, child-rearing literature suddenly embraced what had previously been a significant, but minority, opinion—that parents ought to be less strict with their children. A number of studies at the time supported this point of view. To take one at random that is nonetheless representative, Watson (1957) found children brought up "with an extraordinary degree of permissiveness" to rank significantly higher on several desirable personality measures than did peers reared with strict parental control. Watson's study included a review of the literature on the subject and concluded that there was "considerable convergence" among the different studies that more permissive treatment by parents leads to greater independence and more appropriate forms of aggressiveness in children.

Professional opinion had gradually been shifting toward more permissive parenting since World War I. Wolfenstein (1953) examined the ten issues of the United States Children's Bureau's *Infant Care* from 1914 to 1951. She found substantial changes in the "official" advice given to parents over those nearly four decades. Advice on how to handle several common problems grew progressively more permissive. Masturbation and thumb sucking drew nonrepressive responses by the 1920s. Strictness in weaning was not recommended after the late 1930s. By the 1940s, *Infant Care* recommended more patience and understanding on all of the problems discussed than was the case in 1914.

An authoritarian or dogmatic style was clearly less acceptable to experts by the 1950s than it had been in the early part of the century. Writing at the time, Sears and his co-workers (1957) thought this change was the result of scientific progress, the result, that is, of submitting parenting practices to the objective eye of psychological research, thereby taking this important task out of the hands of folk wisdom and tradition. They noted the high status science enjoyed as the result of a steady string of medical advances since the late nineteenth century. In consequence of this status, "Solution of problems by rational means replaced reliance on tradition, personal experience, and the self-arrogated wisdom of those who had decision-making power" (p. 549). Technique was replacing tradition, in effect, a change that was undoubtedly intended to the good but which, we believe, held an ironically cruel twist.

We might ask why researchers would examine strict versus permissive parenting in the first place. The chief concern was clearly with the rigidity and repressiveness of a strict approach, that such an approach might lack the flexibility needed to be adaptive. This concern reflects the bias of a rapidly changing society that flexibility in the face of change is desirable. Permissive parenting can be seen as part of a general cultural orientation toward what Mead (1949) called the situational approach to life, the attitude that each new situation is a discrete entity, unrelated to what came before or to what comes later, and requiring full and immediate adaptation. When one situation is left for another (home for work, church for the club), little is carried over. Each situation is addressed as if its demands and rules were valid in themselves without reference to broader aims and values. Mead referred to the "atomization" of experience that results from the situational approach: "Relationships disappear, and experience is broken down into small, discrete bits which may be given temporary meaning in any one of a thousand patterns but which lack coherent relationship to any one pattern" (p. 30).

It is no accident that those approaching the issue from the standpoint of scientific technique would find themselves on the side of a more permissive, and therefore more flexible, approach. Scientists and technicians are, after all, authors of change in any society, and they can be expected to gravitate toward a parenting style that would offer the greatest number of options (and thus the greatest flexibility) to the growing child. However, the exact parenting style endorsed by the experts is not nearly as important as the fact that scientific experts were moving into the child-care arena, challenging and displacing tradition and personal experience. Reliance on experts for child-rearing advice, and the attendant move away from tradition, are part of the general move toward a more situational approach to life, which must disentangle itself from tradition as part of being open to each new situation.

This ascendancy of the professional expert in child rearing began to place subtle pressures on the average parent. There was, for example, René Spitz's (1945) truly ominous warning that deficiencies in early mothering skills could have "unavoidable and irreparable psychiatric consequences" (p. 73). Therapists still hear mothers worry aloud that they may have made some fatal error that will ruin their children in an unforeseen way, reminiscent perhaps of the way earlier generations worried they might have unknowingly committed the unforgivable sin against the Holy Ghost. Certainly the burgeoning literature in the late 1950s on the "schizophrenogenic mother" did very little to ease the minds of those who were beginning to wonder if they had the expertise to bring up healthy children. A television advertisement run by *Parent* magazine through much of the 1980s illustrates the pressures still being placed on young mothers. It said, "Every day a mother has to make important decisions that affect her baby's life—she has to know what to do."

A latent message in the welter of child-rearing advice since the 1950s is that parenting is a field in which technical information is available and therefore a field in which there is a correct and an incorrect way. Previously, child rearing was thought of as a matter of cultural values and wisdom, not as a technical field. What it means to be a parent is quite different when parenting depends on knowledge and technique as opposed to wisdom and tradition. Only relatively recently have theorists begun to raise questions about the undermining of parents' confidence and the potentially woeful effects of being brought up by parents who lack faith in themselves (e.g., Chessick 1977, Harrison and Delano 1976, Van den Berg 1972). In 1957, Sears and colleagues wrote that "the rational problem solving of science" had replaced traditional wisdom. This was intended to improve the fate of the young, and there are undoubtedly aspects of child care that have benefited from scientific attention. Research, however, has not led to new traditions—that is, to consensual approaches that parents can follow automatically for no better reason than, "this is how we do it." When there is a tradition to follow, there is a stable context in which individuals can experience their identities as parents. They have the chance to *be* parents, to exercise an office that places them in an ongoing and constant scheme of things. In a sense, it does not matter whether child-rearing traditions are wise or foolish; it is a benefit to children to be brought up by people who feel that they know what they are doing and who are supported in their identities as parents by participation in a tradition.

Parents cannot, however, feel certain of themselves when they are, in effect, following the latest advice. In such a circumstance, the parents are turned into actors, following a script that, even if learned by rote, is still only a script. Between parent and child lies the script, and in a sense the script is the real parent. The child's personality is affected by such parental uncertainty or, worse, by persons who are essentially behaving *as if they are parents.* The problem lies in the child's identification with the parents: The child cannot truly identify with a script, that is, with parents who are acting out roles because they lack traditions on which to ground their identities as parents. The problem lies in what the child internalizes when the parents are primarily acting their parts rather than being parents.

Wheelis (1958) reasoned that what is internalized is an image of one's parents as conformers to what is recommended. At first glance, this may not seem to be different from identifying with parents who represent a community or family tradition. However, the two are experienced very differently. Conformity in a small, homogeneous community is not experienced as such but, rather, as adherence to principle, as doing one's duty. When the homogeneous community is replaced by the global village, where one is poised to expect constant change, conformity is experienced as "going along" and "fitting in" (p. 92). Soon after World War II, Reider (1950) noted just this change; he wrote that normality had replaced morality as the criterion of adequate behavior. This change makes the object of identification more impersonal for the young child, more difficult to distinguish from the common mass that is conformed to.

To use classical terms, the result is a weakened and less personal superego, since the parent who is the object of identification looks less and less like an authority or rule giver and looks more and more like an expert or source of information. Those who sought changes in child rearing in the 1950s generally sought a less repressive social world for the young child. A weakened superego gives less repression internally as well. Much more is thinkable without guilt or anxiety, and therefore a far wider range of options can be objectively considered. If such things could be measured, those who grew up learning to trust their native inclinations and abilities rather than firmly set external (parental) limits would surely show an enlarged ego and a shrunken superego compared to their parents' generation. This change equips the individual for life in modern society; the ego is the personality structure that adjusts to the demands of the external world. A strong superego constrains the child not to adapt to circumstances that are at odds with the parents' values and traditions. Thus, the ability to adapt rapidly and easily is considerably reduced by a strong superego. As the superego declines in influence, ego is given a freer hand, the individual is more plastic, and the requirements of the situational approach to life are better served.

The price of this increased adaptation is a diminished sense of personal identity. The superego is not only the agency that represses impulsivity and the drives; it is also the foundation of identity. The superego is comprised of identifications with key figures and therefore with their standards and values. Superego formation is one of the first sources, therefore, of a sense of "this is what I am like" or "I am the kind of person who does these things but not these other things." These internalized images and standards not only help manage the drives but also define the self in the early years and are the foundation for later, more mature identifications. If, however, the child's identifications are with parents who are uncertain of themselves as parents and who are chiefly conforming to what is expected of them, the child derives little basis for identity or definition.

Greenson (in Weiss 1966) remarked that many parents only act as if they were parents but do not behave as real parents. Such individuals, he believes, might be expected to produce children who are as-if personalities. We believe that Greenson's intuition is sound. As parents lose confidence in themselves as authorities, their child's superego is weakened due to having weaker objects of identification. There should be either of two results: heightened impulsivity and freer expression of drives on the one hand or a less constrained ego on the other. The former course (presumably occurring with individuals whose native aggressiveness is higher) leads to psychopathy and need not concern us here. The latter course (presumably occurring with individuals whose constitutional aggressiveness is lower) inevitably leads in an as-if direction: As ego replaces superego, adaptation replaces identity. The result is that conformity is built into the personality. This is a conformity that is not based on communal values, however, and therefore is conformity for conformity's sake.

We are suggesting, with Greenson, that as-if parents are more likely to produce as-if children. In our view, the key variable is whether parents are able to take themselves seriously in their office as parents and, in turn, to take their children seriously. When we say that parents must take themselves seriously as parents, we mean that they must have confidence that they can deal with their children without damaging them unduly. When we refer to being able to take the child seriously we mean that the child's gestures, movements, and noises come to have relevance or meaning for the parents, have a place in their world, and matter to the parents. (Ironically, one of the things it means to take the child seriously is knowing when not to take him or her seriously, being able to ignore, for instance, the angry child's "I hate you!") When parents take themselves and their children seriously, they are in position to engage the child intimately and to demand without fear that their values and standards become part of the child's life. They are able to present themselves as models or as objects for identification.

Parental confidence is precisely what is undermined by the social changes we have been discussing. When parents lack confidence, they become afraid of the tasks before them with their children, worrying chiefly that they will harm the child or that they will do something that might bring criticism. Parents who lack confidence focus on behaving with their children in ways that will be acceptable to others or in ways that could be justified and explained to others. Often this comes to include making sure that nothing potentially upsetting occurs between parent and child. An unconfident parent will necessarily be uneasy with the child's intense feelings. These impinge on the parents and seem to call for some response, but the very intensity of the emotion makes the parents feel that something very important is afoot and that they do not know what to do. The easiest response is not to see the child's inner states (moods, feelings, urges) at all.

This is the situation we outlined in Chapter 3, where we proposed that as-if pathology results from repeated parent–child interactions in which the child's inner world remains invisible and undefined. The child then becomes a reflection of this invisibility, as it were. When the parents cannot see the child's inner world, that world eventually withers and is no longer there to be seen. All that remains is appearance.

AS-IF THERAPY

Just as the social environment for child rearing has changed, so, too, has the environment in which therapists ply their craft. It will be no surprise to most of those reading this work that there is nowadays an emphasis on shorter treatments. Occasionally, someone tries to argue that this change is supposed to benefit the patient by making therapy more focused and efficient. Everyone knows, however, that the driving force behind this change is economic; briefer treatment is less expensive treatment (unless it leads to multiple brief treatments or otherwise unnecessary inpatient stays). Whether patients benefit from the change will depend on whether their problems are amenable to brief work and whether their therapists are competent in what they try to do.

On the one hand, there is nothing magical about a long treatment, and no responsible person advocates a lengthy therapy in every case. There is no doubt that some treatments could have ended earlier than they did without harm to the patient. On the other hand, it is sheer fantasy to suppose that brief treatment is all every patient needs. Such a position—if anyone apart from a managed-care employee actually holds it—could be built, we believe, only on the cynical assumption that therapy does no good anyway and that therefore a short treatment is no more ineffectual than a seemingly interminable one.

Of course, we do not hold such a position; we hold the hardly radical opinion that some patients need a little work and some need a lot. Common sense suggests that patients who enter treatment functioning at a fairly high level and experiencing well-defined symptoms are more likely to benefit from brief therapy, while those suffering personality-level pathologies are much less likely to receive what they need from a short treatment. It is also worth mentioning that even intact, well-functioning patients may need more help than one would expect in a society that teaches less and less about relationships and finds the emotional life to be an impediment to adaptation. In such a world, marriages, parenting, and feelings can be unexpectedly and tenaciously problematic.

The problem of who should receive a long and who a short treatment and the question of who pays for either will eventually work itself out. If psychotherapy is an enterprise worth preserving, patients and therapists will find the means to preserve it. The question of who should or should not pay is not one we can resolve here. What is of more immediate concern to us is that the nature of therapy is subtly being changed by changes in the marketplace—much as the situational approach to life has gradually changed what it means to be a parent. Therapists are bound to experience themselves and their work very differently in a world that stresses speed. Just as social changes have made as-if personality development more likely, current pressures on therapists make it more likely that therapists will feel pressed toward what might be termed as-if therapy.

The pressure to work faster or to define patients' problems so that brief therapy seems plausible impacts how therapists experience themselves and what they believe they might be able to offer those who come to their offices. The therapeutic relationship is less likely to be important in a world of brief psychotherapy. To begin with, the relationship between therapist and patient is experienced differently when the end is always in sight. Time is an essential ingredient if another person is to become personally significant; there must be history and shared experiences before we can become a meaningful part of another person's life. Only individuals whose boundaries are porous and who lack a sense of privacy can feel deeply attached after one or a few encounters. Treatments that are known by both parties to be brief are therefore far less likely to make the therapist personally important to the patient. This is true even if we compare an open-ended treatment that ends relatively quickly with treatment that is designed to be brief; when the future of a therapeutic relationship is bounded only by the willingness of the parties to be involved with one another, the therapist is experienced differently—as potentially more important—than if the relationship is known to end at some fairly near point.

The dynamic therapies have assumed a rather different situation. The therapeutic relationship is the context and in many ways the centerpiece of dynamic psychotherapy. The therapist's interventions simply do not mean the same thing when those interventions must stand entirely by themselves versus when they occur in the midst of an ongoing and significant relationship between patient and therapist. The question then arises: If the relationship stops being the centerpiece of treatment, what will take its place?

The answer is that technique becomes the central factor in therapy if the relationship is not. By technique we mean an orderly and predictable set of interventions based entirely on presenting symptoms and complaints. This is a situation that at least appears more scientific, since the interaction between therapist and patient is more controlled. There is less discretion for the therapist and therefore more homogeneity to treatments. Similar presenting complaints will consequently draw the same responses from the therapist, and this situation is bound to seem more logical and organized to an outsider. The cost of the appearance of science is that the therapist becomes a technician, someone following a script or a series of steps laid out in advance to address a circumscribed set of issues or symptoms. We should add that it is not only the short-term therapies that might lead to too great an emphasis on technique; long-term treatment modalities are not really less prone to becoming caricatures of their original intent. This may occur whenever therapists use technique to replace, first, openness to the patient and, second, the willingness to meet the patient's pathology without demanding that the patient be able to make the therapist feel better. In today's climate of training and practice, however, we believe it is the short-term treatments that are especially at risk to become dominated by technique. There is no freedom to such relationships, we believe, and as is always the case when there is no freedom, the people involved behave mechanically, even if they are earnest and sincere in what they do.

There are several consequences. First, patients and therapists automatically assume that psychic pain is bad and must be remedied. When time is of the essence (but not essential), the goal automatically becomes making the patient as functional as possible. Consequently, anything that makes the patient unhappy is by definition a problem that must be solved, and self-understanding is irrelevant. The effect of this is that the inner life is something of an unwelcome distraction, an impediment to functioning. The problem with this attitude, as we see it, is that there is no selfhood without pain. Life entails suffering, and an individual who cannot suffer is perpetually in retreat. If therapy comes to regard emotional pain as a problem, rather than as a fact of life to be known and faced, then therapy is engaged in taking persons away from themselves and fragmenting their experience.

Of course, it is always possible to say (with Freud) that therapy is aimed at neurotic pain, not at ordinary human suffering. This is a distinction that can be made in theory, but it is perhaps too neat a distinction to survive life as it is lived. Events that occasion ordinary human suffering tend also to bring out whatever is neurotic in us. The problem is that neurosis is not some isolated or well-circumscribed segment of the individual. As first Angyal (1965) and, more recently, Shapiro (1989) have proposed, neurosis is, rather, an expression of the whole person. Isolating neurotic pain from ordinary pain may therefore be one of those things that is easier to say than to accomplish. In addition, a therapy that tries to get rid of neurotic suffering without understanding how it is an expres sion of the person who is suffering is bound inevitably to regard all pain as neurotic, because pain is an impediment to rapid adaptation. Even if the distinction between neurotic pain and ordinary suffering could be maintained in theory, it would collapse in practice in the face of any approach to life stressing rapid adjustment.

Second, when technique rather than the therapeutic relationship is figural, the patient identifies with technique rather than with the therapist. We believe that this identification encourages patients to view themselves impersonally, as though their problems were alien to themselves as persons, like viruses or other outside entities that had invaded them. The patient is then involved in an effort to disown something that is integral to who he or she is. The more distant the patient becomes from unwanted elements of experience, the more successful the treatment seems. The patient is seen as *having a problem* instead of *being troubled.* Whenever difficulties are defined as something the patient has or possesses, the problem has been detached from the patient as a person. When, by contrast, the difficulty is seen as an expression of who the patient is, the patient is assigned responsibility for creating change, as opposed to waiting passively for the therapist to solve the problem. Patients who identify with the therapist are in position to accept such responsibility and will do so as an expression of wanting to be like the therapist. By contrast, patients who identify with their therapist's techniques are by definition learning to define themselves as those who *have* problems and who therefore are looking for ways to have the problems taken away from them.

Third, the therapist is not in a position to be spontaneous. Therapists who follow a script or a narrowly defined treatment plan can ill afford to take their eyes off the desired goal. Spontaneity runs the risk of deviating from the treatment plan, or script, leaving the therapist unsure what to do next or introducing an unwanted complication to the interaction. Patients must be seen as illustrations of a category if they are to be addressed with a controlled technique; the greater the spontaneity, the more the individual starts to leave the category, showing traits that do not fully fit the technique. Unfortunately, the absence of spontaneity will handicap therapists who seek to know their patients in any detail, as individuals. Spontaneity is required if we want to know another person; there must be freedom to invite the other to be something more than a complement to how we choose to behave and there must be freedom also to step away from the other person's definition of us.

This is not to say that therapists can know their patients only if sessions lack discipline and focus, nor is it to say that technique is somehow antithetical to competent work. The issue is: What should be figural? We believe that technique, discipline, and control are essential to good treatment, but these must be in the service of treatment, not the equivalent of treatment. Technique is the tool, not the entirety, of therapy. When technique is the focus of therapy, the patient is automatically pressed toward those patterns of interaction allowed by the technique. Whatever about the patient lies outside the parameters of the technique will necessarily be lost to sight if technique is taken to be the essence of therapy—the patient who is being treated becomes only a fragment of the individual who has come to therapy.

The problem with these consequences is that they are not terribly far from characteristics associated with the as-if personality and serve to make therapists more mechanical, plastic, and uninvolved. With an excessive emphasis on technique, therapists behave in a stereotyped manner and press patients into relatively narrow parameters, saying, in effect, that the patient can be whatever sort of individual matches up with what the therapist is comfortable with, but cannot violate these limits. The whole intention of what we call as-if therapy seems to be keeping the patient and the patient's pathology under control and, ultimately, manageable. As long as the patient is controlled, the therapist need not be challenged or pushed as a person.

We suspect that all therapists go through a period when they are as-if therapists. During training, there is a time when we all model ourselves after our mentors or those we have studied, speaking and behaving in ways that are not (yet) our own. This period of imitation is a necessary first step to identifying with those we admire and hope to emulate. We cannot stay at the level of imitation, however. Just as the young child moves beyond concrete behavioral imitations of the parent, so must student therapists find their own singular voices even as they remain within the system of thought and discipline learned from their models. As-if therapy occurs when therapists never move past the level of imitation.

In our experience, there are two forms of this sort of perpetual imitation. First, there are therapists who never move beyond a fairly limited and circumscribed set of interventions, saying essentially the same things to nearly everyone in their caseloads. By remaining with these familiar and comfortable interventions, such therapists are never challenged by their patients or made to wrestle with themselves in any meaningful way. An example would be therapists who think of themselves as empathic and whose technique consists largely of making soothing, overly sympathetic and comforting remarks. Other examples would include therapists who rely on a jargon gleaned from popular culture, such as those working on ''co-dependency'' or the ''inner child.'' In these examples, these therapists offer the appearance of understanding. The underlying intent, however, is to arrange a scenario in which the patient can substantiate the therapist's attempt to appear competent. The patient's part is to act as though he or she has been helped, suppressing any doubts to the contrary. We refer to this sort of therapy as imitation because both patient and therapist seem engaged in trying to learn a prescribed set of interactions.

The second type of perpetual imitation we have seen occurs when therapists objectify their patients. Earlier, we described patients who identify with their therapist's technique rather than with the therapist, learning thereby to think of themselves as *having* problems as opposed to *being* troubled. Therapists who allow and perhaps even encourage this in their patients are engaged in pseudo-therapy, we believe. It is an easier matter to address the patient's problems as though they were discrete entities separate from the person of the patient. Such an approach means that the therapist's own subjectivity is not called into play or challenged; nothing is personal, and so the therapist is never vulnerable or, for that matter, even uncomfortable. Rather, the therapist is in the role of expert, following a preset script or treatment plan. The script or plan lies between the therapist and the patient, leaving the appearance of a shared world but without the risks.

One of us recently encountered a couple whose previous therapist had set up a contract to address their respective concerns. The wife's complaint was that her husband did not help with household chores, such as taking out the garbage, while the husband wanted his wife to be more sexually available. The resulting contract called for the couple to have sex after the husband had taken out the garbage a certain number of times. The contract failed to help; the husband complained that his wife did not seem very interested in sex, even though there was more sexual activity between them. The wife noted that this was not part of the contract, saying, "You're not very excited about the garbage either." In this case, what is most striking is the apparent reasoning of the original therapist, who seems to have viewed the presenting complaints as quite separate from the persons making the complaints and also from their life as a couple. This is an example, we believe, of circumscribing problematic behavior and applying a preset technique with little willingness to understand the persons involved. It may be understood as a type of imitation whereby a predetermined strategy is applied almost by rote rather than on the basis of an experience-near understanding.

A frequently seen corollary of this type of as-if therapy is an emphasis on feeling good. The idea seems to be that the patient should experience heightened self-esteem and avoid a sense of failure. In the real world, of course, self-esteem must be rooted in achievement, and failure is a fact of life that must be faced and felt. Nonetheless, when emotional pain is defined as problematic, it is easy to move toward a pattern of interaction that is primarily designed to reduce the patient's tension level. Unhappily, this robs therapists of one of their most effective tools; it is hard to imagine any genuine treatment in which the therapist must take care not to produce tension or distress in the patient. In addition, it ought not be the therapist's task to make the patient feel better. This task would place the therapist in a position of constantly having to react to the patient's signs of distress, in the process communicating to the patient that distress cannot be tolerated.

Therapy should offer that which culture fails to provide. In Freud's time, this meant offering psychic freedom to persons whose (at the time) unthinkable thoughts and wishes brought them into conflict with an era of rigid social structure and stifling morality. In our day, stifling morality is hardly the problem, and freedom (in the sense of license) does not seem to be a scarce commodity. Indeed, there may be too much cultural license, or too little constraint. It can be hard to know who one is when little seems deviant and unacceptable. The fluidity of Western society complicates the individual's efforts to gain self-definition. It may fall to therapy to provide some of the most basic elements of life, constancy and a basis for identity.

We do not believe that as-if therapy is likely to provide such elements. The key variable in as-if therapy is that the approach is imposed on the patient from outside, if we may put it that way. Neither those who rely on a few, familiar interventions nor those who objectify their patients are responding to what actually goes on between therapist and patient. The therapist's approach is preconceived in both cases, imposed on the patient with little willingness to remain open to the unexpected or to what does not fit the therapist's script. This means that the therapist will not see the patient's inner world, or that web of private meanings and intentions that may define the individual. Rather, as-if therapists focus on altering only that which is visible within their particular framework. With such an approach, other elements of the interaction with the patient will remain invisible, a circumstance that essentially duplicates the sort of parent–child interaction leading to as-if personality development.

References

Akhtar, S. (1992). *Broken Structures: Severe Personality Disorders and Their Treatment*. Northvale, NJ: Jason Aronson.

Angyal, A. (1965). *Neurosis and Treatment: A Holistic Approach*. New York: Wiley.

Bach, S. (1977). On the narcissistic state of consciousness. *International Journal of Psycho-Analysis* 58:209–233.

Basch, M. F. (1985). Interpretation: toward a developmental model. In *Progress in Self Psychology*, vol. I, ed. A. Goldberg, pp. 33–42. New York: Guilford.

Blanck, G., and Blanck, R. (1974). *Ego Psychology: Theory and Practice*. New York: Columbia University Press.

Cameron, N. (1963). *Personality Development and Psychopathology: A Dynamic Approach*. Boston: Houghton Mifflin.

Camus, A. (1955). *The Stranger*, trans. S. Gilbert. New York: Alfred Knopf.

Capponi, A. (1979). Origin and evolution of the borderline concept. In *Advances in Psychotherapy of the Borderline Patient*, eds. J. LeBoit and A. Capponi, pp.63–147. New York: Jason Aronson.

Chasseguet-Smirgel, J. (1984). *Creativity and Perversion*. New York: W. W. Norton.

Chessick, R. (1977). *Intensive Psychotherapy of the Borderline Patient*. New York: Jason Aronson.

Cohen, C., and Sherwood, V. (1989). Becoming a constant object for the borderline patient. *Bulletin of the Menninger Clinic*, 53:287–299.

_____ (1991). *Becoming a Constant Object in Psychotherapy with the Borderline Patient*. Northvale, NJ: Jason Aronson.

289

Deutsch, H. (1942). Some forms of emotional disturbance and their relationship to schizophrenia. *Psychoanalytic Quarterly* 11:301–321.

Dorr, D., Barley, W., Gard, B., and Webb, C. (1983). Understanding and treating borderline personality organization. *Psychotherapy: Theory, Research, and Practice* 20:397–404.

Erikson, E. (1959). *Identity and the Life Cycle.* New York: International Universities Press.

Fairbairn, W. R. D. (1952). *Psychoanalytic Studies of Personality.* London: Tavistock.

Fleming, J. (1975). Some observations on object constancy in the psychoanalysis of adults. *Journal of the American Psychoanalytic Association* 23: 743–759.

Fraiberg, S. (1969). Libidinal object constancy and mental representation. *The Psychoanalytic Study of the Child* 24:9–47.

Freud, A. (1937). *The Ego and the Mechanisms of Defense.* London: Hogarth.

Freud, S. (1920). Beyond the pleasure principle. *Standard Edition* 18.

Gardner, C., and Wagner, S. (1986). Clinical diagnosis of the as-if personality disorder. *Bulletin of the Menninger Clinic* 50:135–147.

Green, A. (1977). The borderline concept. In *Borderline Personality Disorders: The Concept, the Syndrome, the Patient,* ed. P. Hartocollis, pp. 15–44. New York: International Universities Press.

Greenson, R. (1958). On screen defenses, screen hunger, and screen identity. *Journal of the American Psychoanalytic Association* 6:242–262.

Grinker, R., Werble, B., and Drye, R. (1968). *The Borderline Syndrome: A Behavioral Study of Ego-Functions.* New York: Basic Books.

Gruen, A. (1968). Autonomy and identification: The paradox of their opposition. *International Journal of Psycho-Analysis* 49:648–655.

Grunberger, B. (1989). *New Essays on Narcissism,* trans. D. Macey. London: Free Association Books.

Gunderson, J., and Singer, M. (1975). Defining borderline patients: An overview. *American Journal of Psychiatry* 132:1–10.

Harrison, S. I., and Delano, J. (1976). The status of prevention in the education of child psychiatrists. *Child Psychiatry and Human Development* 7:3–21.

Hoch, P., and Polatin, P. (1949). Pseudoneurotic forms of schizophrenia. *Psychoanalytic Quarterly* 23:248–276.

Jacobson, E. (1961). Adolescent moods and the remodeling of psychic structure in adolescence. *Psychoanalytic Study of the Child* 16:164–183.

_____ (1964). *The Self and the Object World.* New York: International Universities Press.

Katan, M. (1958). Contribution to the panel on ego distortion. *International Journal of Psycho-Analysis* 34:265–270.

Kernberg, O. (1967). Borderline personality organization. *Journal of the American Psychoanalytic Association* 15:641–685.

_____ (1975). *Borderline Conditions and Pathological Narcissism.* New York: Jason Aronson.

Khan, M. (1960). Clinical aspects of the schizoid personality: affects and technique. *International Journal of Psycho-Analysis* 41:430–437.

Kierkegaard, S. (1962). *The Present Age and on the Difference between a Genius and an Apostle,* trans. A. Dru. New York: Harper & Row.

Laing, R. D. (1960). *The Divided Self: A Study of Sanity and Madness.* London: Tavistock.

Laing, R. D., and Esterson, A. (1964). *Sanity, Madness and the Family.* London: Tavistock.

Laplanche, J., and Pontalis, J. (1973). *The Language of Psychoanalysis,* trans. D. Nicholson-Smith. New York: W. W. Norton.

Mahler, M., and Furer, M. (1968). *On Human Symbiosis and the Vicissitudes of Individuation, Volume II: Infantile Psychosis.* New York: International Universities Press.

Mahler, M., Pine, F., and Bergman, A. (1975). *The Psychological Birth of the Human Infant.* New York: International Universities Press.

Malatesta, C., and Haviland, J. (1983). Learning display rules: The socialization of emotion in infancy. *Child Development* 53:991–1003.

Marcuse, H. (1964). *One Dimensional Man.* Boston: Beacon.

McDevitt, J. B. (1975). Separation-individuation and object constancy. *Journal of the American Psychoanalytic Association* 23:713–742.

Mead, M. (1949). Culture change and character structure. *Social structure.* Oxford: Oxford University Press.

Meissner, W. (1984). *The Borderline Spectrum*. New York: Jason Aronson.

Miller, A. (1981). *Prisoners of Childhood: The Drama of the Gifted Child and the Search for the True Self,* trans. Ruth Ward. New York: Basic Books.

Millon, T. (1981). *Disorders of Personality: DSM-III: Axis II*. New York: Wiley.

Modell, A. (1963). Primitive object-relationships and the predisposition to schizophrenia. *International Journal of Psycho-Analysis* 44:282–292.

Nayman, S. (1991). Temporality and the self: A phenomenological study of the narcissist, the schizoid, and the as-if personality. *Psychoanalysis and Contemporary Thought* 14:479–503.

Pontalis, J. (1981). The birth and recognition of the self. In *Frontiers of Psychoanalysis: Between the Dream and Psychic Pain,* pp. 126–147. New York: International Universities Press.

Reich, A. (1953). Narcissistic object choice in women. In *Annie Reich: Psychoanalytic Contributions,* pp. 179–208. International Universities Press: New York, 1973.

Reider, N. (1950). The concept of normality. *Psychoanalytic Quarterly* 19:43–51.

Reisman, D., Denny, R., and Glazer, N. (1955). *The Lonely Crowd*. New York: Doubleday.

Ross, N. (1967). The "as if" concept. *Journal of the American Psychoanalytic Association* 15:59–82.

Schachtel, E. (1959). *Metamorphosis: On the Development of Affect, Perception, Attention, and Memory*. New York: Basic Books.

Sears, R., Maccoby, E., and Levin, H. (1957). A study of child rearing. In *Readings in the Psychology of Human Growth and Development,* ed. W. Baller. New York: Holt, Rinehart, & Winston, 1962.

Shapiro, D. (1989). *Psychotherapy of Neurotic Character*. New York: Basic Books.

Sherrod, L. (1981). Issues in cognitive-perceptual development: The special case of social stimuli. In *Infant Social Cognition: Empirical and Theoretical Considerations,* eds. M. E. Lamb and L. R. Sherrod, pp. 11–36. Hillsdale, NJ: Lawrence Erlbaum.

Sherwood, V. (1987). The schizoid personality in light of Camus's actor. *Bulletin of the Menninger Clinic* 51:158–169.

———— (1989). Object constancy: The illusion of being seen. *Psychoanalytic Psychology* 6:15–30.

_____ (1990). The first stage of treatment with the conduct disordered adolescent: Overcoming narcissistic resistance. *Psychotherapy* 27:380–387.

Southwood, H. M. (1973). The origin of self-awareness and ego behavior. *International Journal of Psycho-Analysis* 54:235–239.

Spitz, R. (1945). Hospitalism: An inquiry into the genesis of psychiatric conditions in early childhood. *The Psychoanalytic Study of the Child* 1:53–74.

_____ (1957). *No and Yes: On the Genesis of Human Communication.* New York: International Universities Press.

Spitz, R., and Wolf, K. (1946). The smiling response: A contribution to the ontogenesis of social relations. *Genetic Psychology Monographs* 34:57–125.

Stern, D. (1985). *The Interpersonal World of the Infant.* New York: Basic Books.

Stone, M. (1986). *Essential Papers on Borderline Disorders.* New York: New York University Press.

Sullivan, H. S. (1947). *Conceptions of Modern Psychiatry.* Washington, DC: William Alanson White Institute.

Uzgiris, I. (1974). Patterns of gestural and vocal imitation in infants. In *The Competent Infant,* eds. J. L. Stone, H. T. Smith, and L. B. Murphy, pp. 599–604. London: Tavistock.

_____ (1984). Imitation in infancy: its interpersonal aspects. In *Parent-Child Interaction and Parent-Child Relations in Child Development. The Minnesota Symposium on Child Psychology,* vol. 17, ed. M. Perlmutter, pp. 1–32. Hillsdale, NJ: Lawrence Erlbaum.

Van den Berg, J. H. (1972). *Dubious Maternal Affection.* Pittsburgh: Duquesne University Press.

Watson, G. (1957). Some personality differences in children related to strict or permissive parental discipline. *Journal of Psychology* 44:227–249.

Weiss, J. (1966). Clinical and theoretical aspects of "as if" characters. *Journal of the American Psychoanalytic Association* 14:569–590.

Wheelis, A. (1958). *The Quest for Identity.* New York: W. W. Norton & Co.

Winnicott, D. W. (1955). Clinical varieties of transference. In *Through Paediatrics to Psycho-Analysis,* pp. 295–299. New York: Basic Books, 1975.

——— (1960). The theory of the parent-infant relationship. In *The Maturational Processes and the Facilitating Environment*, pp. 37–55. New York: International Universities Press.

——— (1967). The mirror role of mother and family in child development. In *The Predicament of the Family: A Psychoanalytical Symposium*, ed. P. Lomas, pp. 26–33. New York: International Universities Press.

Wolfenstein, M. (1953). Trends in infant care. *American Journal of Ortho-Psychiatry* 27:120–130.

Wright, K. (1991). *Vision and Separation*. Northvale, NJ: Jason Aronson.

Zilboorg, G. (1941). Ambulatory schizophrenia. *Psychiatry* 4:149–155.

Index

Absence of self, as-if persona-
lity/schizoid phenomena
and, 50–51. *See also* Self
Acting, family adaptation and,
79–80
Adaptiveness, quiet borderline
personality, 24
Adolescence, developmental
factors and, 53–54
Affect
absence in variability of,
diagnosis, normalcy and
treatment, 132–133
as-if personality and, 5, 7–9,
43
developmental factors and, 9
family adaptation and, 79–80
quiet borderline personality
and, 14, 22
schizoid phenomena and, 44
Akhtar, S., 55, 78
Alien self, stranger anxiety and,
67
Aloneness
as-if personality and, 12, 45
identity diffusion and treatment, 216–222

precocious ego development
and, 169–170
Amiability, diagnosis and,
127–128
Angyal, A., 282
As-if personality. *See also*
Quiet borderline
personality
as borderline condition,
51–53
continuum concept and,
39–43
culture and, 265, 269–288.
See also Culture
etiology of, 59–86. *See also*
Etiology
false-self and, 48–50
identity disturbance and,
53–56
normalcy and, 28
problem of, 5–12
schizoid phenomena and,
43–51
theory and, xiii–xiv
Authenticity, quiet borderline
personality, 22–23. *See also*
Genuineness

Authority
  as-if personality and, 8
  family adaptation and, 81, 82
Autonomy
  failure of constancy and, 74
  mirroring and, 73

Bach, S., 68
Basch, M. F., 65
Blanck, G., 19
Blanck, R., 19
Body focus
  dependency on therapist,
    building of, 184
  treatment approach,
    resistance of compliance,
    115–117
Borderline personality. See also
    As-if personality; Quiet
    borderline personality
  as-if personality and, 6, 51–53
  etiology of, 73–74
  literature on, 37–38
  quiet patient and, 12–15
  wanting and, 106–107
Brief therapy
  culture and, 279, 280
  impossibility of, 94–95

Cameron, N., 214
Camus, A., 270
Capponi, A., 51
Chase, L., 11
Chasseguet-Smirgel, J., 167,
    214, 215
Chessick, R., 275
Cohen, C., xiv, 6, 61, 95,
    100–101, 106, 183
Commitment
  conflict and, 217–218

culture and, 271
identity and, 211–214
Compliance
  failure of constancy and,
    74–75
  resistance of, treatment
    approach and, 113–119
Conflict
  as-if personality and, 8
  commitment and, 217–218
  intimacy and, 217
  quiet borderline personality,
    23–24, 32
  triadic relationships, as-if
    personality and, 128–130
Conformity, culture and,
    277–278
Confrontation, patient response
    to, diagnosis, normalcy and
    treatment, 135–136
Confusion, dependency on ther-
    apist, question of, 175–182
Continuum concept, as-if
    personality and, 39–43
Countertransference, patterns
    in, diagnosis, normalcy and
    treatment, 136–138
Culture, 269–288
  as-if personality and, 265
  identity and change, 269–272
  parenting and, 272–279
  therapy and, 279–288

Defenses, as-if personality/
    schizoid phenomena and,
    46–47
Delano, J., 275
Dependency
  as-if personality/schizoid
    phenomena and, 47

plasticity and, 216
precocious ego development
    and, 167, 173–175
quiet borderline personality,
    21
on therapist
    building of, 182–187
    question of, 175–182
Depersonalization, failure of
    constancy and, 72
Detachment, schizoid
    phenomena and, 45
Deutsch, H., xiii, xiv, 5, 6, 7–8,
    11, 12, 13, 28, 31, 32, 38,
    39, 40, 42, 43, 46, 51, 55,
    56, 99, 126, 135, 213, 218,
    272
Developmental factors. See also
    Mirroring; Parenting
    adolescence and, 53–54
    affect and, 9
    facial expression and, 62–65
    false self and, 49
    identity and, 209–210
    mirroring and, 9–10, 68–69
    normal/as-if personality
        compared, 171
    precocious ego, quiet border-
        line personality, 19–23,
        165–170
    schizoid phenomena and, 44
Diagnosis
    as-if personality and, 12–13,
        123
    normalcy and treatment,
        132–138. See also
        Normalcy and treatment:
        diagnosis
    quiet borderline patient and,
        96–101

Differentiation,
    pseudo-differentiation,
    quiet borderline
    personality, 27–34
Dorr, D., 51
Drug abuse, diagnosis, normalcy
    and treatment, 134–135
Drye, R., 51

Ego, culture change and,
    276–277
Ego development, precocious,
    quiet borderline
    personality, 19–23. See also
    Precocious ego
    development and treatment
Ego ideal, as-if personality/
    schizoid phenomena and,
    47
Ego psychology, as-if
    personality and, 7
Emotion. See Affect
Empathy, treatment approach
    and, 101–102
Erikson, E., 53, 54
Esterson, A., 60
Ethnicity, normalcy and
    treatment, 140–141
Etiology, 59–86
    child as family protector,
        83–86
    family adaptation and, 76–83
    internalized object relations
        and, 61–65
    object constancy and, 65–76
        failures of, 70–76
        mechanism of, 65–70
    overview of, 59–61
Externalization, as-if personality
    and, 11

Facial expression. *See also*
    Mirroring
    developmental factors and,
        62–65
    treatment approach,
        resistance of compliance,
        115–116
Fairbairn, W. R. D., 43, 44, 45
False self, as-if personality/
    schizoid phenomena and,
    48–50
Family adaptation, quiet border-
    line personality and, 76–83,
    176
Family protector role, etiology
    and, 83–86
Fantasy, as-if personality and,
    219, 220
Fixation, as-if personality and,
    42
Fleming, J., 68
Fraiberg, S., 67
Freud, A., 7, 42
Freud, S., 7, 65–66, 287
Frustration, mirroring and, 73
Furer, M., 63

Gardner, C., 16, 38, 42, 51, 53
Gender identity, as-if person-
    ality and, 55
Generational difference
    identity and, 214–215
    perversions and, 215
Genuineness. *See also*
    Authenticity
    absence of, identity diffusion
        and treatment, 225–228,
        229
    treatment approach and,
        103–104, 111–112

Green, A., 52
Greenson, R., 11, 12, 40–41,
    277, 278
Grinker, R., 51, 53
Gruen, A., 74
Grunberger, B., 61, 167
Gunderson, J., 52, 53

Harrison, S. I., 275
Haviland, J., 63
Hoch, P., 6
Hollowness, diagnosis and, 98,
    132–133
Hostility, borderline personality
    and, 52
Humor, identity diffusion and
    treatment, 237–239, 240

Identification
    as-if personality and, 6–7
    quiet borderline personality,
        24
Identity
    as-if personality and, 12
    commitment and, 211–214
    culture change and, 269–272
    developmental factors and,
        209–210
Identity diffusion
    as-if personality and, 53–56
    quiet borderline personality,
        27–34
Identity diffusion and treatment,
    209–262
    aloneness and relatedness,
        216–222
    case example transcript,
        243–262
    overview, 209–215
    pseudo-relatedness, 222–243

manifestation of, 222–228
therapy of, 228–243
Id psychology, as-if personality
and, 7
Imitation
as-if personality and, 53
quiet borderline personality,
24, 32
Imperfection, identity diffusion
and treatment, 239–240
Inauthenticity. *See* Authenticity
Independence, appearance of,
precocious ego develop-
ment and treatment,
172–175. *See also*
Dependency
Infancy. *See also* Developmental
factors; Mirroring; Parenting
mirroring, 9–10
object relations, internalized,
etiology and, 61–65
Internalization, as-if personality
and, 11
Interpersonal relationships. *See
also* Pseudo-relatedness;
Relatedness
as-if personality and, 221
identity and, 209
pseudo-relatedness, quiet
borderline personality,
23–27
Intimacy
conflict and, 217
dependency and, 178–179
precocious ego development
and, 168
quiet borderline personality,
24–26, 218–219
Isolation, schizoid phenomena
and, 45

Jacobson, E., 42, 168

Katan, M., 41
Kernberg, O., 51, 52, 54, 73
Khan, M., 11, 17, 43, 45, 46,
47, 48, 180
Kierkegaard, S., 272
Klein, M., 7
Kohut, H., 101

Laing, R. D., 60, 66, 170
Language
dependency on therapist,
building of, 183–184
family adaptation and, 81
Laplanche, J., 8
Life-style discrepancy, normalcy
and treatment, diagnosis,
134–135

Mahler, M., 63, 66, 68
Malatesta, C., 63
Marcuse, H., 272
Maturity
identity and, 212–213
precocious ego development
contrasted, 166–167
McDevitt, J. B., 67, 68
Mead, M., 273–274
Meissner, W., 11, 31, 43, 45,
47, 51, 52, 54
Miller, A., 65, 71
Millon, T., 43
Mimicry, quiet borderline per-
sonality, 24, 32
Miniature adult role, precocious
ego development and treat-
ment, 165–172
Mirroring. *See also* Parenting
abnormal, 10

Mirroring (*continued*)
  developmental factors and,
      9–10, 68–69
  facial expression and, 62–65
  object constancy and, 65–70
  reciprocal nature of, 9–10
  treatment approach and, 115
Modell, A., 51, 52
Morality
  as-if personality and, 55
  as-if personality/schizoid
      phenomena and, 46–47
  identity diffusion, quiet
      borderline personality,
      27–28
Mutuality, lack of, therapeutic
    relationship, 223

Narcissism
  as-if personality and, 45
  of parents
    as-if personality and,
        41–42
    quiet borderline personal-
        ity, 21–22, 23
  relatedness and, 216–217
Nayman, S., 40, 55, 94
Negative transference, xv
Noisy borderline personality.
    See Borderline personality;
    Quiet borderline personality
Normalcy
  appearance of, quiet border-
      line personality, 16–19
  as-if personality, 28
  diagnosis and, 123–124
  identity diffusion and treat-
      ment, 241–242
Normalcy and treatment,
    123–161

case example transcript,
    141–161
diagnosis, 132–138
  affective variability, absence
      of, 132–133
  confrontation, patient re-
      sponse to, 135–136
  continuation of therapy
      question, 138
  countertransference pat-
      terns, 136–138
  life-style discrepancy,
      134–135
  personal questions, patient
      response to, 133–134
ethnicity and, 140–141
first impressions, 126–132
overview, 123–126
referral and, 138–139

Object constancy, 65–76
  failures of, 70–76
  mechanism of, 65–70
  treatment approach and, 101
Object relations
  affect and, 9
  internalized, etiology and,
      61–65
Occupation. *See* Vocation
Oedipal conflict, identity and,
    214

Parenting. *See also* Develop-
    mental factors; Mirroring
  as-if personality and, 41–42
  culture and, 272–279
  false self and, 49
  family adaptation and, 76–83
  object relations, internalized,
      etiology and, 61–65

precocious ego development,
quiet borderline personality, 20–22
schizoid phenomena and, 44
Passivity, quiet borderline
personality, 23–27
Peek-a-boo game, 69
Peer relations, precocious ego
development and, 169
Perception, mirroring and, 63
Personal questions, patient
response to, diagnosis,
normalcy and treatment,
133–134
Plasticity
dependency and, 216
diagnosis, normalcy and
treatment, 134–135
quiet borderline personality,
23–27
Polatin, P., 6
Pontalis, J., 8, 31, 50, 51, 72
Precocious ego development
child as family protector role
and, 83–86
quiet borderline personality,
19–23
Precocious ego development
and treatment, 165–206
case example transcript,
187–206
dependence on therapist,
175–187
building of, 182–187
question of, 175–182
independence, appearance of,
172–175
miniature adult role, 165–172
Projective identification, relatedness and, 219–220

Promiscuity
as-if personality and, 55
diagnosis, normalcy and
treatment, 134–135
identity diffusion, quiet
borderline personality,
28, 213
treatment approach and, 110
Pseudo-differentiation, quiet
borderline personality,
27–34
Pseudo-relatedness, 222–243.
See also Interpersonal
relationships; Relatedness
identity diffusion and
treatment, 228–243
manifestation of, 222–228
quiet borderline personality,
23–27
Psychosis, borderline
personality and, 6

Quiet borderline personality.
See also As-if personality
as-if personality and, 6
borderline personality and, 6
clinical characteristics of,
15–34
appearance of normalcy,
16–19
overview of, 15–16
passivity, plasticity, and
pseudo-relatedness,
23–27
precocious ego develop-
ment, 19–23
pseudo-differentiation and
identity diffusion,
27–34
described, 12–15

Quiet borderline personality
(*continued*)
family adaptation and, 76–83
treatment approach, 93–119.
See also Treatment approach

Rapprochement stage, mirroring
and, 66
Reality
failure of constancy and,
70–71
mirroring and, 9, 10, 66, 67
Reality testing, quiet borderline
personality, 31–32
Referral, normalcy and treatment, 138–139
Regression, as-if personality/
schizoid phenomena and, 47
Reich, A., 41, 42
Reider, N., 276
Reisman, D., 38
Relatedness, identity diffusion
and treatment, 216–222.
See also Interpersonal
relationships;
Pseudo-relatedness
Repression, as-if personality
and, 8
Resistance
absence of, identity diffusion
and treatment, 225
quiet borderline patient and,
97–98
wanting and, 106–107
Resistance of compliance,
treatment approach and,
113–119
Responsibility
family adaptation and, 82

identity diffusion and
treatment, 232–233
Ross, N., 11, 12, 38, 40, 41, 42,
43, 271

Schachtel, E., 61–62
Schizoid phenomena, as-if
personality and, 43–51,
127–128, 170, 180–181
Schizophrenia, as-if personality
and, 7
Screen identity, as-if personality
and, 40–41, 43
Sears, R., 273
Secrecy, schizoid phenomena
and, 45
Self
mirroring and, 63
stranger anxiety and, 67
Self-sufficiency
appearance of, precocious ego
development and
treatment, 172–175
quiet borderline personality,
22
Separateness, normalcy and
treatment, 140–141
Separation anxiety, mirroring
and, 66
Separation-individuation
failure of constancy and,
70–72
rapprochement stage of, 66
Seriousness, treatment approach
and, 104–113
Sexuality
as-if personality and, 55
diagnosis, normalcy and
treatment, 134–135
identity and, 212

identity diffusion, quiet borderline personality, 27–28, 213
treatment approach and, 110
Shapiro, D., 282
Sherrod, L., 62
Sherwood, V., xiv, 6, 9, 17, 61, 95, 100–101, 106, 183, 215
Silence (of therapist), quiet borderline personality and, 17, 99
Singer, M., 52, 53
Southwood, H. M., 62
Spitz, R., 63, 67, 274
Spontaneity
absence of, diagnosis, normalcy and treatment, 133
family adaptation and, 79–80
therapeutic relationship and, 283–284
Standing still concept
borderline personality and, 95–96
quiet borderline personality and, 96–97
Stereotyping, identity diffusion and treatment, 234–235, 236
Stern, D., 62, 63, 64, 65
Stone, M., 12
Stranger anxiety, mirroring and, 67–68
Subjectivity, treatment approach and, 108–109, 114–115
Submission
as-if personality and, 8
family adaptation and, 81
Sullivan, H. S., 219
Superego
as-if personality and, 8

as-if personality/schizoid phenomena and, 46–47
culture change and, 276–277
quiet borderline personality, 28

Termination, as-if personality and, 6
Therapeutic relationship. See also Treatment approach
as-if personality and, 102–103
as-if personality/schizoid phenomena and, 45–46, 47–48
culture and, 279–288
mutuality, lack of, 223
quiet borderline personality and, 13–15
Time-limited therapy
culture and, 279, 280
impossibility of, 94–95
Time sense
absence of, identity diffusion and treatment, 232
as-if personality and, 55, 95
Treatment approach, 93–119
diagnosis and, 96–101
genuineness in, 101–104
identity diffusion and, 209–262. See also Identity diffusion and treatment
normalcy and, 123–161. See also Normalcy and treatment
overview of, 93–95
precocious ego development and, 165–206. See also Precocious ego development and treatment

Treatment approach
(*continued*)
    resistance of compliance and,
        113–119
    seriousness and, 104–113
    standing still concept and,
        95–97
Triadic relationships, as-if
    personality and,
    128–130

Uzgiris, I., 63

Van den Berg, J. H., 275
Verbal skills, quiet
    borderline personality
    and, 18
Vocation
    identity and, 212

quiet borderline personality,
    29–30, 213–214

Wagner, S., 16, 38, 42, 51, 53
Wanting
    narcissism and, 217
    resistance and, 106–107
Watson, G., 272
Weiss, J., 11, 12, 31, 40, 51,
    277
Werble, B., 51
Wheelis, A., 270, 276
Winnicott, D. W., 43, 48, 49,
    62, 63, 77
Wolf, K., 63
Wolfenstein, M., 272
Wright, K., 71, 72

Zilboorg, G., 6